Wild About Wildflowers

Extreme Botanizing in Crested Butte, Wildflower Capital of Colorado

Katherine Darrow

"Bread feeds the body, indeed, but flowers also feed the Soul."

– The Koran

Let wildflowers
feed your soul!
Kathy D

This book is dedicated to
Brooke Warren and Orion Pendley

"Stay together, Learn the flowers, Go light."

from "For the Children" by Gary Snyder

First published in 1998 by Heel and Toe Publisher, Fort Collins, CO.

Published and distributed by
WildKat Publishing Co.
P.O. Box 12017
Glendale, AZ 85318
wild_kat@cox.net

Layout Design and Production: Kathy Carr
Cover and Interior Design, Illustration p. 115: Leanne Canty.
Cartoon Illustrations: Kristen Anderson
Text: Katherine Darrow
Science editors: Bruce Bartleson, David Inouye, Vinnie Rossignol, Amy Taylor, Kevin Taylor
Copy editors: Erika Perloff, David Barker, Esther Darrow, Mary Ellen Harte

Front cover landscape photograph: Rosy Paintbrush on Frigidaire Pass by Jannette Runge.

Darrow, Katherine
Wild About Wildflowers: Extreme Botanizing in Crested Butte, Wildflower Capital of Colorado
—2nd Edition
Includes bibliographical references and index.

Preassigned LCCN: 2006925204
ISBN: 9780977971800

Printed and manufactured in Korea through P. Chan and Edward, Inc.
www.pchaninc.com

Contents

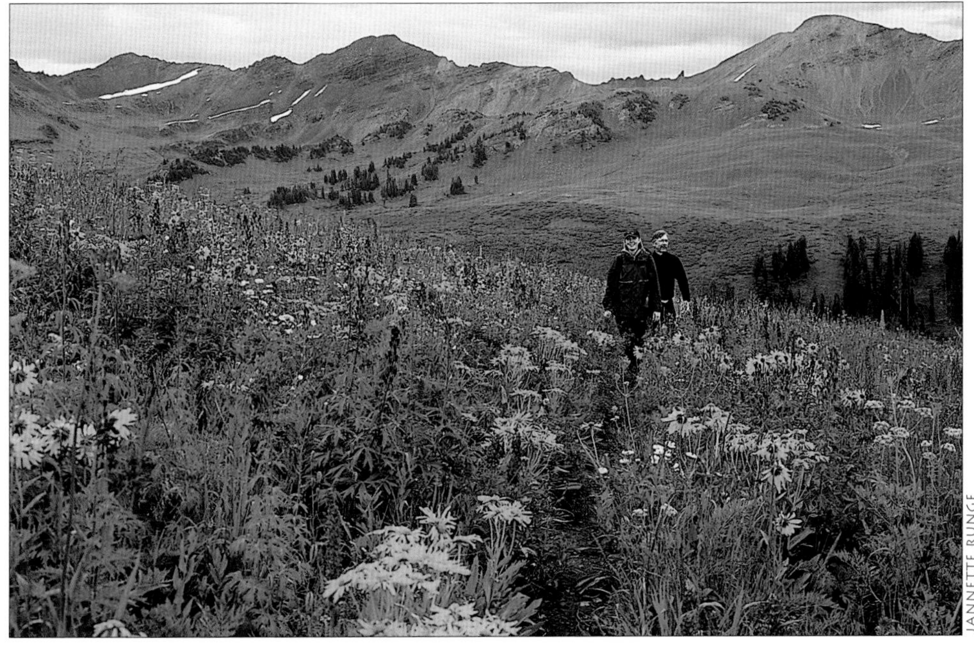

JANNETTE RUNGE

Preface to the 2nd Edition

Since the creation of the first edition of Wild About Wildflowers in 1998 much has changed, both in the great wide world, as well as in the small world of this book that you hold in your hands. It is hard to imagine that in 1998 the Internet was just beginning to surge into common usage and digital photo technology was only recently available. Reflecting both of these technologies, this "new and improved" 2nd edition of Wild About Wildflowers features mostly new and twice as many photographs, including contributions from talented photographers Jannette Runge, David Inouye, Mel Harte, Wendy Brown and Gale Pickett.

Eighty new species, including seven more plant families, have been added along with updated taxonomic names and information on the plants. The book has been re-formatted to a slightly larger size, with a sturdier binding and handy color reference section. The new cover and interior graphic design by artist Leanne Canty greatly enhance the visual appeal and readability.

Fortunately, Crested Butte and the surrounding landscape have largely remained the same over the years, lush and splendid with wildflowers throughout the summers and with plenty of trails to take you far into the backcountry right from town. I hope that *Wild About Wildflowers* will help you to learn about and enjoy this amazing landscape even more.

Acknowledgements

Scores of people have been involved in this project since its conception in my mind as a child. Actually seeing it to completion has been a bit like giving birth. To all of the following people I am indebted for assisting me through the labor and delivery:

Many praises go to all of my editors for their patience, advice, thoroughness and efficiency. On the first edition, David Barker, Paul Rich and Susie Geer; for the second edition, Kevin Taylor, Amy Taylor, Erika Perloff , Vinnie Rossignol, Mel Harte, Soozie Darrow and David Inouye.

The 2nd edition has traveled far, and been in the hands of many people I will never meet, from slide scanners to printers and handlers in Korea, to shipping dockhands in Los Angeles. This is amazing to me.

Ron Siepel at Ritz Camera in Glendale, Arizona provided excellent slide scanning services.

Cindy Peer, press coordinator with P.Chan & Edwards helped to make the book production stress free.

Without Kathy Carr, I would still be lost in a Quark manual. Kathy's patience and knowledge are extraordinary. She also was my most faithful cheerleader in the home stretch in the production of both the first and second editions; a billion thanks to you, Kathy!

Sandy Fails has been my most enduring "muse of writing." Her ability to find peace within chaos, humor in every moment and strength to keep moving when everything seems impossible have helped to inspire me to complete this project and to know that, yes, I can write!

Special thanks goes to my numerous partners in botanizing, especially my daughter Brooke, husband Tom and the dozens of people who joined me on guided tours over the years. Many other friends contributed in their own special ways; Erika Perloff, Lisa Acree, Janis Huggins, Kate Watkins, MJ Simmons, Polly Hays, Wendy Brown, Nancy Wicks, Joni Clark, Andrea Heller, Michele Simpson, Paula Lehr, Gay Austin, Carla Bunch, Karen Taylor, Lorraine Pappalau and Stephanie Keeler all helped to fuel this project with their positive spirits and friendship.

There are also innumerable people who helped make this revision happen by merely asking, "When are you going to reprint this book?!?" Bill Kastning, Dottie Machurek and Lee Renfrow lead the pack in this regard. Without their persistent encouragement this book would not be here. Whoever offered old copies of the first edition on E-bay for $99 also deserves a bit of credit!

Huge thanks goes to my partner, Tom Pendley, who provided technical support and foot massages when needed.

Most of all, I cannot express enough gratitude to my parents, Dan and Soozie Darrow, who taught me to love wild things and to my sister, Karie, who has always been there to give encouragement.

Foreword

In 1988 I stepped off a bus from Guatemala for a summer of biology classes in Gothic, Colorado. Having majored in math and physics in college, the main thing I knew about biology was that I'd much rather be an ecologist working in the Rocky Mountains than a physicist drinking coffee in some small cement cubicle in a big city. And while numbers came naturally, it took me many summers to start to get the hang of the wildflowers. I remember sitting in one of Gothic's old cabins scribbling my list of plant names conjuring images of the flowers in my mind's eye, determined to get a handle on the profusion of the area's wildflowers. With such a diversity of wildflower species it certainly seemed a hopeless, though appealing task. And I remember the disparaging remark of one visiting botanist when I asked what family the delicate little purple flower belonged to, "Boraginaceae, but what do you care? You are never going to remember that." Of course his remark made certain that at least one family, with its characteristic of scorpioid flower arrangement, stuck in my head.

Truth be told, after close to twenty summers of scratching my head, looking through herbarium collections and learning to use dichotomous keys, I've finally started to get an eye for the wildflowers. Wildflowers are something that you can devote your life to, as numerous scientists at the Rocky Mountain Biological Laboratory have demonstrated. I have watched many individuals, from small kids to retired engineers to highly trained botanists, learn the local wildflowers. They all have their own way of learning and getting to know the flowers. However, whenever someone new to the area asked me how to get started, I inevitably sent them in search of the previous version of this book.

We are fortunate that Kathy has taken the time to revise and expand her wildflower book, and to put it back into print. Kathy has filled this updated version with more photos, stories, and species descriptions. This book is a wonderful companion for both the experienced botanist and the newcomer looking to have a better understanding of the wild profusion of colors that fill the valleys around Crested Butte. And my advice is not to worry about how much botany there is to learn. Rather, revel in the world of beauty and complexity that awaits you, with this book in hand, of course!

Ian Billick, Director
Rocky Mountain Biological Laboratory

JANNETTE RUNGE

Introduction to Extreme Botanizing

Whether you are practicing extreme botany as an artist, mountain biker, research biologist, photographer or hiker, the landscape surrounding Crested Butte, the official Wildflower Capital of Colorado, is one of the best places for anyone who is looking for a "wildflower rush." With over eight hundred plant species, 6,500 vertical feet of habitat and over 850,000 acres of wilderness to explore, there is clearly some world class botanizing to be experienced in this remote cul-de-sac of Colorado. Even more importantly, access to natural areas is as easy as walking out your front door or hopping on a bike to the nearest trail, whether you want to explore sagebrush valleys or discover wildflowers on the alpine tundra.

Extreme botanizing is about having a passion for wild plants. As with any extreme sport, this may require endurance, risk and special skills. Wildflower enthusiasts are challenged to endure long journeys in search of moments of intense beauty, to take on the risks associated with exploring the outdoors and to hone their skills of observation and inquiry. More importantly, extreme botanizing is about understanding plants as living beings that are vital to our own lives as well as the wild places they inhabit. This book offers a blend of science, ethnobotany, poetry, art and folklore that I hope will inspire botanists of all levels to reach new heights in their knowledge and appreciation of wildflowers.

In general, the month of July is when you'll see the most spectacular wildflower show in the Crested Butte area. But the full season begins in late March when pasque flowers start poking through spring snow, and lasts until October, when the first hard frost of winter snuffs the last wild gentians. Predicting the wildflower season can be difficult, because it all depends on location, precipitation and temperature extremes. Following a winter of slightly above average snowfall, we can expect a slightly above average wildflower display. However, if spring has been relatively dry and warm, lower elevation wildflowers will need some extra summer rain to reach their potential.

Always inquire locally for up-to-date information on trails and wildflowers. Displays change from week to week, depending on frost, winds, and seasonal moisture levels. Keep in mind that what looked magnificent two weeks ago may already be going to seed, especially if the season is dry. The best wildflower displays often follow in the tracks of the most recent snowmelt. Rocky, south-facing slopes low in sagebrush country are always the first to bloom, because that is where the snow disappears first and soils warm fastest. By late July, when snows have melted off the high peaks, the alpine tundra is putting on its best show. Moist, south-facing mountain meadows at lower elevations tend to keep wildflowers the longest, until the first snow falls again in October.

As they say in the world of extreme sports: *"Life is not measured by the number of breaths we take, but by the moments that take our breath away."* My wish for you is that you will count among your life's precious moments those spent among wildflowers. May you experience the awe of wading through a field of lupines; curiosity about the lusty relationship between pollinators and wildflowers; sensual bliss from the sweet, spicy fragrance of little bee balm; enchantment at the intricate beauty of fairy slipper orchids; reverence for each tiny seed and how just one can transform into an entire forest of aspen trees; and astonishment while thinking about how all of this wildness is interconnected.

Go for it!

Crested Butte
Wildflower Capital of Colorado

In 1988 and 1989, Colorado Governor Roy Romer signed resolutions designating the Crested Butte area as the wildflower capital of the state. In 1990, the designation was made official in a resolution passed by the State Senate.

Senate Joint Resolution 90-18

CONCERNING THE DESIGNATION OF THE CRESTED BUTTE AREA AS THE WILDFLOWER CAPITAL OF COLORADO.

WHEREAS, The Crested Butte area lies in the breathtaking Colorado Rocky Mountains and has sheltered perfect conditions for wildflowers of many varieties; and

WHEREAS, Each summer for thousands of years the beautiful mountains and valleys in the Crested Butte area have blossomed with countless species of wildflowers of every shape and hue imaginable to dazzle our senses; and

WHEREAS, The Rocky Mountain Biological Laboratory, which is located in the Crested Butte area, has brought in researchers for over sixty years to study the local populations of the many plant species that reliably bloom each year; and

WHEREAS, Local appreciation of the area's beautiful wildflowers has prompted an annual celebration known as the Crested Butte Wildflower Festival which attracts travelers and wildflower lovers from all over the country; now, therefore,

Be It Resolved by the Senate of the Fifty-seventh General Assembly of the State of Colorado, the House of Representatives concurring herein:

That the Crested Butte area is hereby designated the Wildflower Capital of Colorado.

The Landscape

Geography & Geology

The area featured in this book encompasses the high peaks and river valleys surrounding the town of Crested Butte, in Gunnison County, Colorado. This includes the West Elk and Elk Mountains, plus the major drainages including Coal Creek, Slate River, East River, and their tributaries, collectively known as the Upper East River Valley. Crested Butte sits at an elevation of 8,885 feet, with surrounding elevations ranging from 7,500 feet near the town of Almont to over 14,000 feet at the summit of Castle Peak. Although I have specifically referenced trails and locations within this region, most of the plants discussed in this book are found throughout the southern Rocky Mountains and some even grow wild on other continents.

The geology of the area is very diverse. Volcanoes, uplift, massive erosion, inland seas and glaciers have all played a role in forming the landscape. The spectacular panorama surrounding Crested Butte is composed of igneous, sedimentary and metamorphic features, all shaped by the wind, water, ice and frost that continue to sculpt the mountains and valleys daily. Variation in the type of rock, as well as aspect, drainage, moisture and temperatures, determine which plants can grow where. In fact, plant communities are often classified based on soil types, which are determined largely by geology, above all other factors. Some of the major formations and landmarks are described here.

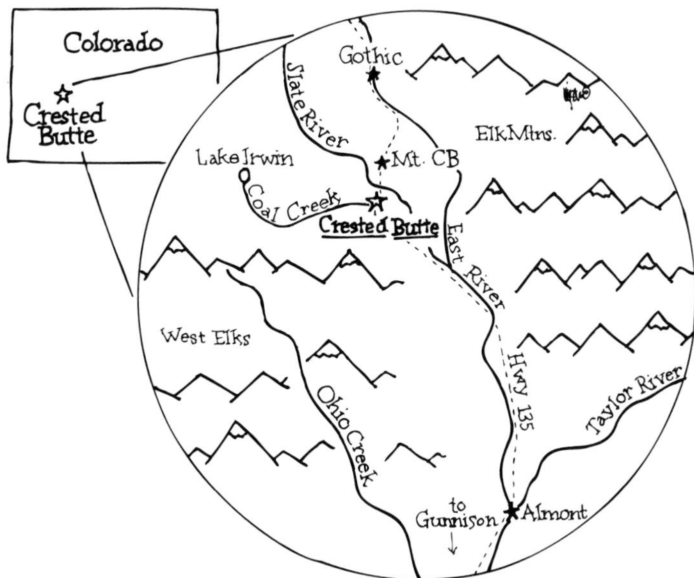

Crested Butte is located in the middle of Colorado's mineral belt, a source of ores and deposits that attracted the first settlers to the region. Although coal was the foundation of wealth for Crested Butte, other ores, including silver, gold, zinc, lead and molybdenum have also been mined in the surrounding mountains. The high quality coal is part of the Mesa Verde Formation, formed when vast swamps and marshes dominated the region around seventy million years ago.

Beneath the Mesa Verde Formation, the valley floors around Crested Butte are composed of Mancos Shale, a soft rock made of silts and mud that filled an inland sea that existed between about 100 million and 70 million years ago. Evidence of this is found in the fossil shells and limestones that can be found near Crested Butte. Over 5,000 feet of shales interbedded with layers of limestone accumulated during the time when the vast Mancos Sea occupied most of Colorado. Although the shales are overlaid by the sandier coal-bearing Mesa Verde Formation, they are well exposed near the bases of nearby mountains. Much of Mt. Crested Butte is built on beds of shale.

Throughout geologic history, inland seas have inundated the region, in between various episodes of mountain uplift and erosion. The shallow marine environments resulted in the formation of several layers of limestone, created by the slow accumulation of shells from ocean creatures ranging from microscopic diatoms to giant clams. Where mountains have been formed from the uplift of these sedimentary rocks, limestone can be found at the summit of high peaks. Many endemic alpine plant species are restricted to limestone-derived soils.

Rising out of the valley are massive granite intrusions known as laccoliths. Gothic Peak, Crested Butte Mountain and Whetstone Mountain are all laccoliths. Laccoliths formed when huge bodies of magma bubbled up from beneath the surface and intruded into the overlying sedimentary layers, forming a mushroom shaped body of rock. Of course, this happened over the course of many millions of years, between 10 and 70 million years ago, combined with erosion of the overlying sediments.

Many of the surrounding peaks are made of sediments eroded from older mountains called the Ancestral Rockies, comprised of two huge mountain ranges, the Ancestral Front Range and the Ancestral Uncompahgre Uplift. Most of the Elk Range, including Castle Peak, Teocalli Mountain, Avery Peak and the Maroon Bells are made of Maroon Formation, a purplish-red conglomerate of cobbles and sandstone that washed out of the ancient mountains that dominated the landscape 300 million years ago. Over 10,000 feet of sediments accumulated as these mountains eroded to plains.

About 70 million years ago, forces within the Earth began to create the existing, or Modern Rocky Mountains. The convergence of two plates of the earth's crust effectively crumpled the surface, pushing the sediments of the Ancestral Rockies up into the new mountain ranges of Colorado. The thrusting, faulting and folding of the Earth's crust that uplifted the Modern Rockies is referred to as the Laramide Orogeny.

The Modern Rockies have already undergone a tremendous amount of erosion, enough to create significant layers of red sediment known as the Wasatch Formation. These layers have been consolidated and uplifted to form newer mountains, which in turn, have been intruded by magma

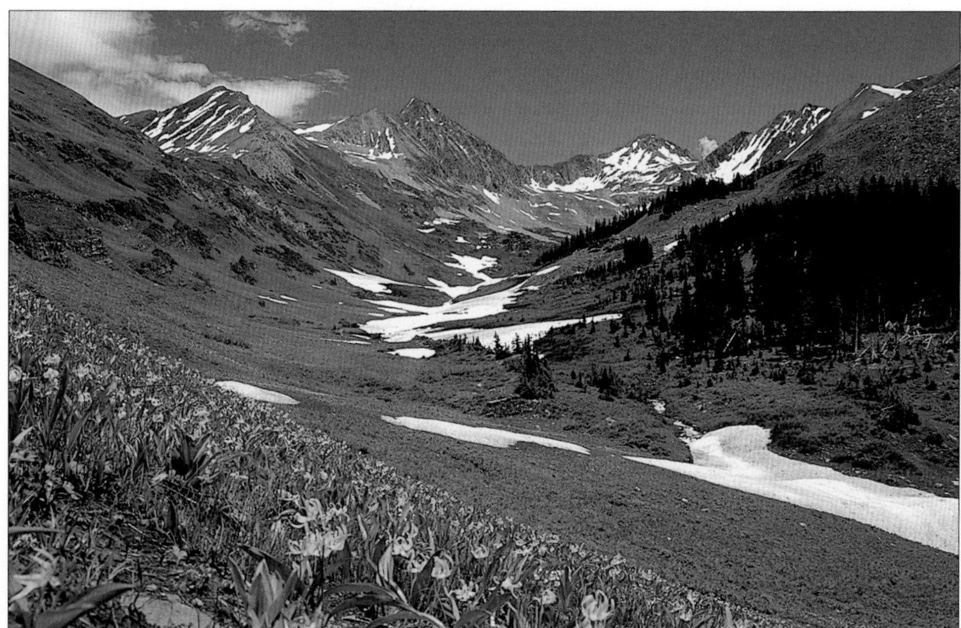

to form extensive mineral-rich stocks, dikes and sills (35-30 million years ago). These intrusives are part of the Colorado Mineral Belt, a band of mountains stretching from Durango to northwest of Denver. This is the origin of the Ruby Range, which includes Ruby Peak and Mount Owen above Lake Irwin, Augusta Mountain, Mineral Point and Cascade Mountain near Paradise Divide, and Mt. Emmons, which rises above the town of Crested Butte.

Further south in the West Elks, remnants of a volcanic episode in the Gunnison Basin have eroded to form cliffs and peaks. The West Elk Breccias are rocks made of ash and volcanic fragments spewed out in massive explosions and mud flows that occurred about 30 million years ago. The epicenter of this activity was near West Elk Peak (13,035 feet), the highest in the range.

Glaciation, wind, frost-heaving and the erosive forces of water continue to sculpt the ever-changing landscape. This is the foundation for the soils and microclimates that create the environment for the growth and evolution of our native plants.

DAVID INOUYE

Climate

Three characteristics sum up the climate in the Crested Butte region: sunny, cold and snowy. Over 300 days of the year you can count on sunshine, but any morning of the year you may wake up to find frost. Local gardeners hope for at least forty-five frost-free days in the growing season. Average high temperatures in the summer are in the upper 70s, while summer nighttime temperatures dip to an average low of 38 degrees. In the winter, the average daytime temperatures are in the 20s, but early mornings at 20 degrees below zero are not uncommon during the darkest months.

The average annual snowfall is 225 inches, or roughly twenty feet of the white stuff. There is some snow on the ground at least seven months of the year and it is not unusual to have a blizzard in July! Snow makes up about two thirds of the annual precipitation, which totals approximately twenty-seven inches on average (roughly one foot of snow equals an inch of rain). The other third comes as late summer rains, typically drenching and cooling the mountains during afternoon thunderstorms.

With this severe climate, it is a wonder any plants (or people!) thrive here at all. This combination of low temperatures and relatively low precipitation defines much of the area as a cold desert. The lingering snowpack is what allows lush vegetation to grow in mountain meadows and forests, as it slowly releases water throughout the short growing season.

Plant Communities

There are seven distinctive plant communities found in the Crested Butte area. Each type is defined by the dominant trees, shrubs or grasses that grow there. However, hundreds of other plant species create the mosaic of life that we know as a forest, meadow or wetland. Within each community there are smaller microhabitats, or areas where certain soil, moisture and light conditions create a more specialized environment that determines which plants and animals live there.

The major plant communities tend to occur in broad bands depending on the elevation. As you ascend from the valley floors, there is a steady decrease in temperatures and increase in precipitation. These changes are also affected by solar exposure, so that the elevation range of major vegetation communities is generally higher on warmer, drier south-facing slopes than on cooler, moister north-facing slopes. East and west-facing slopes are more influenced by prevailing winds and storm patterns. Following are descriptions of the main plant communities you'll encounter as you climb just about any peak in the area:

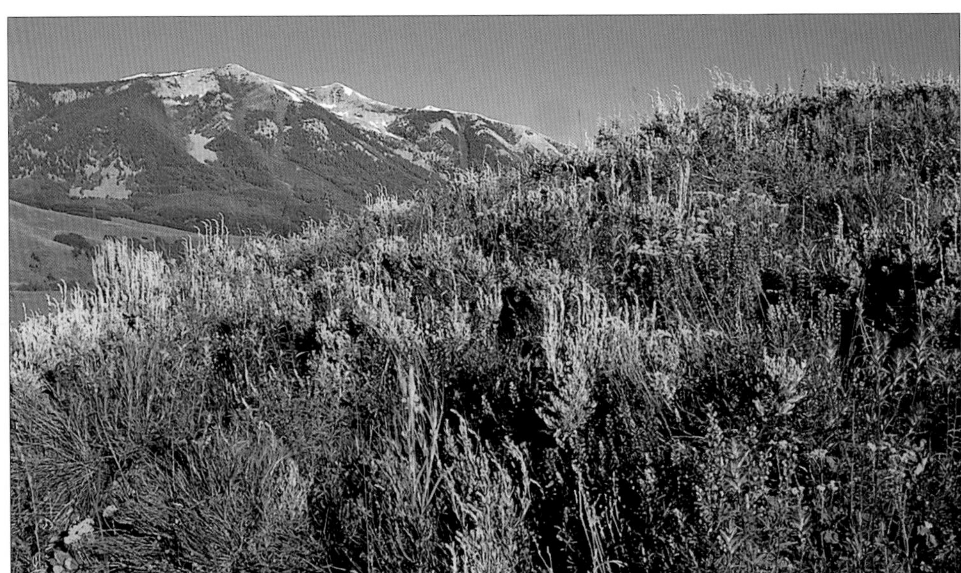

Sagebrush Community

In the Crested Butte area, the diverse sagebrush community is near its upper elevational limits, bordered by aspen and coniferous forests and intermingled with grasslands and wetlands. Over a third of the vegetation between 8,500 and 9,500 feet around Crested Butte is dominated by sagebrush, although much has been converted to hay meadows and housing developments. Patches of sagebrush can be found in sunny, well-drained locations from the valley bottoms to beyond treeline above 12,000 feet.

Many people view these blue-green vales as treeless wastelands, passed by as "nothing but sage" that is of little economic value unless removed and replaced with grasses for grazing or real estate development. To others, sagebrush country evokes the legend and romance of the American West, its rugged pioneers, cowboys and Native Americans. For wildflower enthusiasts, it is a fascinating place to explore. Blended in with the blue-gray softness of sagebrush are over one hundred other species of native plants. If you take time to wander amid the sagebrush around Crested Butte, you will find a flora that is often more colorful than the bordering aspen groves, more diverse than the nearby coniferous forests and a lot easier to get to than the alpine tundra! Some of the plants unique to the sagebrush community are broomrape, crimson paintbrush, dwarf lupine and arrow-leaf balsamroot.

Aspen Forest

Aspen forests of the surrounding Elk and West Elk mountain ranges are some of the most extensive in the Southern Rockies. Aspens have the widest distribution of any native North American tree, with nearly three million acres in Colorado alone. These are also the only deciduous trees that forms vast forests in the high, cold mountains.

Unlike most other parts of Colorado, aspen forests, rather than pinyon-juniper woodlands, blend into the sagebrush community at lower elevations around 7,500 feet. At their upper limits around 10,500 feet, aspens are usually replaced by Englemann spruce and subalpine fir forests. However, they will grow at all elevations below treeline, including moist patches within the sagebrush valleys, on up to 12,000 feet, where extreme winds and year-round frost reduce the vegetation to low-growing tundra species.

Although aspen forests are generally regarded as successional vegetation, destined to be replaced in time by coniferous forest species, much of the aspen in the Crested Butte area are stable communities. A long-term aspen forest has many age classes of aspen trees, from saplings to mature individuals, with only a few shade tolerant trees, such as spruces and firs, in the understory.

Other aspen forests are seral communities, meaning that they are short-lived (one or two centuries) forests being gradually replaced by longer-lived vegetation types. In seral aspen forests, the trees are mostly one or two age classes, with growth of more shade tolerant trees in the understory. Eventually, the aspen saplings are outcompeted by spruces and firs or other conifers, transforming the area to an evergreen forest. Sometimes an aspen stand is continuously changed by disturbance, such as periodic avalanches and rockslides, which maintains an open environment that favors regeneration of aspen clones over the growth of evergreen seedlings.

The understory of an aspen forest is usually very lush with a variety of shrubs such as elderberry, snowberry and shrubby cinquefoil. Early spring wildflowers like glacier lily, spring beauties and violets are rapidly overtaken by the luxuriant growth of other plants such as meadow rue, osha, wild geranium and sweet cicely.

Lodgepole Pine Forest

Like the aspen forest, lodgepole pine communities grow in a broad elevation range, from around 7,500 feet to treeline in the southern Rockies. This is also a seral community, meaning that lodgepole pine is a pioneer species, regenerating quickly in response to disturbance, such as fire, and is gradually replaced by more shade tolerant trees. Lodgepoles dominate on drier, rocky sites whereas aspen are usually found on moist, fertile and more organic soils.

Rapid and prolific growth of lodgepole seedlings following a major disturbance usually results in a thick, shaded forest, leaving little light or nutrients for other plants to flourish. Common juniper, kinnikinnik, myrtle blueberry, and buffalo berry are typical shrubs in the understory of lodgepole pine forests. Other pioneering and drought tolerant plants such as fireweed, arnica and pussytoes are also common.

For more about lodgepole pines, see page 28.

Mountain Meadows

Within and between the aspen and spruce-fir forests are the colorful and diverse mountain meadows. Although the diversity of showy wildflowers in these meadows overwhelms the senses, these areas are dominated by grasses. Tall bunch grasses like nodding bromes, slender wheatgrass, Letterman's needlegrass, Idaho and Thurber fescue are the matrix within which the more colorful wildflowers thrive. Breathtaking displays of aspen sunflower, larkspur, Indian paintbrush, lupines and blue columbines draw wildflower enthusiasts to mountain meadows in midsummer.

Mountain meadows develop where fine sediments have accumulated and where disturbances have prevented the invasion of longer-lived trees. In the absence of disturbance, a meadow may be gradually replaced by an aspen forest, which in turn may be replaced by spruce-fir forest. However, the poor drainage of the soils favors grasses and wildflowers.

JANNETTE RUNGE

Spruce-fir Forest

The most extensive forests from about 9,500 feet to treeline are dominated by deep-green Engelmann spruces and subalpine firs. Both trees can grow to massive proportions, sometimes towering over 120 feet high, up to three feet in diameter and living up to five hundred years. Extensive wildfire or insect infestation can return the ancient forest to the pioneering communities of aspen or lodgepole pine, but otherwise spruces and firs will sustain themselves for centuries, as their seedlings thrive in the moist, shady environment created by other trees.

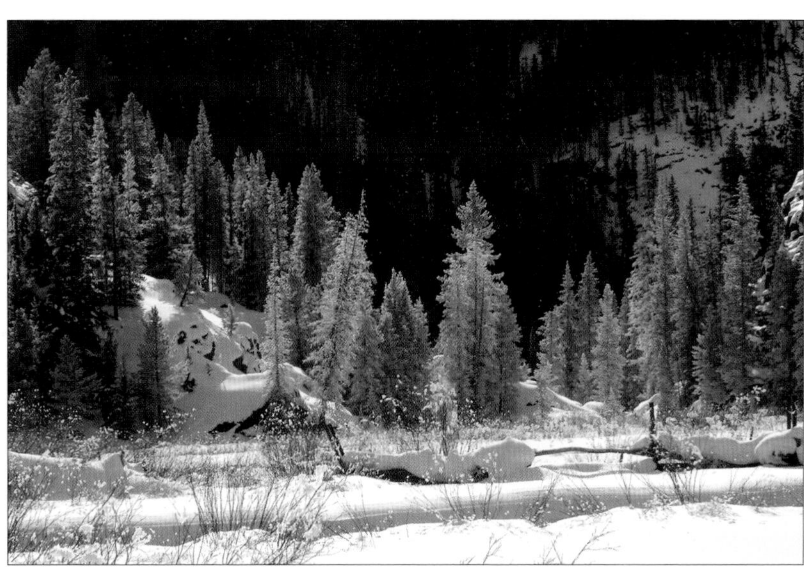

Spruce-fir forests grow at higher elevations, where annual snowfall, and therefore the overall moisture, is usually greater than lower elevation plant communities. Moisture availability is also greater than in alpine regions, where high winds blow away much of the snow. Because the deep snowpack in a spruce-fir forest is protected by shade, it melts off slowly. Deep drifts may remain late into summer, especially on north-facing slopes.

The combination of shade and late snowmelt create an open understory, although it is often strewn with the dead, decaying trunks of trees. These become "nurseries," or nurturing environments for the seeds of other plants to germinate and grow. Gray-green lichens called old man's beard drape the branches of older trees, giving the forest a mysterious air. Shade and moisture also make the spruce-fir forest the most ideal environment for mushrooms to grow. In August and September, look for dozens of colorful and bizarre fungi on the forest floor.

This is the dominant forest at treeline, where trees have been shaped by severe winds into dwarfed and flagged *krummholz*, meaning "twisted timber" in German (see p. 26). As the snow melts around krummholz, felt-like mats of black fungus are visible on the lower branches of these trees. The snow fungus (*Herpotrichia* spp.) contributes to the formation of lopsided *krummholz* stands, infecting and killing the lee side branches where snow accumulates and persists late into summer.

Flagged trees and krummholz at treeline.

Alpine Tundra

The word tundra is derived from a Russian word, meaning "land of no trees." This applies both to arctic and alpine regions where climatic conditions of wind, frost and a short growing season make it impossible for trees to become established. The only "trees" that can be found in this extreme environment, snow willow and arctic willow, are reduced to low growing mats no more than a few inches high. Arctic and alpine plant communities around the world share many of the same species. Over 45% of the alpine plants found in the Rocky Mountains also grow in mountain ranges throughout the northern hemisphere.

An interesting feature of the alpine tundra is that for nearly every plant species you see in the valleys below, there is a miniature to match on the tundra. Sometimes this may be the same species, dwarfed by the more extreme environmental conditions. Others are entirely different species, cousins of lower elevation plants, with special adaptations to the alpine environment. Low growing mats and cushions, insulating hairs, waxy layers on the leaves, protective pigments and extensive root systems are just some of the adaptations common in alpine plant species that enable them to endure a climate of intense wind, sun, frost and drought found at higher elevations.

Although most of the vegetation is below ankle height, the alpine tundra can be one of the most fascinating and diverse environments to explore. Distinctive microhabitats support different types of plants. Some are specialized to grow on rocky slopes and ridges; others thrive in snowmelt basins where the ground may only be snow free for a few brief weeks in the middle of the summer. Colorful meadows flourish where the land is blown clear of snow most of the winter. Some of the plants found only on the tundra are alpine sunflower, moss campion, arctic gentian, sky pilot and alpine spring beauty. Many others, including blue columbines, fireweed, rock jasmine, snowball sandwort and wallflower, can be found in a wide range of habitats and elevations, from sagebrush to tundra.

Wetlands and Riparian Communities

Wetlands and riparian areas form distinct plant communities within each of the broader vegetation types. Marshes and fens are areas where water remains at or near the surface all or most of the year; the main difference between these two types of wetlands is that marshes have mineral soils and fens have organic soil accumulation. Although the soils in a wetland may appear to be dry, they are saturated just below the surface. Riparian communities are wetlands that occur along rivers, streams, ponds and lakes.

Wetland and riparian communities are the most biologically diverse and productive plant communities. A healthy wetland community will have up to two or three times the number of plant species found in adjacent forests, meadows or shrublands. In turn, the abundance of wildlife is also greatest here, from mud-loving insects, to nesting birds, to beavers and fish that live in the water. Over 90% of wildlife species use wetlands at some point in their life cycle. Wetlands also function to cleanse and store the water that supports the flora and fauna.

Unfortunately, because wetlands comprise only about 3% of the land in Colorado and water is a coveted resource in the semi-arid west, these habitats are also the most threatened and abused. Draining and filling for agriculture and development, overuse from grazing and recreation, and fragmentation of water systems by subdivision of the land, has gradually degraded wetlands throughout the state. Because of this, wetlands are the only habitat types regulated by government agencies and laws, including the Army Corp of Engineers, the Environmental Protection Agency and the Clean Water Act.

Due to the abundance of public land around Crested Butte, as well as the protection by private citizen groups such as the Crested Butte Land Trust, this region's wetlands and riparian systems are relatively intact and healthy. In fact, the Slate River Wetlands, north of the town of Crested Butte, have been identified as one of the highest quality riparian systems in Colorado.

Willows, sedges, rushes and grasses dominate the wetland vegetation in marshy areas, mingled with wildflowers such as elephantella, bog orchids, iris, blue-eyed grass, marsh marigolds and cow parsnip. Along streams and rivers, many species of shrubs and trees are common, including shrubby cinquefoil, elderberry, gooseberry, bog birch, alder and cottonwood. In subalpine and alpine wetlands, rivulets are lined with Parry's primrose, brookcress, monkeyflowers and shooting stars.

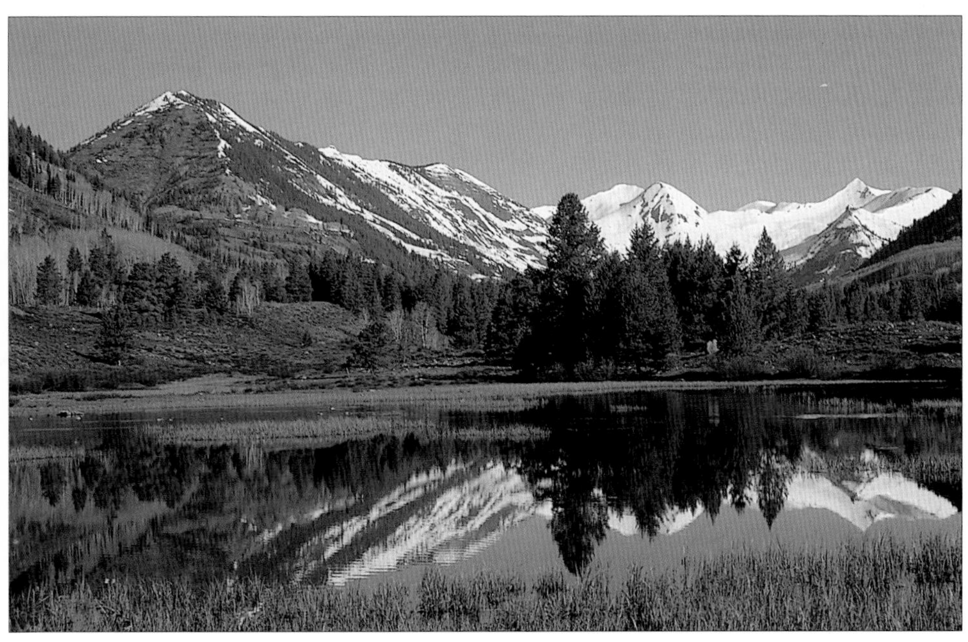

Plants and the Law

Picking Posies

People often ask whether it is illegal to pick wildflowers on public lands, especially in designated wilderness. The question reminds me of a Far Side cartoon in which an over-sized daisy presents a bouquet of human babies as a gift to his lover. I tend to return the legal question with a philosophical one: Should we pick wildflowers? Response to this depends on personal values and particular circumstances.

However, the legal question has an uncomplicated answer. It is not illegal, although it is strongly discouraged, to pick flowers in the National Forest or wilderness areas. Collection of a whole plant or tree is illegal though, unless a special permit has been issued, such as for Christmas trees, for research or for commercial purposes. To collect without a permit is considered poaching, just as hunting is without a license.

The National Park Service has a different policy. It is illegal to collect, pick or willfully damage any native plant in a National Park or Monument. For instance, a ranger could issue a warning or fine for wildflower picking at Black Canyon of the Gunnison National Park. The Colorado blue columbine, the state flower, is also legally protected wherever it grows on public lands, though it is not considered rare.

Threatened, endangered and sensitive species are protected from any kind of collection on public lands, including harvesting seeds or picking flowers, through the Endangered Species Act. One problem with this is that few people know which plants are legally protected. Endangered plants may be very abundant where populations do exist, so sheer numbers of flowers is not necessarily a good indication of the rarity of a species. A bigger problem with the Endangered Species Act is that it does not protect plants on private lands, as it does with animals. This means that unless landowners are very conscientious, there is no legal recourse for protection of rare plants should a private landowner see fit to destroy them.

Beyond the legal ramifications, however, I believe it is more important to honor the life of every native plant. Picking wildflowers leaves less forage for wildlife and for other people to enjoy. Most importantly, picking flowers ends an opportunity for that plant to produce seeds. When we remember that the biological purpose of flowers is to carry life into a new generation, the act of picking them becomes more profound.

How To Pick A Wildflower

There are many ways you can pick a wildflower.
You can lie on your stomach
in a meadow
and watch it grow.
You can stare at it
through a magnifying glass
to better discern each leaf.
You can paint it,
sketch it, etch it
in whole, or just in bloom.
You can take its picture then blow the picture up
larger, Larger, LARGER
and hang it on the wall.
Or you can pinch the stem between your fingers,
separate it from the Earth
and kill it.

– Carolyn Richter

Rare Plant Protection

Over 10%, or over three hundred species, of Colorado's native flora are at risk, due mostly to habitat loss and degradation from human activities and development. Two dozen plant species are listed as endangered, threatened, rare or sensitive in Gunnison County. Many of these are alpine species that have very specific habitat requirements and therefore have extremely small populations. Others are rare because of their popularity with plant collectors.

Most people are aware of the accelerated loss of tropical rainforests and the endangerment of wildlife species such as tigers, whales and giant pandas, i.e. the "charismatic megafauna." These are topics for entire curricula in public schools, mass media reports and stamp collections. There is far less education and awareness of what goes on in our own backyards with regard to habitat degradation and native species protection. When it comes to plants, the "enigmatic microflora," most people would be hard pressed to name one species that is rare or endangered, even though there are over five hundred plants on the U.S. Threatened and Endangered Species list.

Colorado Buckwheat, *Eriogonum coloradense*

For more information on this rare plant, see page 147.

The individual species, however small, in every ecosystem are equally important whether they play a role in the colorful, lush drama of the Amazon or in a remote mountain wetland in Colorado. You can do your part by learning about rare native species and their habitats near where you live and in the places you visit, and by finding out how you can to help ensure their continued survival. In this book, I do not pay special attention to rare plants of the region. Two excellent books have been published on the rare plants of Colorado by the Colorado Natural Heritage Program and The Colorado Native Plant Society. To purchase the *Colorado Rare Plant Field Guide*, contact the Colorado Natural Heritage Program. The second edition of *Rare Plants of Colorado* is available at local bookstores or through the Colorado Native Plant Society. For more information, visit their respective websites at www.cnhp.colostate.edu and www.conps.org.

"When we try to pick out anything by itself, we find it hitched to everything else in the Universe."

– John Muir

The Weed Management Act

A weed is generally defined as any plant that is growing where we don't want it to. In the context of a natural ecosystem, a weed in North America is any non-native species that was introduced after European settlement. Noxious weeds are those that aggressively reproduce and take over the land in the absence of their natural predators and diseases. Invasive introduced species present a threat to native plants and habitats, degrade agricultural land, decrease the quality and quantity of wildlife habitat, and negatively impact aesthetic and recreational values of natural areas.

Because of the threat to agriculture, wildlife, native vegetation and general ecosystem health, federal, state and county Weed Management Acts have been passed. Funding for education and management is provided to assist agencies and private landowners in eradicating and preventing noxious weed invasions.

One thing all of these plants have in common is that they are closely associated with human activities. The seeds of many were carefully collected and nurtured so that European settlers would have familiar flowers as well as important medicinal and edible plants with them when they migrated to North America. Others have been distributed unwittingly, traveling in soil used as ballast on ships, hitching onto animals, including humans, and then continuing their ride via cart or train. Every time a plow or bulldozer is laid to the earth, brand new habitat is created for these opportunistic species. Each trail, road and pasture provides a corridor and open ground for weeds to expand their colonization.

Among the enemies are some beautiful and even very useful plants; dame's rocket, butter-and-eggs, ox-eye daisy and tansy are a few of the plants on the Colorado State and Gunnison County noxious weed hit lists. Others considered obnoxious rather than noxious include dutch clover, dandelion and scentless chamomile. Altogether there are nearly seventy noxious weeds listed in Colorado and over thirty-five listed in Gunnison County.

Landowners and managers are required by law to minimize disturbance to native vegetation, re-seed with native or non-invasive species and remove targeted noxious weed species from their land under the various Weed Management Acts. To learn more about what noxious weeds might occur near you and what you can do to prevent them from spreading, call your local Weed Commission. For Colorado, visit the state website for noxious weed management at www.ag.state.co.us/CSD/weeds.

Ox-eye Daisy
For more information see page 44.

Dame's Rocket
For more information see page 74.

Using This Book

Organization

Wildflower guides are organized in many different ways: by flower color, alphabetically by common name, by habitat type, by seasonal appearance and by plant family. Each of these organizational schemes has its pitfalls and attractions. I chose to organize by plant family for a variety of reasons. Number one, learning about plant families leads to an understanding of plant geography and evolution and therefore, how life all over the planet is connected. This is also the easiest way to find out more about other plants you discover when you travel to other areas, whether it is Colorado, Georgia, Costa Rica or Europe.

Nearly eighty plant families are found in the Crested Butte area and over eight hundred species recognized. Of these, 48 families and 242 species are presented in photos in Wild About Wildflowers. Because all species could not be included, I developed a rating system based on three criteria: 1) how common the plant is, 2) how showy or noticeable the plant is and 3) whether the plant had something of special interest about it ecologically, biologically, medicinally or otherwise.

The plants in this book are organized in alphabetical order by the Latin names, first by plant family and within each family by species. Color bars are used to spotlight each family and species within each family group. These colors are not indicators of flower color, but an organizational tool to help users recognize where a new family begins, and the species described within each family group. The color bars rotate through seven different hues as you move through the families.

To help locate plants there are three different indices you can use in the back of the book.

Color Thumbnails: On pages 206-213, small photos of flowers and cones have been organized roughly by color, with a reference to the page where you will find more information about that plant.

Plant Family Key: On pages 214-216 there is a simple taxonomic key to plant families in this book.

Family and Species Index: Pages 217-221 list all the main common and Latin names of families and species in the book in alphabetical order.

Latin Lingo, Taxonomic Terms and Common Names

For most people, except young children interested in dinosaurs, the scientific names of plants and animals can seem intimidating and incomprehensible. We forget that familiar words like *Brontosaurus* and *Chrysanthemum* are scientific names. For many reasons, I encourage readers to learn the scientific as well as common names of plants. By learning both you will access a wealth of information including myths and legends associated with plants, habitat information, medicinal and edible uses, expedition history and basic plant characteristics. For each family and species discussed in this book, I have attempted to decipher both scientific and common terms.

Many different species may have the same common name. For example, "buttercups" refers to over 400 species in the genus *Ranunculus.* By contrast, a scientific name, such as *Ranunculus glaberrimus*, applies to only one species. The scientific name gives us a common language with which to speak about plants. This is important if we want to understand and discuss evolutionary relationships, plant ecology and plant geography. Many common names may also be given for one species, which further complicates matters if people are trying to communicate about the same plant. This can be critical, for instance, if we want to understand herbal medicine, where identifying, gathering and using a certain species could have very significant effects if not done correctly.

Taxonomy is a system of classification based on evolutionary relationships. In biology, every living thing is classified first to the broader group of organisms, or Kingdom, to which it belongs. This book features the Plant Kingdom. At the other end of the spectrum, each organism is recognized as a certain species. The name given for a species consists of a genus and specific epithet. The genus (plural is genera), or first name, is generally a noun, while the specific epithet, or second name, is an adjective. For example, the Latin name for marsh buttercup is *Ranunculus alismifolius,* meaning "plant that grows where frogs live, with long slender leaves."

Within this hierarchical system, related species are part of a larger grouping known as a genus and closely related genera are grouped into families. The family is a larger group that is mostly based on similarities in reproductive structures, i.e. flowers and fruits. I have chosen not to go into great detail to describe the anatomy and morphology that unites a family, genus or species. As you begin to recognize various species of plants and understand their "gestalt," or suite of characters, the natural groupings that taxonomists recognize will become apparent.

Scientists attempt to assign only one "correct" scientific name to each plant species, but continual changes in our understanding of plant relationships, based on new technologies in genetics or reviews of botanical literature, often lead to a long list of names being associated with a single species. The International Congress of Botanical Nomenclature (ICBN) has established certain rules and principles for naming plant species. Botanists often differ in their approach to taxonomy, sometimes classifying each other as "lumpers" (those who tend to group plants together) and "splitters" (those who tend to recognize small differences as separate taxonomic groupings). Therefore, the literature is not always consistent, because not all experts agree. However, scientific names are still much more standardized than common names.

The science of taxonomy is a living discipline, in which our concept of evolutionary relationships between living things is continuously changing and becoming better understood. I have used Hartman and Nelson's *Checklist of the Vascular Plants of Colorado* (2001) as the taxonomic standard for this book. William Weber's *Colorado Flora: Western Slope* (2001) is also widely recognized by botanical enthusiasts in the state; Latin names that differ from Hartman and Nelson are included in parentheses for each species. Where names of families or genera have been revised, I have included alternative names that are commonly used. Readers who are interested in understanding the taxonomy of local flora more thoroughly are encouraged to consult Weber's *Colorado Flora* plus the companion text, *Catalog of Colorado Flora.*

Edible and Medicinal Plants

Although edible and medicinal uses of native plants are described for many species in this book, the details of identification and preparation are not. Positive identification of plants is essential if you are planning to eat them or use them for medicine. For more specifics on medicinal preparation and uses, I recommend Michael Moore's book, *Medicinal Plants of the Mountain West*. The most comprehensive book on edible plants for the Rocky Mountain region is H.D. Harrington's *Edible Native Plants of the Rocky Mountains*. For accurate identification of species, Weber's *Colorado Flora* is the most thorough. The author and publisher assume no responsibility for the effects of edible and medical uses of plants described in this book.

Ferns and Fern Allies

Pteridophyta

Over 12,000 species of ferns and other spore-producing relatives, such as horsetails, quillworts, club-mosses, spike-mosses and adder's tongues, grow in all types of environments around the world. These plants are most diverse in warm, humid environments such as rainforests and deciduous forests. In the cold, dry climate of the southern Rocky Mountains, there are a dozen or so ferns and fern allies.

Without going into details of the reproductive cycle and anatomy of these primitive plants, it is interesting to note the millions of spores produced by a single individual of any of these species. On the backs of the leaves of a lady fern for instance, there are little brown dots called sori, or fruit dots. In Greek, sorus means "heaps," and sori is the plural of sorus. Here on the fern are heaps of tiny one-celled spores. When fortunate enough to land in the proper soil and moisture conditions, a spore will grow into a little heart-shaped plant called a prothallus, which then grows into a new fern. None of these plants produce true flowers, so are recognized primarily by the shapes of their leaves and patterns of sori.

Fearn is an Old English word for wing or feather. Likewise, the scientific name is derived from the Greek word *pteron*, also meaning feather. Both describe the shape and feel of many fern leaves, which are also known as fronds.

Giant Lady Fern *Athyrium alpestre (A. distentifolium)*

These lush, robust ferns grow up to a meter high, forming huge clumps on rocky soils near treeline. The generic name, *Athyrium*, means "shield-less," referring to the fact that some species lack the covering of the sori found on many ferns, also known as an *indusium* in botanical lingo. *Alpestre* means "of the mountains." This species is alternatively known as *A. distentifolium* which describes how huge or "distended" the leaves become. One place you can easily find these is in the Poverty Gulch drainage on the way up to Daisy Pass (see page 202 for trail description).

Rock Brake *Cryptogramma acrostichoides*

Look for rock brake ferns tucked among boulders and cliffs at high elevations. One kind of frond looks leafy, the other kind looks spiky. The spiky one is the fertile frond, with sori wrapped up inside the curled leaflets. The leafy fronds photosynthesize but produce no spores. *Cryptogramma* means "hidden line," describing how the spores are curled inside the leaf edges. The species name translates to "hairy-lipped," referring to the fringed tips of the fronds. Like many fern species, rock brake is common throughout the world, as spores are easily distributed by wind and water and can endure environmental extremes.

Horsetail *Equisetum arvense*

Horsetails are common around the world and are miniature evolutionary remnants of what used to be dominant life forms in Carboniferous forests, as pictured in dinosaur dioramas. The great coalbeds upon which the town of Crested Butte was founded were once towering horsetails, along with other ancient species of oversized fern allies. Today there are still tree-like species in Amazonia that grow to twenty feet tall. This species rarely grows to more than two feet high and is common along forest streams, marshes, irrigation ditches and wet fields.

The Latin name, *Equisetum arvense,* translates directly to "horsetail of the field," describing the appearance of the sterile shoots of this globally common species, which has whorls of leaves growing from each joint on the stem. The fertile shoots look very different, lacking leaves or chlorophyll. They appear as pinkish or yellow stalks with a cone-like spore-producing tip.

Scouring rush is another common name for these plants, which were used by pioneers to scour pots and pans. The whole plant has a lot of silica in it, which you can feel if you rub a stem against your fingernail like an emery board. This quality has benefitted resourceful cabinet makers, who use horsetails as a very fine grade polisher. Horsetail is also sold as a medicinal herb to treat urinary tract problems, since it is a mild diuretic.

As a child, I remember spending afternoons pulling apart the hollow, jointed stems of horsetail and putting them back together like a long puzzle. The pieces made good little straws or whistles as well, inspiring the folk name "paddock pipes."

In addition to the field horsetail pictured here, there are three other species of *Equisetum* found in the area, all of which lack the branched sterile stems and bear spore-bearing strobuli at the tip of unbranched green stems.

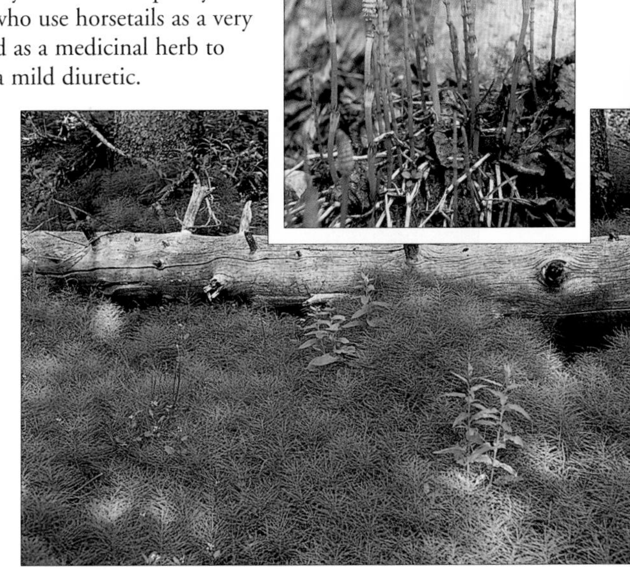

Cone-bearing Plants

Gymnosperms

Long before true flowers evolved, the first true seeds were born on cones, rather than within fruits. Plants bearing cones with "naked seeds", or Gymnosperms, were part of the dominant vegetation between 250 million and 200 million years ago, along with Ferns and their allies, and thus formed the forests that dinosaurs roamed. Today, the most well-known cone-bearing plants are the "evergreens", or pines, spruces and firs, that make up some of the world's most extensive forests. Other gymnosperm families in Colorado include Mormon Tea (Ephedraceae), a common shrub in desert regions of North America, and the Junipers (Cupressaceae), a group of shrubs and trees with berry-like cones. Ginkgos, cycads and yews are common gymnosperms native to other parts of the world.

Pine Family Pinaceae

In the wintertime, conifers stand out as the dominant trees in the mountain landscape. Most people call them all "pine trees," but in reality, there are ten different conifer species in the Crested Butte area, including spruces and firs, as well as pines. An easy way to begin telling them apart is by feeling their needles. The *spruces* have *sharp, square* needles (in cross-section). They are not cuddly. The needles can be rolled between your thumb and finger. The *firs* have *flat, friendly* needles. If you hug a fir branch, it feels soft. The flat needles do not roll. The *pines* almost always have *plural* needles, i.e. more than one needle attached at one point, in bundles. Some have five, some three, some two. If you smooth them all together you can see that the whole bundle forms a cylinder.

The thick, narrow leaves of conifers are adaptations to the wintry climates where these trees dominate. Small surface areas and a waxy coating reduce water loss in cold, windy environments. The conical shape and flexible branches of these trees, in combination with narrow needles, make them able to handle and shed huge snow loads as well as withstand intense winds that would destroy trees with broad leaves and stiff branches.

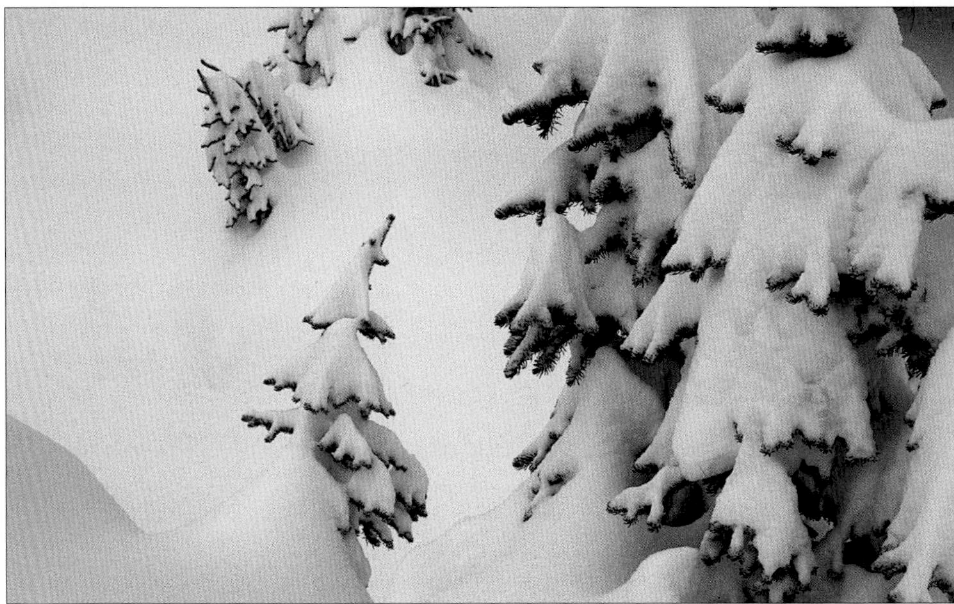

Subalpine Fir *Abies bifolia (A. lasiocarpa)*

The subalpine fir is the only true fir in the Crested Butte area. Besides having flat, soft needles in comparison to the sharp needles of spruce, this tree can be distinguished from spruces by the smooth, silvery bark. Spruce bark is rough and brown-colored.

You can also spot a subalpine fir at a distance by looking for the cones, which point up instead of down from where they are attached to the branches. Because the scales of the cone fall away rather than remaining attached, as on pines and spruces, it is rare to find an intact fir cone on the ground unless it has been dropped by a squirrel when it is still green. At the base of large fir trees and other conifers there are often huge piles of cone scales created by squirrels who feast on the seeds and keep stashes buried for later use. These middens become perfect environments for the growth of fungi, another important item in the squirrel's diet.

For more on spruces and firs, see page 15.

Engelmann Spruce *Picea engelmannii*
Blue Spruce *Picea pungens*

The most common conifers in the high mountains is Engelmann spruce. In mountain towns, the blue spruce is popular as a landscaping tree and is native to the area. The easiest way to tell these trees apart is to look at the cones. Blue spruce cones are nearly twice the size of Engelmann spruce cones, usually three to four inches long versus two to three inches long. Engelmann spruce forms vast forests in association with subalpine fir from about 9,000 feet elevation to treeline. Blue spruce is restricted to moist habitats, and is most common along rivers and streams.

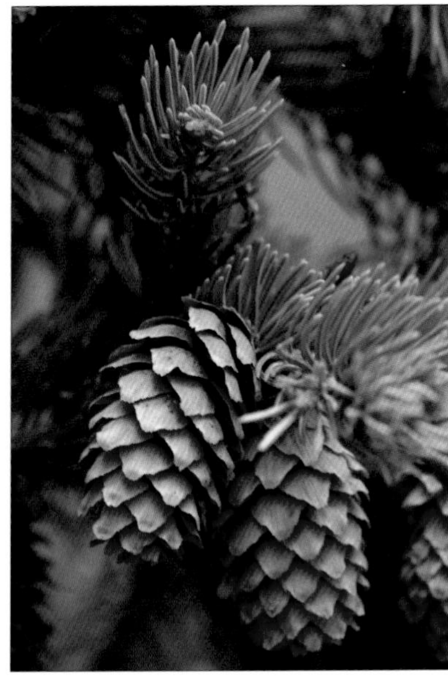

All conifers are wind pollinated. In spruces, the seed-producing cones are usually clustered at the tops of the trees, while the smaller, pollen-producing cones are found on lower branches. This helps to ensure cross-breeding, as pollen will float down-slope to a different tree rather than fertilizing its own cones. This is a common arrangement in firs as well. In the early summer, notice the yellow plume of pollen in the air after brushing against a branch.

Spruces are susceptible to infestations of aphids that lay eggs in the tips of branches, stimulating the growth of cone-like galls. The genus, *Picea*, is derived from the Latin word *pix*, meaning "pitch" or "sap,"which oozes from the damaged bark of these and other conifers. George Engelmann was one of Colorado's 19th century botanists and founder of the Missouri Botanical Garden, a center for international botanical research and one of the world's largest plant collections. *Pungens* means "sharp" or "prickly," which is very true of the sharp, square blue spruce needles.

Lodgepole Pine *Pinus contorta*

Lodgepole pines are well known as "fire trees," because the heat of forest fires is one way that the woody cones can be opened to release the seeds for a new generation. Fire also prepares the soil for the seedlings and helps to create the open, sunny environment in which lodgepole seedlings grow best. This reproductive strategy results in large, thick, even-aged stands of lodgepoles, which have a reputation for being "sterile" forests, leaving little light for other plants to thrive. However, as the forest ages, trees thin out to create a more open forest which subsequently becomes fertile ground for many other plants as well as late successional spruces and firs. Lodgepoles dominate where the ground is drier, particularly on high elevation south-facing slopes. You can distinguish lodgepole from spruce-fir forests at a distance by their color; lodgepoles are a paler, olive-green, while spruce-fir forests are a darker green.

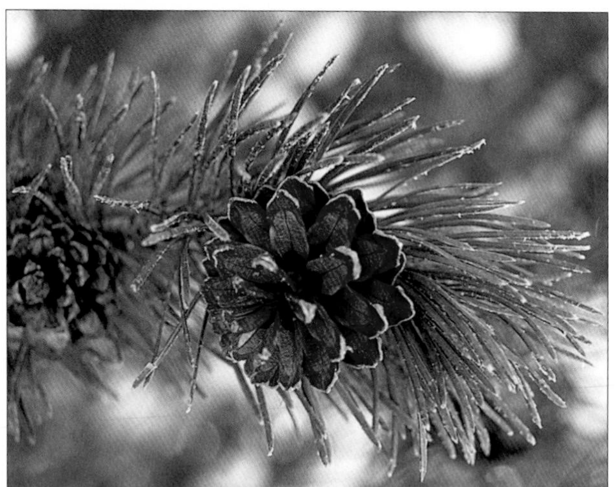

The twisted or contorted needles come in bundles of two and grow all around the loose branches, looking like huge bottlebrushes. Lodgepoles, like other pines, are either predominantly male or female. Clusters of small, pollen-producing cones (shown below) are found at the ends of branches on male trees. Woody, lemon-sized, seed-producing cones (shown left) are found all over the female trees.

The seed-bearing cones are often serotinous, meaning that they are sealed with pitch and open in response to the heat of fire. Age will also cause them to open if a fire doesn't sweep the area after a number of years. Therefore, younger closed cones can be found on some trees along with many open cones. The old, gray cones will continue to cling to a branch long after the branch or tree has died.

The tall, straight trunks of lodgepoles made them a preferred choice as the framework for tepees and for telephone poles. Three other pines grow in the area, but are far less common than the lodgepole: bristlecone pine, limber pine and ponderosa pine. Pinyon pine (*P. edulis*) is conspicuously absent in the Gunnison Basin, apparently because the environment is too cold for their seedlings to become established. A few small stands of pinyon pine can be found in the southeastern part of the basin, probably started from seeds left in caches by Clark's nutcrackers (see page 29). However, drop down any pass out of the Gunnison Basin and you will be in pinyon territory.

Ponderosa Pine *Pinus ponderosa*

Ponderosa pines are common in the American West. Three varieties can be found throughout their range, from Nebraska to California and from British Columbia to northern Mexico. In the southern Rockies, we have *Pinus ponderosa* var. *scopulorum*, the smallest of the three, growing to 150 feet high and three feet in diameter in favorable locations. South of Gunnison there are towering stands of ponderosas, sifting warm sunlight through their long needles and emanating the sweet smell of vanilla or butterscotch from their thick puzzle-like bark. In the Almont Triangle, small groves of ponderosa are scattered along the rocky ridges, marking the upper elevational and northern limits of these trees in the East River valley.

Just north of Almont and across from Eagle Landing, where bald eagles gather to feast on salmon each fall, one distinctive ponderosa pine stands as a sentinel to the valley. This ponderosa pine is quite old for its size, owing to the particularly cold and exposed environment it sunk its roots into. According to estimates from a tree core, this tree has lived for over 250 years. From the looks of the lichen-encrusted shards of crockery, rusted tin cans, blue bottles and old buckets that littered the base of this tree prior to the realignment of Highway 135 in the 1990s, this tree has served as a landmark and campsite for travelers since the late 1800s, when Europeans first discovered the wealth and beauty of this valley.

Nutcrackers

Clark's nutcracker is a common mountain bird closely related to ravens and magpies. Nutcrackers are easily mistaken for woodpeckers, because they have long, pointed black beaks and sometimes use these as tools to peck at tree trunks and extract insects from beneath bark. They are known to store enormous amounts of pine nuts in the ground and are able to carry about a hundred seeds at a time in a special food pouch under their tongue. Observation of nutcrackers has shown that one individual may store up to 35,000 seeds per year, and will retrieve around 70% of their caches through the winter season. Nutcracker stashes are recognized as an important means of seed dispersal for many species of pine trees.

Like the lodgepole pine, ponderosas are a classic "fire tree," adapted to germinate and grow in open, sunny soils. The layer of long, dry needles on the forest floor are a perfect tinder for fire to smolder through the understory of a ponderosa forest. A healthy ponderosa grove, or "park", is very open, with plenty of space between the trees. Thick, corky bark protects the mature trees from fire like a suit of armor, leaving trees only lightly scorched, rather than torched, after a fire. They are also self pruning, meaning that the lower branches drop off as they grow older, leaving healthy branches out of reach of a natural ground fire.

Douglas-fir *Pseudotsuga menziesii*

The Douglas-fir is not a true fir at all but does have soft, flat needles similar to firs. The Latin name, *Pseudotsuga*, means "pseudo-hemlock," a tree that it resembles but from which it is genetically distinct. The cones are easy to identify, having three-pronged bracts sticking out between the scales. One story about the Douglas-fir cones explains how those bracts were created. Once upon a time. there was a huge forest fire. All the animals ran to safety, but the tiny mice could not run fast enough, so they found refuge in the Douglas-fir cones. The cones snapped shut, trapping the mice. Ever since, the tails and feet of the mice can be seen dangling out of the cones!

In the mist-shrouded forests of the Pacific Northwest, the graceful "Doug" is second only to the giant sequoia in size and are adapted to cool, humid north-facing aspects. In the southern Rockies, Douglas-firs are smaller in stature and more drought resistant than those of the northwest. The Rocky Mountain variety is most common in moist ravines, shaded canyons and on cooler north-facing slopes. They are found at relatively low elevations between 6,000 and 9,500 feet and are often mingled with other conifers.

Archibald Menzies was a Scottish naturalist, explorer and physician who was one of the first Europeans to visit the Pacific Northwest in the late 1700s when Douglas-firs were first noted. These trees were also named after a young friend of Menzies, David Douglas. Both may have learned that a handful of fresh Douglas-fir needles boiled in a pot of water makes a delicious, vitamin C-rich tea!

Mistletoe

Leafy mistletoes (*Phoradendron* spp.) traditionally used at Christmas-time are not common in Colorado, but there are many species of dwarf mistletoe, which are parasites of coniferous trees. Dwarf mistletoes (*Arceuthobium* spp.) are mostly leafless, with yellowish-green twigs. They are very host-specific, meaning that each species is found only on a certain species of conifer. Mistletoes are also flowering plants, belonging to the Mistletoe Family, or Viscaceae, which means "sticky."

Unlike the leafy mistletoe, which spread their seed mostly via animal and bird carriers, dwarf mistletoes have the remarkable ability to shoot their seeds like little bullets onto neighboring trees. Seeds have been clocked at ninety feet per second for distances up to fifty feet! The seeds are covered with a sticky glue-like substance that easily adheres to anything they land on. If they land on a twig, they soon germinate and grow roots into the host tree. The parasite causes abnormal growths of the tree called "witch's broom." Mistletoe infections weaken and can eventually kill a tree.

Although these plants have a bad reputation in the timber industry for causing deformities in trees, mistletoe is a native plant and a natural part of the ecosystem. Some research has shown that the presence of mistletoe in a forest correlates with an increase of diversity and abundance of birds. Death of trees by mistletoe creates openings in the forest, thereby providing greater habitat diversity. Mistletoe-infected trees are generally more susceptible to insects, providing more food for birds.

Flowering Plants

Angiosperms

The global diversity of flowering plants is huge, with over 400,000 species recognized, dwarfing that of the gymnosperms (750), ferns (12,000), and mosses (30,000). Their emergence during the Cretaceous period between 145-65 million years ago is linked with the boom in the diversity of mammals and insects that occurred around the same time. The development of the enclosed seed, or fruit, has proven to be a superior strategy for reproduction and survival. Today, we know that human life could not exist without flowering plants, which provide us with food, shelter, fibers and medicines, as well as beauty.

Agave Family Agavaceae

The Agave Family is most prominent in the southwestern deserts of the U.S. and other arid regions around the world. The leaves are usually long, stiff and pointed, forming large rosettes that may grow into a tree-like form. The flowers resemble lilies (see p. 132), with six succulent petals and produce hard-shelled seedpods. The family is of economic importance for the long, strong fibers in the leaves, which are used by many cultures to make cloth and rope, such as sisal. Tequila is the fermented juice of the blue agave, *Agave tequilana*, and other species native to Mexico, where the family is most diverse.

Yucca *Yucca harrimaniae*

This slender-leaved yucca is a reminder that the Gunnison Basin is an arid region, and is a characteristic plant of the Great Basin Desert, which extends west into Utah and Nevada. Yuccas provide a classic story of coevolution and symbiosis, since the plant and its pollinator, a tiny white moth, are dependent on one another for reproduction. The moth, *Tegeticula yuccasella*, lays its eggs in the flower and in the process, also stuffs a ball of pollen down the center of the stigma. This is the only way that the flowers can be successfully pollinated. Ultimately, plenty of seeds mature, providing enough for the plant to reproduce, as well as some for the moth larvae to eat before boring a hole through the seedpod and escaping to continue the cycle.

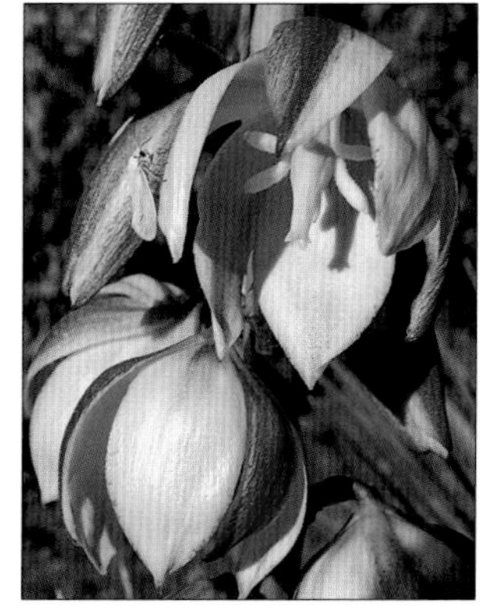

Yucca is also known as Spanish bayonet, because of its sharp-pointed leaves, which can be used as sewing needles. The fibers of the leaves are useful for making twine, the flowers and green seedpods are edible, and the roots can be processed to use as soap, making for an ethnobotanical goldmine that still remains important to indigenous peoples today.

Yucca grows abundantly in the Almont area and further south in the Gunnison Basin where it blooms most abundantly in June.

Parsley Family APIACEAE

One of the most aromatic families of plants is the Parsley or Umbel Family, which is the source of many of our favorite culinary foods and herbs, including carrots, parsnips, caraway, fennel, dill, cilantro and cumin. Ginseng is also closely related and sometimes included in this family. Because of their distinctive aromas, one way to help identify members of this family is to roll a leaf between your palms and inhale its scent.

The meadows and forests of the Rocky Mountains are full of umbels, all easily recognized by their umbrella-shaped flower arrangement and hollow stems. Plants in this family have many tiny flowers arranged together in a sphere or flat disc, creating a larger display to attract pollinators.

Many of these plants are important medicinals and delectable edibles, but **extreme caution is advised in tasting any of these plants, since the umbels also include some of the most toxic members of the Plant Kingdom.** Most ominous is the poison hemlock (*Conium maculatum*), which is famed as the source of the deadly potion that was used to kill Socrates. Although poison hemlock is not among the dozen species that grow in the Gunnison Basin, water hemlock (*Cicuta douglasii*) is fairly common along irrigation ditches and marshes and is equally poisonous.
To distinguish water hemlock from other large umbels, look for horizontal partitions inside the rootstock. Poison hemlock is easily recognized by its purple-spotted stems.

GIANT ANGELICA *Angelica ampla*

Giant angelica is a robust wetland plant growing up to six feet tall and bearing huge round inflorescences the size of a cantaloupe. Angelica is so named because of its diverse healing properties. Today many herbal formulas for women contain extracts from a Chinese species, *Angelica sinensis,* also known as *dong quai*. Extracts from its roots are also used to make various liqueurs, including Chartreuse, Benedictine and vermouth.

According to Susanne Fischer-Rizzi, author of the *Complete Aromatherapy Handbook*, a whiff of the spicy angelica root will aid in the "search for reality" and is "particularly suited for people who need solid ground." She also claims that angelica "has a fiery temperament, and lends us more physical vitality or earthly strength."

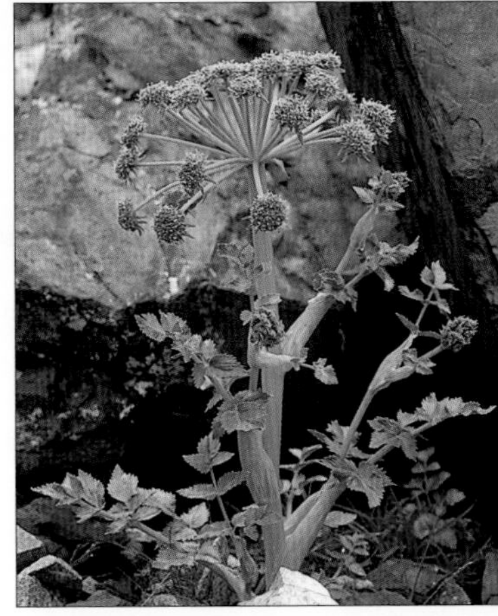

Two species of angelica are common in the southern Rockies. Giant angelica, shown above, is found in wetland areas and along ditches. Look for the dwarf cousin, alpine angelica (*A. grayi*), pictured to the right, on dry, rocky slopes above treeline. Although the stout root of this plant is most potent, caressing the leaves for the therapeutic aroma may be all you need to get grounded. Then the plant can continue to live and spread seed!

Caraway *Carum carvi* Non-native Species

Caraway was introduced to North America as a culinary herb and has rapidly dispersed throughout the country to colonize meadows and pastures. In Colorado, caraway is considered a noxious weed because it is invasive and will displace native plants, especially in wetlands. The species is most abundant along ditches and in hay meadows, creating seas of white in the spring when the flowers bloom.

The plants are biennials, forming rosettes of leaves the first year and flowering the second year. They are easily recognized by the flat-topped clusters of white or pinkish flowers and fern-like leaves. By mid-summer the flowers have turned to hard brown-striped seeds.

The seeds have been used for thousands of years around the world as flavoring in cooking and liquers. Caraway is also useful as a remedy for flatulence. Folk wisdom suggests that caraway will prevent fickleness, so is a powerful ingredient in love potions.

Mary Ellen Harte

Mountain Parsley *Cymopterus lemmonii (Pseudocymopterus montanus)*

This is the most common yellow-flowered umbel in the southern Rockies, and can be found growing in the drier soils of ponderosa pine forests, mountain meadows, aspen forests, as well as the alpine tundra. The plants are highly variable, growing close to the ground in exposed conditions at higher elevations, and up to two feet tall in open meadows. The leaves are finely dissected, and grow from the base of the long, slender flowering stems. These are one of the longest blooming mountain flowers, appearing in early spring and lasting through late summer.

The aromatic leaves can be used as garnish, and taste similar to the garden-variety parsley. Like other members of the family, Rocky Mountain parsley is often pollinated by flies, which are especially attracted to open, flat-topped, yellow clusters of flowers.

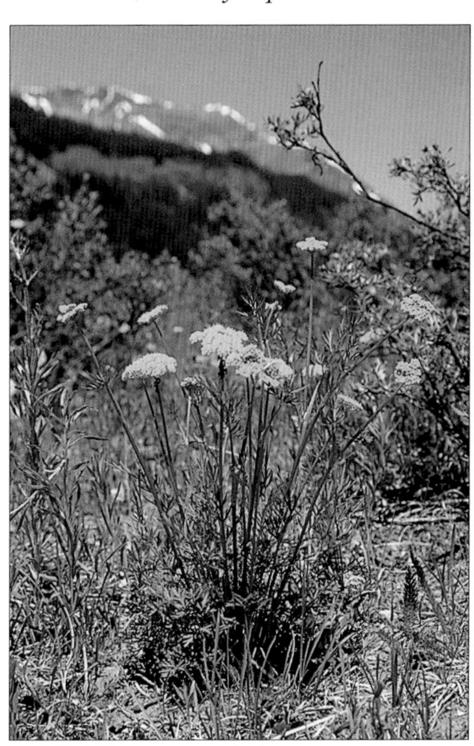

Cow Parsnip *Heracleum sphondylium*

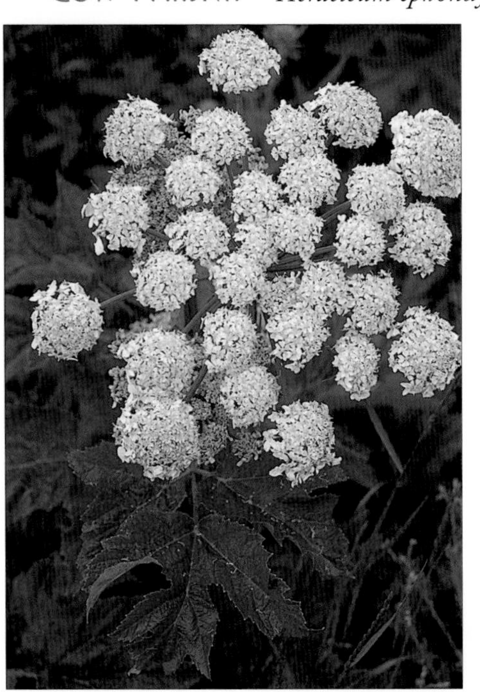

Towering up to six feet tall with flowering heads the size of a platter and leaves that could be used for placemats, these plants are truly of herculean proportions. The Latin name, *Heracleum*, was given for its size and also for its healing properties as a cure for indigestion, which may have been useful for the great demigod. The large parsnip-like root, as well as the rest of the plant, is edible and important forage for bears and elk. Spanish speaking peoples of the southwest call it *yerba del oso*, or bear plant. Cow parsnip grows in wet meadows and along ditches and streams.

Be sure not to confuse this plant with water hemlock (*Cicuta douglasii*) or poison hemlock (*Conium maculatum*), both of which have a similar inflorescence but much divided, fern-like leaves. While cow parsnip is edible, a taste of the other two species can be deadly.

Osha *Ligusticum porteri*

The ferny-leafed, white-flowering oshá has a distinctive sweet, spicy smell. The plant is also known as Porter's lovage, after botanist Thomas Porter who was a member of the Hayden Survey. Europeans have cultivated a closely related species, *Ligusticum officinale*, for hundreds of years as a culinary and medicinal herb. The original lovage was identified in the Liguria region of Italy, from which the Latin, *Ligusticum*, is derived. Oshá looks similar to Queen Ann's lace (*Daucus carota*), another member of the parsley family and a common introduced species in the eastern U.S.

Oshá means "bear," for the massive, dark, hairy root. Tinctures of the root are used around the world as medicine for a long list of ailments. Chewing on a piece of the spicy root is a good remedy for sore throats, coughs, and latent sinus and bronchial infections. Like many in the Parsley Family, the ripe seeds are tasty and a good cure for indigestion.

DAVID INOUYE

The Hayden Survey

Ferdinand Vandiveer Hayden was the leader of the U.S. Geological and Geographic Survey of the Territories between 1867-1879. Many botanists participated in these expeditions, including Townshend Brandegee, John Coulter and Thomas Porter. On a clear day in 1873, Hayden climbed to the top of nearby Teocalli Mountain to get a better view of the surrounding land. Looking west from the summit, he saw two "crested buttes." The name stuck with one mountain, for which the town is named. The other was Gothic Peak, later named for its craggy ridges and buttresses that overshadow the old mining town of the same name, now home of the Rocky Mountain Biological Laboratory.

Indian Biscuitroot *Lomatium dissectum*

These are some of the earliest blooming plants in the area, though the greenish-yellow flowers are not very noticeable. The large finely dissected leaves form lush clumps over two feet tall and are often surrounded by flamboyant displays of lupine in high mountain meadows. *Lomatium* describes the seeds, which have a "little border" or papery wings.

There are eighty species of *Lomatium*, mostly in western North America. Twelve species of biscuit-root are native to Colorado; two are endemic to the state; six grow in Gunnison County. Most are small, ground-hugging plants found in desert/sage-brush areas with well-drained soils and lots of sun.

Native people roasted and ground the large roots into flour to make biscuits. The seeds are also edible and the foliage is important forage for wildlife. Both the root and seeds demonstrate anti-viral and anti-bacterial properties and have been used similarly to oshá (see p. 35), as preventative medicine and cures for influenza and respiratory infections.

> *"Graceful in gesture, with delicate, fern-like leaves, and anise-scented roots that children, like rabbits, delight to nibble, the Sweet Cicely attracts attention by its fragrance however insignificant its flowers."*
>
> – Neltje Blanchan

Sweet Cicely *Osmorhiza occidentalis*

Delicate sweet cicely smells like anise or licorice. The Latin name translates to "scented root of the West." Not only the root, but the leaves and seeds are deliciously sweet smelling and edible. This plant grows in habitats similar to and often side-by-side with its cousin oshá, and is nearly as lush and tall.

A smaller species of sweet cicely, *O. depauperata*, is more of a shade-loving plant found growing in aspen and spruce-fir forests. This kind rarely grows more than a foot high, hence its Latin name, *depauperata*, which means "dwarfed."

Sunflower Family ASTERACEAE

For many wildflower enthusiasts, identifying members of this family entails distinguishing between a bewildering array of "DYC's" or "darn yellow composites." Composite is another name for members of the Sunflower Family and hundreds of them are yellow!

Composites are so named because each flower head is actually composed of many tiny flowers. The common name, sunflower, can refer to any member of the family, but also refers to certain species with large flower heads (more than three inches in diameter) having yellow rays and brown or yellow centers. Two kinds of flowers are found on a sunflower. The outer, more conspicuous petals are called "ray flowers." Each petal represents one individual flower. In the center of a sunflower are numerous "disk flowers." On closer inspection you'll find that each one is a tiny tube-shaped flower. In sunflowers, each of these produces one seed. Some members of the Sunflower Family have only ray flowers, such as dandelions. Others have only disk flowers, such as tansy, pussytoes and sagebrush.

The compacting of many tiny flowers into one "head" is believed to be an evolutionary adaptation which maximizes attraction of pollinators and, thereby, seed production. Apparently, this is a very successful strategy, for composites make up about 10% of the species of flowering plants in the world! Over 24,000 species are recognized on the planet and more than 120 species are found in the Crested Butte area. Composites are common everywhere except for the tropics, where orchids rule. Lettuce and artichokes are culinary members of the family.

Before embarking into the world of sunflower identification, it's helpful to understand a few esoteric terms. Here are the basics of "SUNFLOWERESE":

PHYLLARY: These are modified leaves that enclose the bud of a sunflower head. When you eat artichoke leaves, you are really eating phyllaries. Sometimes they are big and leafy, but most sunflowers have tiny, thin phyllaries.

INVOLUCRE: All of the phyllaries together are called an involucre.

PAPPUS: This is the fluff on a dandelion seed. On some seeds the pappus is absent, or it may be a stiff scale or hook that can hitch to fur or clothing.

DISK FLOWER: These are the tubular flowers found in the center of many sunflowers.

RAY FLOWER: These are flowers with showy petals on the outside of a sunflower. When you play "She-loves-me, She-loves-me-not" with a daisy, you are plucking ray flowers.

HEAD: The head of a sunflower is all of the ray and disk flowers put together.

RECEPTACLE: When you pluck all of the flowers off of the head, this is what is left, like the little button you hold on a stem after you blow all the seeds off a dandelion puff. This is also the "heart" of an artichoke.

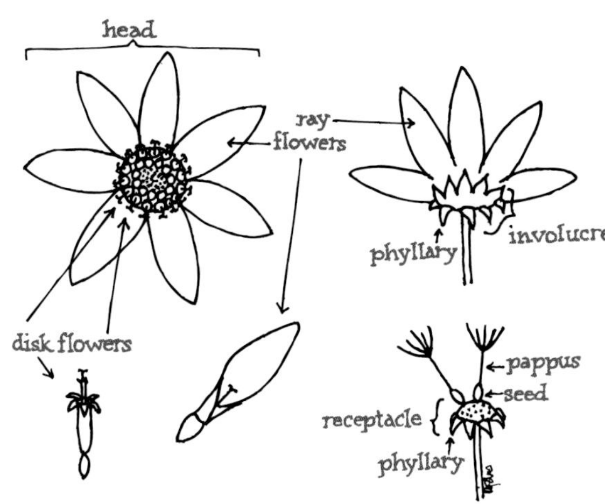

YARROW *Achillea millefolium (A. lanulosa)*

DAVID INOUYE

The Greek warrior, Achilles, was said to have used the leaves of yarrow as poultices for wounds of soldiers in the Battle of Troy. Chiron the centaur, a mythical creature of Greek legend and teacher of medicine, named this plant after his favorite pupil.

Also known as staunchweed and nosebleed plant, the aromatic compounds in the leaves are very effective in stimulating clotting and also have antibiotic and anesthetic properties, as Chiron taught Achilles. A long list of other ailments may be treated with yarrow as well, including flatulence, headaches, hemorrhoids, athlete's foot and hot flashes during menopause. The plant is also used in love charms and as a substitute for hops to flavor beer.

Yarrow is considered sacred in Chinese cultures, where it is also recognized as a powerful medicinal herb and as a source of fragrant oil that can help balance the dual energies of yin and yang. Emperors used fifty sticks made of yarrow stems to make decisions using the ancient divination system of I-Ching. Chinese wisdom claims that *"Yarrow brightens the eyes and promotes intelligence"* when eaten.

Two other common names, plumajillo ("little feather") and milfoil ("many little leaves"), refer to the feathery looking leaves. The stems and leaves of this species are *lanulose*, or covered with soft hairs. Yarrow will grow just about anywhere, being a tenacious pioneer species that spreads by rhizomes as well as by seeds.

> *"By contenting itself with neglected corners of the Earth, the yarrow gives us many valuable lessons on how to succeed."*
>
> – Neltje Blanchan

Pearly Everlasting *Anaphalis margaritacea*

Pearly everlasting blooms in masses in late summer, spreading by rhizomes on dry, rocky slopes and roadsides in upper montane and subalpine areas. The papery white phyllaries are more noticeable than the actual flowers, which are tiny yellow disk flowers. The stems and leaves are soft and fuzzy, or woolly. *Anaphalis* is derived from the Greek word *gnaphallon*, which means "lock of wool." The species name, *margaritacea*, means "pearly," for the smooth phyllaries. Another name for the plant is strawflower, because the flowers preserve nicely when dried, like straw.

Small-leaf Pussytoes *Antennaria parvifolia*

Rosy Pussytoes *Antennaria rosea*

DAVID INOUYE

At least nine species of pussytoes can be found in the southern Rockies, the most common of which are small-leaf pussytoes (upper right) and rosy pussytoes (lower right). Clusters of creamy white or soft pink flowers grow on long stems from a tight mat of leaves. Rosy pussytoes are the most abundant of the genus, growing in many habitats in a broad elevational range. Pussytoes is one of the plants in the Sunflower Family that only has disk flowers. Most are also dioecious, meaning that some plants bear only male flowers and others bear only female flowers; dioecious means "two houses." Females are more common and can also produce seed asexually, as do dandelions, through a process called apomixis. When the flowers first bloom, the stems are fairly short, but bolt up to ten inches tall so that the wind will more easily disperse the fluffy seeds. *Antennaria* is Latin for "antennae," because the pappus resembles insect antennae.

Heartleaf Arnica *Arnica cordifolia*

Heartleaf arnica grows in shaded coniferous forests and is easily recognized by its pairs of heart-shaped leaves and bright yellow flowers. There are at least a dozen species of arnica in the southern Rockies from sagebrush to alpine tundra. Arnicas are easy to recognize because they are one of the only locally native yellow sunflowers that have opposite leaves. Arnicas have the ability to produce seed with or without pollination, greatly enhancing their reproductive capability. They can also reproduce vegetatively by sending out horizontal rootlets that develop buds at their ends, spreading to form large colonies.

Arnicas are best known for their powerful medicinal properties which are used in extracts, salves and poultices to reduce swelling, heal bruises and sprains, and relieve aches and pains. The species most commonly used in commercial salves is *Arnica montana*, which is native to Europe. However, roots and leaves of North American species share similar medicinal capabilities.

Longleaf Arnica *Arnica longifolia*

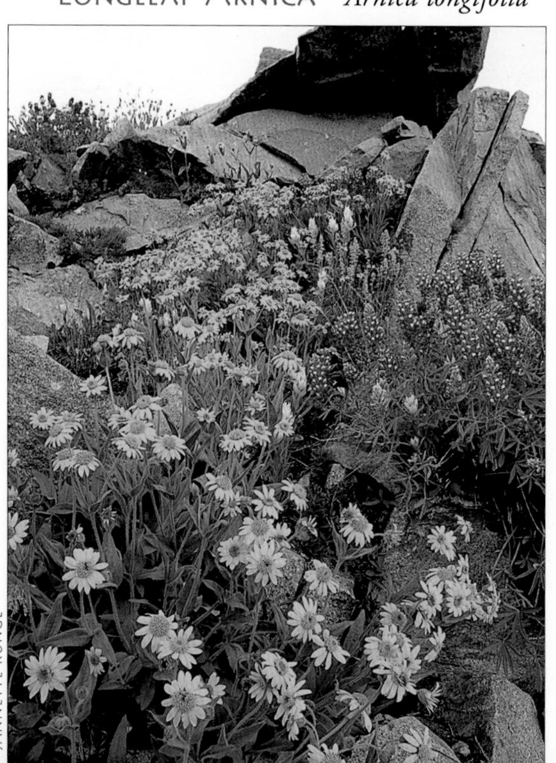

JANNETTE RUNGE

Large clumps of longleaf arnica are common in upper montane and alpine areas on rocky slopes and screefields. Rubbing the leaves releases a sweet aroma. The biochemicals in the plant that are useful medicinals for humans are probably useful in repelling herbivorous insects, fungi and bacteria that could infest the leaves and flowers. Other research suggests that the complex of chemicals that produce various plant scents are a way for plants to communicate with each other, to ensure simultaneous flowering for instance.

Big Sagebrush *Artemisia tridentata*

To know sagebrush and to experience it is, first and foremost, to smell it. Crush some leaves between your fingers, close your eyes, and breathe the intoxicating aroma reminiscent of mint and camphor.

The common term "sagebrush" usually refers to big sagebrush, also known as wormwood or chamisa. The Latin name, *Artemisia*, is after Artemis, the Greek goddess of purity, wild nature and the moon. Artemis, alternately known as the Roman deity, Diana, is also recognized as the goddess of hunting. A world away from ancient Greece, Native Americans are known to have prepared for the hunt by performing a sweat lodge ceremony with sagebrush to cleanse, purify and disguise their human scent. The species, *tridentata*, refers to the three lobed tips of the leaves, or "three little teeth."

The goddess' namesake, Artemisia, was queen of Caria in 350 B.C.; Caria is now part of Turkey. Artemisia is best known for having built one of the Seven Wonders of the Ancient World, the tomb of her husband Mausolus, from which mausoleums are named. Artemisia was also a noted botanist, medical researcher and scholar.

Sagebrush should not be confused with culinary sage, which is an entirely different plant, although they are both often referred to as sage. The cooking herb is a type of mint in the genus *Salvia*, meaning "to save," referring to the plant's healing powers. Native relatives are found throughout the desert Southwest and generally have showy purple flowers. The namesake of Zane Grays' book, *Riders of the Purple Sage*, is different still, probably referring to a shrub in the Snapdragon family, *Leucophyllum* spp., also known as Texas sage.

Despite its wonderful fragrance, sagebrush is NOT recommended for cooking. In fact, the leaves of sagebrush were sometimes chewed by southwest indians to induce vomiting. However, the leaves are beneficial when used in steam baths to treat colds and congestion, and can be burned like incense to treat mild depression and promote vivid dreams.

It may seem odd to the casual observer that sagebrush is in the sunflower family. Unlike most Sunflowers, it has tiny, inconspicuous ball-shaped flowerheads crowded along a slender stem. Sagebrush is wind-pollinated, producing huge quantities of pollen and contributing to the misery of hayfever sufferers in the late summer. Over one hundred species of sagebrush are found in North America, around forty of which grow in the Rocky Mountains. Five other *Artemisias* are scattered from the valley floors to the alpine summits: silver sage (*A. cana*); wild tarragon (*A. dracunculus*); fringed sage (*A. frigida*); prairie sage (*A. ludoviciana*); and Rocky Mountain sage (*A. scopulorum*). For more information on sagebrush, see page 12.

JANNETTE RUNGE

Aster *Aster* spp.

Aster, which simply means "star," is a common name for plants in several genera, including *Aster, Machaeranthera,* and *Heterotheca*. It is also another common name for the entire family, Asteraceae. These species are commonly found blooming late into fall in contrast to their look-alikes, the fleabanes (*Erigeron* spp.; see p. 48), which tend to show up in the spring and early summer. Plants in this genus are most easily distinguished from their cousins by the arrangement of phyllaries. In asters they are in several layers, overlapping like roof shingles. Fleabanes have one or two neat rows of phyllaries that are all the same length and usually narrower than those of asters.

According to Greek legend, asters were created from stardust shed as tears from the goddess Virgo. These plants were considered sacred to all gods and goddesses, who were honored with aster wreaths used to decorate temple altars on festive occasions.

Engelmann Aster *Aster engelmannii (Eucephalus engelmannii)*

Engelmann's aster commemorates one of Colorado's 19th century botanists, George Engelmann. The spruce trees beneath which they often grow also bear Engelmann's name (*Picea engelmannii*). The tall stems (2-6 feet) with white or pinkish, scraggly looking flowers grow in the shade of subalpine coniferous forests in late-summer. These plants spread both by rhizomes, or underground stems, and by seed, creating large, bushy patches.

Leafy Aster *Aster foliaceus*

The purple-rayed flowers of leafy aster are found most commonly in open, sunny meadows. These plants are highly variable in size, and can be anywhere between three inches and three feet tall depending on moisture and soil conditions. The common and scientific names, leafy and *foliaceus,* refer not to the leaves, but the phyllaries, which are broad and leaf-like.

These and other species of Aster are favorite sources of nectar and pollen for bumblebees in the late summer and fall.

Arrowleaf Balsamroot *Balsamorhiza sagittata*

These are some of the earliest spring wildflowers, gilding entire hillsides yellow as they bloom at lower elevations in sagebrush communities. True to its name, both common and Latin, this sunflower has large arrow-shaped leaves and massive, aromatic roots. Individuals may live for over fifty years and bloom yearly from the age of four or five years. From a distance the flowers might be confused with mule ears sunflowers (see page 64), but a look at the leaves will quickly tell you which are which. The leaves of mule ears are shaped like their namesake, while balsamroot leaves are triangular.

Balsamroot, like mule ears sunflower, is often an indicator of heavy clay soils.

Musk Thistle *Carduus nutans* Non-native Species

Beautiful fuschia flowers of musk thistle are indicators of human disturbance, occurring mostly in pastures, roadsides and other areas where soils have been severely changed. These plants are native to Europe and Asia, and are now common all across North America. Although the plants are considered to be noxious weeds, many native species of insects, birds and other wildlife eat the nectar, seeds and succulent stems. Human uses include using fluffy seed hairs to make paper and the inner parts of stems for food.

Dusty Maiden *Chaenactis alpina*

Dusty maiden is one of the members of the Sunflower Family that has only disc flowers. The leaves are covered with sticky hairs that earn the plant its name, since they often are covered with a thin layer of dust. Both the alpine and Douglas dusty maiden (*Chaenactis douglassii*) are common in the Rocky Mountains, thriving on dry, rocky slopes. The two species are distinguished from one another primarily by habitat, with Douglas' being found in sagebrush habitats and alpine dusty maiden growing on the tundra. Leaves of both are grayish green and finely dissected. The flowers are cream colored, sometimes tinged with pink. The rounded shape of the flower head gives it the alternate common name, pincushion flower.

Ox-eye Daisy *Chrysanthemum leucanthemum* Non-native Species

Populations of ox-eye daisy in Crested Butte seem to center on the local cemetery, where they have been planted for over a century to honor the spirits of loved ones. These cheery white flowers were introduced from Europe as an ornamental and have played a role in most of our childhoods to see if "She-loves-me or She-loves-me-not." Like their cousin, scentless chamomile, they are listed as noxious weeds in most of the U.S. and should not be planted in gardens. Daisy is a contraction of "day's eye," for the flower's resemblance to the sun. The Latin name translates to "common white flower."

Rabbitbrush *Chrysothamnus* spp. and *Ericameria* spp.

At the end of summer, as we await the turning of aspen leaves, a subtler gold adorns the valley when rabbitbrush, also known as goldenbush, comes into bloom. There are two genera both commonly called rabbitbrush or goldenbush: *Chrysothamnus* spp. and *Ericameria* spp. A shrubby companion of sagebrush, rabbitbrush thrives on open land all over Colorado. Both sagebrush and rabbitbrush can be indicators of poor soils, where overgrazing and erosion have reduced other vegetation cover and organic matter. Around Crested Butte these shrubs are low-growing, usually not more than knee high; but at lower elevations some species of rabbitbrush may grow to over six feet tall!

The name rabbitbrush undoubtedly comes from its being good shelter and forage for bunnies, although it is probably not more preferred by rabbits than any other shrub. Because of its ability to grow on disturbed land, rabbitbrush is often regarded as a "trashy" plant, wantonly chained and bulldozed along with sagebrush to create more favorable pasture for cattle. Rabbitbrush is an excellent native landscaping plant, offering an attractive shrub that will grow anywhere. The plants are also a source of low-grade rubber, although commercial uses of this have not been promoted.

Sticky Rabbitbrush *Chrysothamnus viscidiflorus*

The most common species in the high mountains (above 7,000 feet) is the sticky-flowered rabbitbrush, *Chrysothamnus viscidiflorus,* which directly translates to "golden bush with sticky flowers." The flowers are not particularly sticky, but the leaves are distinctively twisted, unlike any of the other rabbitbrushes.

Whitestem Goldenbush *Ericameria discoidea (Macronema discoideum)*

Another common rabbitbrush, also known as whitestem goldenbush, is named for the white felt-like hairs that cover the stems. The wavy leaves have a pleasant smell when rubbed between fingers. This plant is very common on the summit boulderfield of Crested Butte Mountain and viewed by hundreds of people every summer. If you stop to catch your breath and take a closer look, you'll also be sure to see a variety of pollinating insects, including beetles and butterflies.

Common Rabbitbrush *Ericameria nauseosus (Chrysothamnus nauseosus)*

At lower elevations, common rabbitbrush is co-dominant with sagebrush. This plant bears the charming Latin description, *Ericameria nauseosus*, after some botanist's distaste for the plant's odor. Again, the Latin seems misplaced, for the plant adds a fresh, spicy aroma to the autumn air.

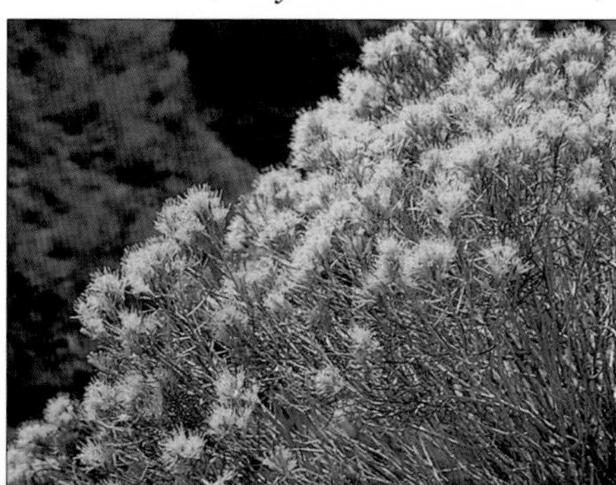

THISTLE *Cirsium* spp.

Thistle is a name used for several genera of plants bearing spiny leaves, stems and flowerheads, but the primary genus is *Cirsium*. Because of their bristly character, most people regard thistles as unwanted plants. However, native species can be an important component of ecosystems, providing forage for many species of wildlife, including a huge diversity of insects, seed-eating birds and root-foraging mammals, such as bears and humans. Survivalists also note thistledown as excellent tinder for starting fires. There are twenty species of native thistles in Colorado, four of which are considered rare and are protected by the state. In addition, Canadian thistle (*C. arvense*) and bull thistle (*C. vulgare*) are two widespread non-native species listed in Colorado as noxious weeds.

Biologists have noticed that there are unanticipated effects of biological control of noxious thistles on natives. A European weevil, a small green beetle with a nose like an elephant, was introduced as part of an integrated pest management (IPM) program to combat the noxious Canadian thistle (*Cirsium arvense*). By laying their eggs in the flower heads, the little beasts are implanting tiny living bombs that will search and destroy thistle seeds. Unfortunately, the IPM effort has done little to stem the tide of invading Canadian thistles, but the beetle thrives quite well on some of the natives.

> *"A symbol of independence and valued for its reputation to protect against negative influences, thistle enhances self-respect and dignity, and the ability to trust your own inner judgement and guidance."*
>
> – From *Flower Power* by Anne McIntyre

DRAGONHEAD THISTLE *Cirsium scopulorum (C. hesperium)*

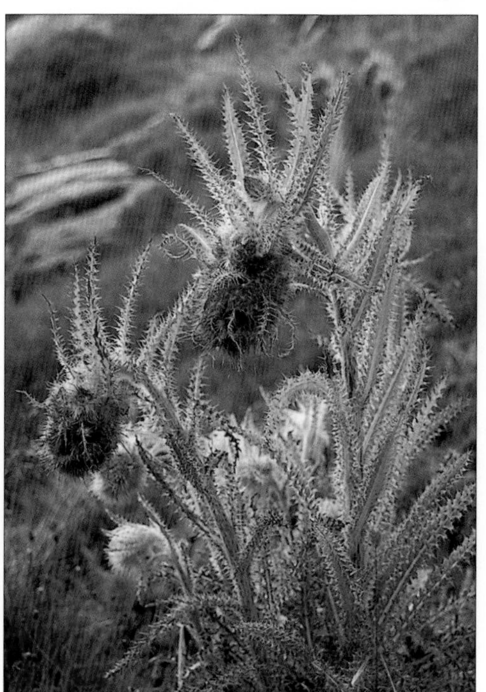

Recognizing thistle species is tricky business, but one that is fairly easy to identify is dragonhead thistle. These robust and very spiny plants grow to three feet tall, and the flowering stem is often nodding with the weight of crowded flowerheads. Most distinctive and spectacular are the leaves, which are so wavy that they are more three-dimensional than flat. The flowers range from yellowish to lavender. This species is most common on rocky slopes in subalpine and alpine meadows. Horses are said to seek out these plants in the high country, earning the plant another folk name, "horse's ice cream cones."

Colorado Thistle *Cirsium tioganum* var. *coloradense (C. scariosum)*

The Colorado thistle takes on two forms: an upright stem up to four feet tall, and a ground-hugging rosette. Also known as elk thistle, this species is found in high mountain meadows up to the tundra. With a good pair of leather gloves, this plant is fairly easy to gather if you want to sample the edible stems and roots, which may be eaten raw or cooked. Flowers range from off-white to pink.

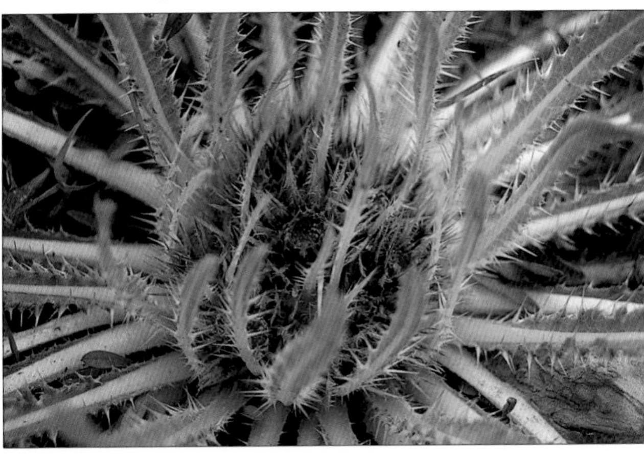

Hawk Moths and Hornworms

Hawk moths are both a horror and delight to gardeners. As larvae they appear as almost pornographic, green caterpillars called hornworms, because of the thorn like appendage on their rear end. Their job is to eat as much as they can, which does not usually make gardeners happy. However, the adult phase of the hornworm is a sphinx moth, which is a beautiful day-flying insect and an important pollinator for many species of wildflowers and garden ornamentals.

The moths are often mistaken for hummingbirds because of their rapid wingbeat and large size. Their long tongues are especially useful for sipping nectar from narrow, tubular corollas like those in the Evening Primrose Family and Sunflower Family. A hornworm feeds on fireweed (p. 132) above; to the left is a sphinx moth feeding on wavyleaf thistle (*C. undulatum* var. *tracyi*), another common thistle that grows in sagebrush areas throughout the southern Rockies.

Fleabane *Erigeron* spp.

Erigeron means "early old man," an apt name for these flowers that bloom in the spring and have downy white seed hairs, as on a dandelion, which resemble the white hair of a geriatric. This is one of the more confusing genera in the Sunflower Family, with over thirty species in our area and more than two hundred worldwide. Fleabane is a name describing its use as a flea repellent; common lore says that burning the plants or hanging them in a doorway will keep away pesky insects. Fleabanes are often confused with asters (see p. 42), which tend to bloom later in the summer and also tend to have fewer, broader ray flowers. The quickest way to tell the difference between asters and fleabanes is to look at their phyllaries. Asters have overlapping rows of phyllaries, sort of like shingles, while those of fleabanes are in one or two neat rows.

Coulter's Fleabane *Erigeron coulteri*

Coulter's fleabane has white ray flowers, and is found mostly in wet meadows or near streams among willows.

Pink-headed Fleabane *Erigeron elatior*

Pink-headed fleabane grows in lush clumps in upper montane and subalpine meadows and commonly grows waist high in wetter meadows. *Elatior* means "tall." The phyllaries are covered with soft pink hairs, giving them their common name. When the flowers bloom, the rays at first appear pink, then white.

Trailing Fleabane *Erigeron flagellaris*

Trailing fleabane is common in dry meadows and among sagebrush. These are the smallest of the fleabanes, with thin white or pinkish ray flowers. Like strawberry plants, they spread by stolons, which can form roots when they touch down. *Flagellaris* means "with tails," referring to the long, thin stolons.

Wandering Fleabane *Erigeron peregrinus*

Wandering fleabane has purple ray flowers, and is most common in wet meadows and along streams in upper montane and subalpine. The ray flowers are broader than most fleabanes, making them resemble asters.

"Be like the flower;
turn your faces to the sun."
– Kahlil Gibran

Showy Fleabane *Erigeron speciosus*

Showy fleabane is one of the most common of the local purple-flowered *Erigerons*, and grows in large clumps from sagebrush hills to subalpine meadows.

These flowers are susceptible to late spring frosts; if the snow melts early the buds develop before the danger of frost is past and may then be killed. The flowers are an important nectar source for the Mormon Fritillary butterfly (*Speyeria mormonia*).

Aspen Sunflower *Helianthella quinquenervis*

The most abundant sunflower in the Crested Butte area is the aspen sunflower. These flowers are a paler yellow than all the others and like the alpine sunflower (p. 53), tend to always face east. *Helianthella* translates to "little sunflower," another common name for the plant. However, they are hardly little, sometimes reaching over four feet high and blooming in extravagant displays that dominate the mountain meadows in mid-summer. The specific name, *quinquenervis*, refers to five dominant veins in the leaves, one way to distinguish them from other yellow sunflowers. The flower buds are very sensitive to frost, so if there are few flowers in July, it may be that a hard frost in June nipped them. This happens most commonly in years with early snowmelt.

"Flowers changed the face of the planet.
Without them, the world we know, even man
himself, would never have existed.
Francis Thompson, an English poet,
once wrote that one could not pluck a flower
without troubling a star.
Intuitively, he had sensed like a naturalist
the enormous interlinked complexity of life.
Today we know that the appearance
of the flowers contained also the equally
mystifying emergence of man."

– Loren Eiseley

Rocky Mountain Biological Laboratory researcher, David Inouye, has discovered a fascinating relationship between ants and the aspen sunflower. Look at a bud or flowerhead and chances are you will find ants walking around. They are foraging for nutritious nectar that is secreted by the leafy bracts of the flower head. In return for this "reward," ants provide a valuable service of chasing away herbivorous insects and egg-laying flies. Inouye has found that without ant guards, seed loss to insect predators can increase up to eighty percent. Above, a tephritid fly is busy laying eggs; when the eggs hatch, the larvae will eat the seeds. Below, an ant gathers nectar.

Golden Aster *Heterotheca villosa*

Golden aster is a low, shrubby plant covered with bright yellow flowers when in bloom. It grows on dry, exposed, rocky or sandy areas from sagebrush to upper montane. The Latin name translates to "two different seed types, with long soft hairs." This fuzz is not on the seeds, but all over the stems and leaves.

Gardening with Natives

One way to enjoy wildflowers closer to home is to collect and plant wild seeds. Look for mature seedpods and gather them in cloth or paper bags. Seeds are alive and need air circulation, so plastic bags are a poor choice for storage. Keeping them outside is preferable, because most wild seeds in the high mountains need to over-winter in the cold ground before they can germinate. If you are broadcasting seed over a large area, mix them with sand to help spread them. This works especially well for fluffy seeds like fireweed and asters.

Most importantly, know what species you are collecting. Make sure you are not collecting seeds of a rare plant and thereby decreasing the chance for that population to flourish in its natural habitat. Avoid cultivating noxious weeds in your area or they will take over your garden! Pay attention to the natural habitat of the plants you are trying to grow. No matter how hard you try, you will not have much luck growing elephantella in dry, sandy soils or mule ears sunflower on the north, shady side of your house. Collect only those seeds that are plentiful and compatible with the soil, light and moisture conditions on your land. Be sure to observe collection regulations in parks and preserves.

Many native plants are also available at local garden centers.

Alpine Sunflower *Hymenoxys grandiflora (Rydbergia grandiflora)*

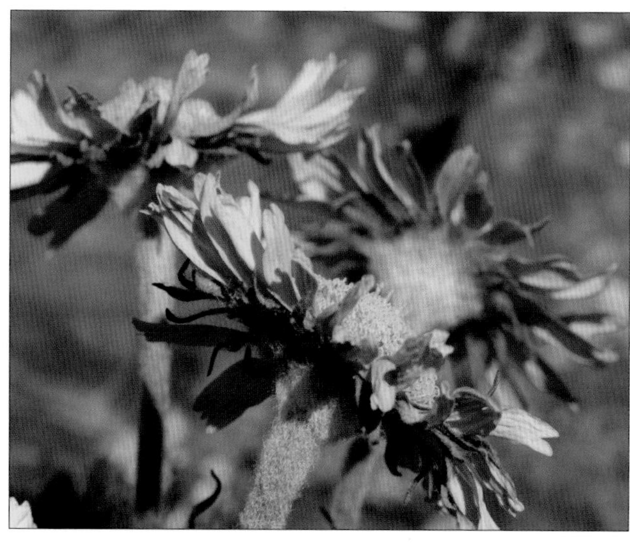

One flower that celebrates the mountain summits most exuberantly is the alpine sunflower. Like the mule ears sunflower that covers slopes below, alpine sunflowers often blanket exposed alpine ridges with thousands of blooms. They especially thrive on limestone, which is the bedrock of many of the mountains in the Elk Range, as on Fossil Ridge and Cement Mountain.

This species is easy to recognize, being the largest yellow sunflower found in alpine habitat. The heads are three to four inches in diameter, looking animated and oversized on a three to six inch tall stem. The stems, leaves and flower heads are covered with long, soft white hairs, an adaptation to protect the plant from frost, drying winds and intense sun in the alpine climate. This white-haired and wizened air has earned the plant another folk name, "old man of the mountains."

Most intriguing about the alpine sunflower is that the flowers always face the rising sun, or eastward. The are also monocarpic perennials, which means that they live for many years just as roots and leaves before they finally flower, produce seed and then die. Like other plants that use this reproductive strategy, such as green gentian, alpine sunflowers bloom *en masse* some years and hardly at all in other years.

Sneezeweed *Hymenoxys hoopesii (Dugaldia hoopesii)*

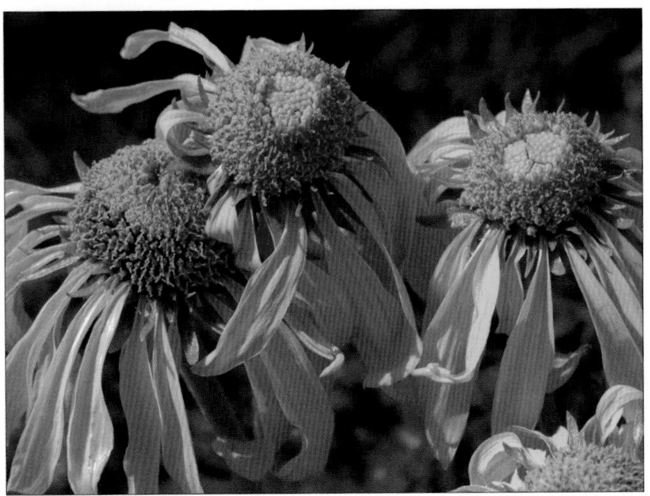

Named for the use of its dried and powdered flowers for snuff, this tall, dark yellow or almost orange sunflower is found in wetter parts of mountain meadows. Another common name is swamp sunflower. The ray flowers often appear droopy, in comparison to its look-alike, curly-headed golden-weed (p. 56). Sneezeweed is known in ranching country for its poisonous effects on sheep and other livestock, causing "spewing sickness."

Hymenoxys means "pointed membrane," referring to the sharp pappus scales found on the ripe seeds. The alternate Latin genus honors Dugald Stewart, who was a Scottish philosopher in the late 1700's. Thomas Hoopes was a 19th century prospector in the Pike's Peak region. Sneezeweed is also known as Helen's flower (*Helenium hoopesii*) after Helen of Troy, the Greek beauty born of Leda, queen of Sparta, and Zeus, the king of gods. The flowers are said to have sprung up from the ground where Helen's tears fell. Herbalists also call this plant *yerba del lobo* and use it like arnica, as a treatment for sprains, bruises and sore joints.

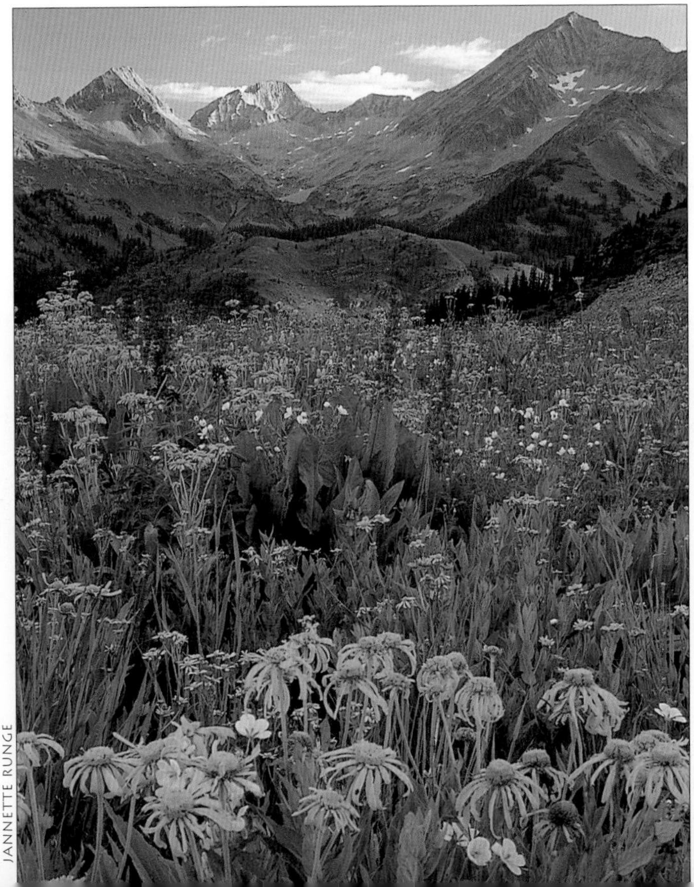

JANNETTE RUNGE

Purple Tansy Aster *Machaeranthera canescens*

Purple tansy asters are one of the latest of summer-blooming wildflowers, adding splashes of purple to the landscape well into September. These plants do well in disturbed and poor soils, so are abundant along roadsides. The generic name means "sword-like anther." Tansy asters are also easy to recognize by their sticky, curly, overlapping phyllaries. This species is described in Latin by its grayish-white, or *canescent*, seed puff.

Scentless Chamomile *Matricaria perforata* Non-native Species

These pretty white daisies are one of the many ornamental and medicinal herbs that were intentionally brought from Europe by early settlers. Although residents of North America for over a century, scentless chamomile may not have arrived in Crested Butte until the late 1970s, when their proliferation along roadsides seems to have coincided with the deposit of fill dirt trucked in for the town's sewage treatment plant. Now they thrive all along Highway 135 and are some of the last flowers you'll see blooming, even after the first few snowfalls in October.

Scentless chamomile is different from the medicinal species used in teas, although both can be used as a mild sedative and for curing a case of the "grumpies." You can smell the difference. In fact, the old species name for this roadside weed was *Matricaria inodora*, meaning "odorless." The medicinal or German chamomile, *Matricaria recutita*, has a strong sweet smell in its broader-leaved, fern-like foliage. *Matricaria* means "of the womb," referring to its use for soothing belly-aches. The species name, *perforata*, describes the glands or tiny holes on the leaves that secrete the medicinal oils. The common name is derived from Greek, *khamaemelon*, meaning "earth apples," because some species smell like ripe apples.

Scentless chamomile is an annual or short-lived perennial and spreads rapidly through the dispersal of its abundant seeds. This plant is so prolific that you probably don't want to plant it in your garden because it will quickly take over.

Curly Goldenweed *Pyrrocoma crocea*

The Latin name for this sunflower means "tawny mane, saffron yellow," because of its brownish pappus, or seed hairs, and brilliant yellow flowers. Sometimes mistaken for sneezeweed (p. 54), it is distinguished by perky petals and broad curly phyllaries, as opposed to droopy petals and thin phyllaries of its look-alike.

Curly-headed goldenweed grows in mountain meadows and does well in disturbed sites, so it is often seen along roadsides. Because it is a drought hardy colonizer, this plant is an excellent choice for native plant gardening!

WENDY BROWN

Goldenglow *Rudbeckia laciniata (R. ampla)*

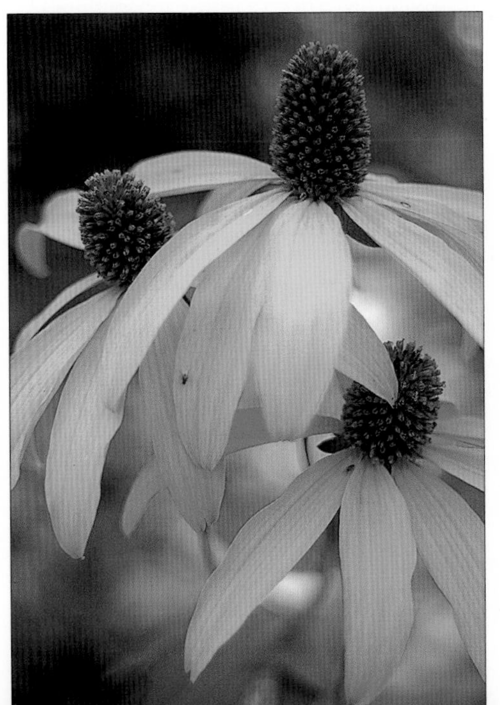

Goldenglow can be found growing in wet soils and is common along irrigation ditches, shaded aspen forests and along mountain streams from lower sagebrush to subalpine meadows. Growing to over six feet tall, the large flowerheads do seem to glow atop the robust stem. The large leaves have three to seven lobes. This plant, as well as the rayless coneflower, is related to the well-known brown-eyed Susan (*Rudbeckia hirta*), which is common at lower elevations in grasslands and disturbed areas across North America. Like its cousins, the foliage of goldenglow is toxic to livestock, so it remains uneaten in areas that may otherwise be heavily grazed. The seeds are important food for birds and small mammals.

Rayless Coneflower *Rudbeckia occidentalis*

You might think these flowers have lost their petals, but what you see is what you get: dark purply-brown cones of disc flowers, blooming late in summer and growing up to four feet tall. Patches of coneflower are usually buzzing with bees, which are attracted by the abundant nectar and pollen.

This species is endemic to southwestern Colorado, but locally abundant on the west side of Kebler Pass. The genus is named after a father and son team of botany professors, Olaf Rudbeck, Sr. and Jr., who both taught at the University of Uppsala, Sweden in the early 1700s. Carolus Linnaeus was one of their predecessors at Uppsalla and is renowned as the father of taxonomy. *Occidentalis* means western.

Pocket Gophers

When the snow melts each spring, curious tube-shaped earth formations called "eskers" appear in mountain meadows. These are the work of pocket gophers, small rodents that tunnel below ground all year round while foraging for succulent roots. During the summer, earth from the gopher tunnels is pushed to the surface, creating small mounds.

In the winter the gophers create tunnels in the snow and then fill these snow tunnels with earth. Named for the fur-lined pouches on the outside of their cheeks, pocket gophers play an important role in mountain ecosystems by aerating the soil and facilitating water percolation. Gophers also have an influential role in determining the diversity and abundance of plant species in meadows where they forage.

GROUNDSEL *Senecio* spp.

The genus *Senecio* is one of the largest in the world of plants, with nearly 3,000 species identified and over one hundred of them in North America. Indeed, this is one of the most difficult genera and definitely in the category of DYC's (darn yellow composites)! *Senecios* manifest in many different forms, from dwarf alpine plants to an enormous tree-like plant found in the mountains of Kenya. Depending on which taxonomic reference you use, the genus may be subdivided into *Ligularia* spp. and *Packera* spp. The *Ligularia* group shares the characteristic of nodding flowerheads. The *Packeras* tend to be smaller in stature than the *Senecios*. (Although Hartman and Nelson separate out *Packera*, I am including this genus with *Senecio* to illustrate the close taxonomic relationship.) All are characterized by a single neat row of thin phyllaries enclosing the usually yellow flowers. There are at least eighteen species recognized around Crested Butte, plus many hybrids. The Latin name means "old" or senescent, and refers to the fluffy white hairs or pappus of the seeds, which resembles an old man's beard. You will also see this group referred to as ragwort or butterweed because of their scruffy yellow flowers.

The common name, groundsel, is a twist of the Old English word *gundeswelge*, which literally means "pus swallower." This lovely term comes from the medicinal use of groundsel in poultices to heal wounds. However, ingesting the plant can cause severe liver damage due to the presence of poisonous alkaloids. *Senecios* in all parts of the world have been the culprits for various ailments in livestock that eat them.

DAFFODIL SENECIO *Senecio amplectens (Ligularia amplectens)*

Daffodil senecio has large, nodding flowers and is common on the upper slopes of Crested Butte Mountain and other open, rocky areas. *Amplectens* means "clasping," for the way the leaves are attached to the stem. The leaves are slightly succulent and have rounded teeth on the edges.

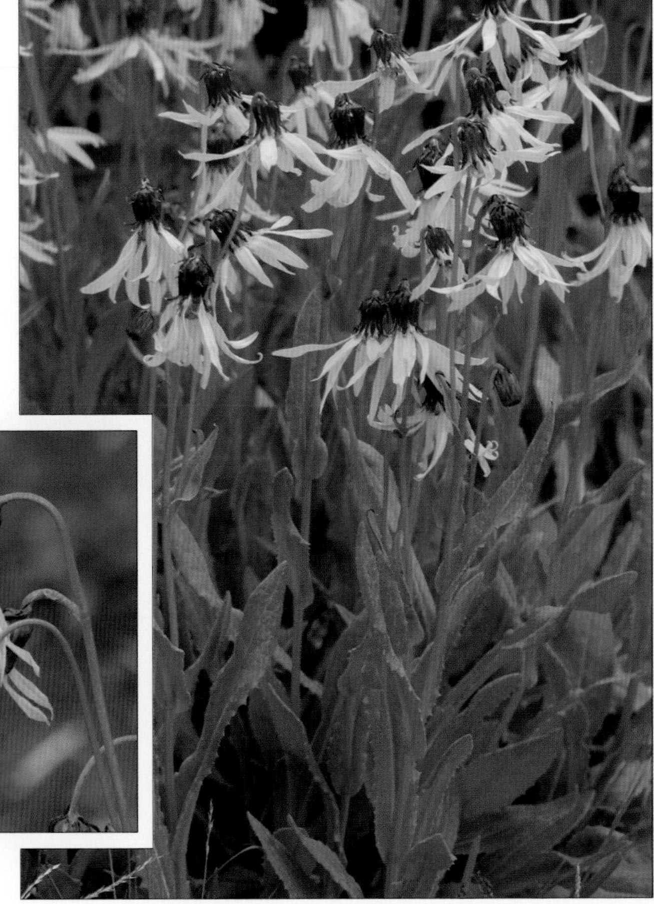

Black-tip Senecio *Senecio atratus*

Black-tip senecio grows in robust clumps on rocky subalpine areas. This species is named for the dark tips on the phyllaries. *Atratus* means "dressed in black." The large leaves and stems, however, are covered in soft white hairs.

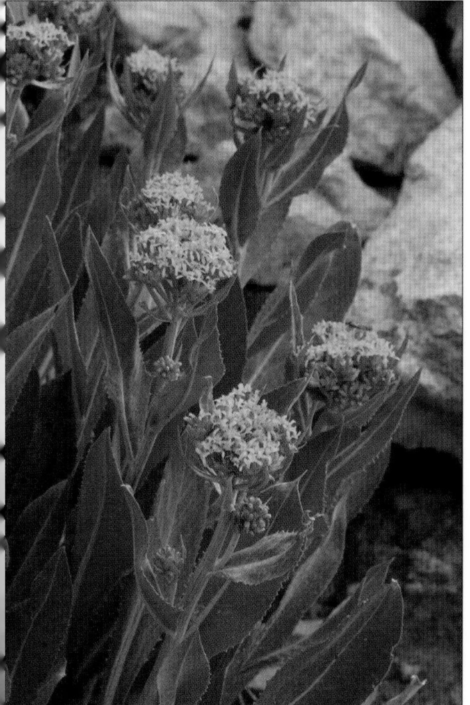

Nodding Groundsel

Senecio bigelovii (Ligularia bigelovii)

Nodding groundsel is common along ditches and streams and is easily recognized by the nodding, rayless flowers.

Saffron Senecio *Senecio crocatus (Packera crocata)*

Saffron senecio is one of the few Rocky Mountain wildflowers that has a deep orange-yellow, or saffron color. Look for them among the shrubby cinquefoils in wet bottomlands or along streams.

Fremont's Senecio *Senecio fremontii*

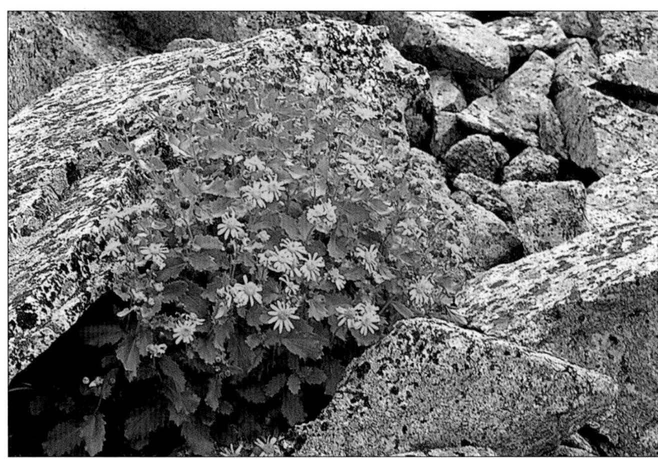

Fremont's senecio grows in lush clumps on alpine scree and talus where snowmelt runs close beneath the surface. The succulent leaves are slightly toothed.

Sawleaf Senecio *Senecio serra*

One of the tallest and easy-to-recognize groundsels is the sawleaf senecio. The fine teeth on the edge of the leaves resembles a saw, hence the species name, *serra,* Latin for "saw." These lush plants are often found near streams, in wet mountain meadows or near aspen forests.

Alpine Groundsel *Senecio soldanella (Ligularia soldanella)*

Alpine groundsel blooms in late summer on talus fields and scree in the alpine tundra. The thick, almost succulent leaves are often tinged with red. This pigment, known as anthocyanin, is found in many alpine plants and provides some protection for the plant from ultra-violet radiation, acting as sort of a botanical sunscreen. The presence of anthocyanin also protects plants from frost damage by enhancing absorption of heat. Because it has a higher concentration of sugars than other plant pigments, anthocyanin reduces the freezing point of tissues. This is the same pigment that colors autumn leaves.

COMMON TANSY *Tanacetum vulgare* NON-NATIVE SPECIES

Tansy is a native of Europe, probably brought to North America as an ornamental that doubles as a culinary herb, medicinal plant and insecticide. Also known as feverfew, bitter buttons and scented fern, the dried leaves were once used as a "strewing herb," i.e. strewn about the floors of a house to repel insects such as fleas, lice and ants. The Latin name, *Tanacetum*, is derived from the Greek word *athanatos*, meaning immortal, because it was also used to help preserve dead bodies, which were rubbed with leaves or laid in a bed of the herb in a coffin. A tea made from the plant is also reputed to render immortality. As a medicinal herb, tansy has been used to expel worms, relieve flatulence and cure gout.

Another translation of the Latin name is "tenacious," which would describe the way tansy takes hold of the land, spreading by runners and generally taking over any piece of bare ground it sets root into, thus earning it status as a noxious weed. Entire vacant lots and alleys in Crested Butte are filled with tansy's lush, fern-like leaves. *Vulgare* means "common." Flowers and leaves have also been popular as flavoring for puddings, cakes and eggs in Europe. In Colorado, tansy blooms are a sign of the end of summer.

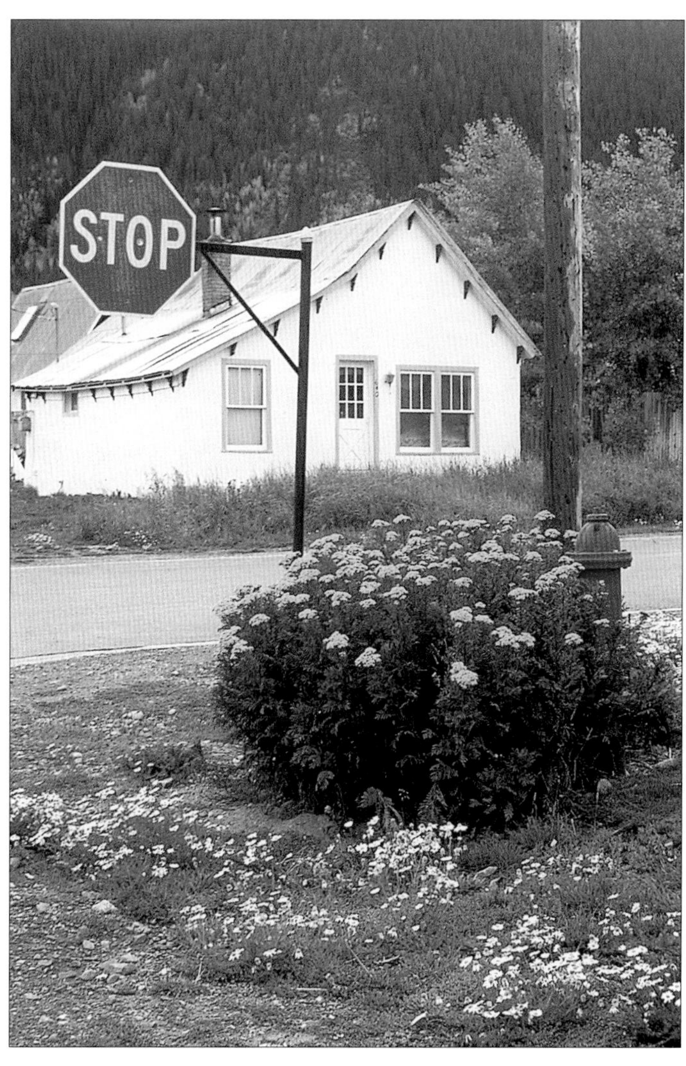

Alpine Dandelion *Taraxacum ceratophorum*

MARY ELLEN HARTE

There are three native dandelions in the Rocky Mountains, though the common one is descended from European migrants. The Colorado natives are found growing on the alpine tundra, mostly above 10,500 feet (*T. ceratophorum, T. eriophorum, T. lyratum*). Around the world, over fifty species of dandelion are recognized.

This native dandelion can be distinguished from the non-native by more succulent leaves with fewer teeth on the edges, leafy phyllaries and wider ray flowers on the flowerhead. Although this species is generally restricted to the alpine tundra, the ubiquitous common dandelion may be found growing on the tundra as well, so it is not ulikely that there are hybrids.

Common Dandelion *Taraxacum officinale* Non-native Species

DAVID INOUYE

Dandelions have become the target of much industry, both chemical and physical, as most people consider them a blight on their lawns. However, if we relax our preconceptions, they are really quite beautiful and also very useful plants. Some are purposely cultivated for their edible roots and leaves and are also harvested for medicinal purposes as a diuretic and liver tonic. This is communicated in the Latin name, *Taraxacum officinale*, which means "bitter herb used for medicine." Those are the likely reasons that Europeans decided that dandelions would be an excellent plant to bring with them to the New World.

After a magnificent spring display, dandelions turn to fields of fuzzy white "blowballs." One of the reasons dandelions are so abundant is that they can produce seed without sex. The technical term for this is "apomixis" or "parthenogenesis." This means there is no need for pollen to create seed; the seeds develop from unfertilized ovules (or eggs). Actually, dandelions can "do it" both ways, as evidenced by the abundant yellow dust, or pollen. However, pollination is not necessary for seed production, so almost every dandelion produces a full head of seed to send on the wind and populate whatever open ground can be found. They will sometimes even ripen seeds after the flower has been picked.

Recipe for Spring Greens

Trim and wash 1 lb. dandelion greens. Slice 2 ripe tomatoes. Thinly slice 2 scallions. Mix 4 T. vinegar, 1 1/2 t. honey, 1 clove minced garlic, 1/2 t. ground pepper. Fry and crumble 6 slices of bacon. Away from the stove, add greens to hot bacon fat and stir until slightly wilted. Toss in the vinaigrette. Arrange tomato slices on a plate. Mound dandelion greens on top and sprinkle with bacon and scallions. Olive oil and toasted sunflower seeds can be substituted for bacon and fat.

Salsify *Tragopogon dubius* Non-native Species

Salsify is another spectacular "weed," producing baseball sized "blowballs" or seedheads. Like its cousin, the dandelion, salsify was intentionally imported from Europe, primarily for culinary purposes. The long taproot resembles a parsnip and can still be found for sale in some groceries. When cooked, the root tastes vaguely like oysters, earning the alternate name, oysterplant. Those who appreciate the culinary value of salsify can find seeds sold for vegetable gardening. The milky juice is also reputed to relieve indigestion. However, these plants will easily establish in a variety of habitats, though they are most successful in disturbed soils, such as roadsides and pastures. Another common name is goatsbeard, for the shape of the phyllaries, which droop down after the flowers have been pollinated. Nobody remembers what "salsify" means!

David Inouye

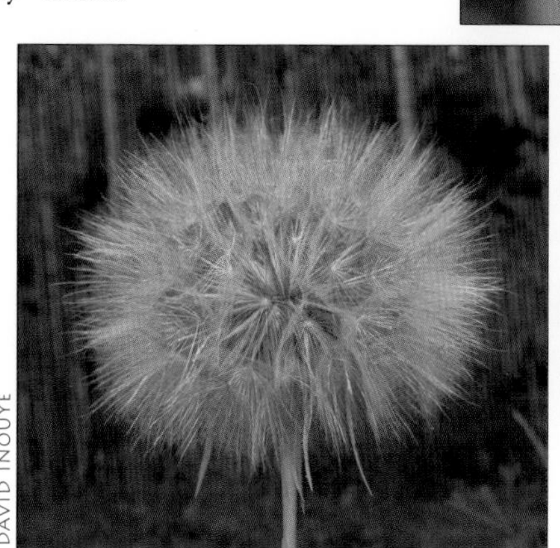

David Inouye

Showy Goldeneye *Viguiera multiflora (Heliomeris multiflora)*

This is the smallest of the dominant yellow sunflowers, with flower heads about two inches across. These plants are delicate, with 20-30 flowerheads per plant, hence the Latin name, *multiflora*. The genus, *Heliomeris*, means "sun" (*helio*) and "part" (*meris*) in Greek, which is where another common name, sunspots, comes from. Blooming late in the summer, they sometimes fill whole meadows with their cheerful blossoms. They often grow with showy fleabanes (p. 49) in a spectacular display of purple and yellow flowers. The genus honors Alexandre L. Viguier (1790-1867), who was a physician and botanist in Montpelier, France. Interestingly, prior to the 1900s, most doctors had a background in botany, since many remedies are derived from plants, so it was important to be able to identify them as well as understand their medicinal properties.

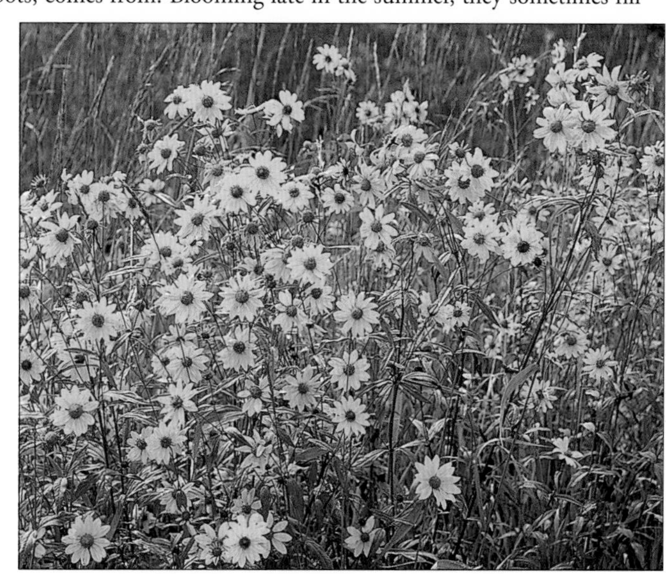

Mule Ears Sunflower *Wyethia amplexicaulis*

Mule ears are easy to identify by the large, smooth leaves that are the size and shape of their namesake. Most of the leaves are found at the base rather than along the stem. These have big, showy flowerheads, sometimes six inches across, and grow in huge clumps near aspen and sagebrush. In the early summer mule ears are the dominant wildflower on many south-facing hillsides. Like its cousin, arrowleaf balsamroot (p. 43), this plant has a long stout taproot that is edible when roasted or boiled. The flowers and seeds are important forage for wildlife.

The genus is named for Nathaniel Wyeth, a western explorer and fur-trader in the early 1800s, while *amplexicaulis* means, "embracing the stem," describing how the leaf bases are attached.

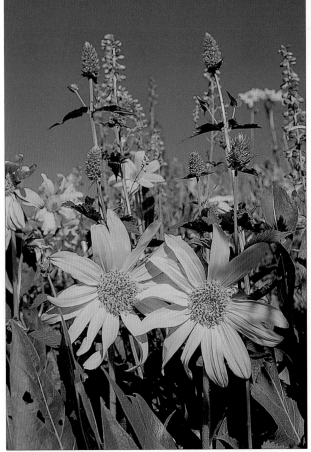

Most of the populations of mule ears sunflower in the Elk Mountains are hybrids of this species and a lower elevation species, Arizona mule ears (*Wyethia arizonica*). Arizona mule ears have hairy leaves and stems, petioled leaves, single flowers and are frost intolerant. The hybrid is somewhat hairy like Arizona mule ears, and has the clasping leaves, multiple flowers per stem and cold-hardiness of *W. amplexicaulis.*

Barberry Family BERBERIDACEAE

Members of this family are considered "living fossils," having survived in northern temperate climates since Tertiary times, up to 30 million years ago. In the Rocky Mountains this was a time of great geologic activity, including the uplift and erosion of present mountains and production of igneous intrusions that created Colorado's mineral belt. Many of the barberries are spiny shrubs found in the foothills of mountain ranges throughout western North America, as well as in Asia and South America. The family also includes the soft-leaved May apple (*Podophyllum peltatum*), a common species in the understory of northeastern deciduous forests.

Some of the holly-like shrubs are cultivated as ornamentals. Unfortunately, one of these, the common barberry (*Berberis vulgaris*), is the obligate alternate host of black stem wheat rust. This fungus destroys acres of grain crop each year. Extermination of common barberry, on which the fungal spores are produced, is one way to prevent wheat rust from spreading. On the other hand, common barberry is also the source of berberine, which has antibacterial and antiviral properties. Barberry fruit and roots have been used as an effective herbal remedy for centuries, especially in Europe.

HOLLY GRAPE *Mahonia repens*

This plant is easily identified by its thick, sharp-pointed, holly-like leaves, bright yellow flowers and succulent purple berries. Holly grape is a low-growing evergreen shrub, spreading by rhizomes in the understory of open coniferous forests and among sagebrush. The leaves turn to flaming reds, oranges and deep purples in the fall, inspiring the Hispanic name, *yerba de sangre*, or "herb of blood." Some other names used for this plant are mountain holly, creeping barberry and Oregon grape. The Latin name, *Mahonia*, honors Bernard MacMahon, a friend of western botanist Thomas Nuttall. *Repens* describes the "creeping" nature of the rhizomes.

Holly grape and its shrubby relatives, found in other parts of Colorado, are credited as "one of the most beneficial medicinal plants of the West" by herbalist Michael Moore. A tea made of the dried roots has been used for centuries as a liver and blood tonic, laxative, treatment for rheumatism, fever reducer, antibacterial skin wash and, more recently, as an antidote for hangovers. The plant is also said to be an effective charm against ill-intentioned witches.

Jelly or wine can be made from the berries or they may be eaten raw. A bright yellow dye made from the roots and stems has been used by Native Americans in weaving and basketry. Holly grape berries are also important food sources for many species of wildlife.

Birch Family BETULACEAE

Birches are common wetland and riparian trees and shrubs in north temperate regions around the world. Paper birch *(Betula papyrifera)* is legendary for its use in making canoes. Birch wood is harvested to make furniture and plywood. Hazelnuts and filberts are the fruit of *Corylus* spp., trees native to Eurasia and cultivated primarily in Turkey, where more than 75% of the world's hazelnut production comes from. In the U.S., hazelnut orchards are most abundant in the Pacific Northwest. All species in this family are monoecious, having separate "male" (pollen-bearing) and "female" (seed-producing) flowers on the same plant, and are wind-pollinated.

ALDER *Alnus incana*

Alder trunks

Silvery-barked alders line many mountain streams and ponds. The seed-bearing catkin looks like a tiny pinecone. The roots have nitrogen-fixing nodules, similar to members of the Pea Family, making these trees important contributers to the nitrogen available in soils. Alders spread rapidly by rhizomes, creating thickets along streams, which is important cover for wildlife.

Male catkins

Female cones

BOG BIRCH *Betula glandulosa*

Along slow streams and marshy areas, bog birch blends with willows and contributes bright orange foliage to fall colors in wetland valleys. Bog birch is a low-growing shrub up to four feet high, with roundish, waxy leaves. The twigs and leaves are excellent forage for deer, elk and moose.

Borage Family BORAGINACEAE

The gestalt of the Borage Family comes from a combination of the rough hairs that cover many of the plants, and the coiled, or scorpioid arrangement of flower stems. When in bud, the stem is curled like a scorpion's tail. As the plant blooms, the tail uncurls. Another distinctive characteristic is the arrangement of four seeds or nutlets in the fruit, which are often equipped with barbs or hooks. The name borage is derived from the Latin word *burra*, which means "rough hair." A second interpretation comes from the Arabic term *abu 'arak*, which, if rolled around in your mouth, could also come out as borage. *Abu 'arak* means "father of sweat," applied especially to common borage (*Borago officinalis*), which is used as a medicinal tea to increase perspiration, thereby bringing out ailments. Comfrey (*Symphytum officinale*) is also in this family and is commonly used as a poultice or in salves to help heal wounds.

Included within the Borage Family are species that were once considered to be in a separate group known as the Waterleaf Family (Hydrophyllaceae). This placement differs from the 2001 version of the Colorado Checklist (Hartman and Nelson) that maintains the Waterleaf Family.

ALPINE FORGET-ME-NOT *Eritrichum nanum (E. aretioides)*

One of the rewards of climbing certain alpine peaks is to discover a patch of alpine forget-me-nots. They are found on dry, rocky alpine ridges, forming mats or cushions of small, fuzzy leaves. The mounds are sprinkled with periwinkle blue flowers to match the color of Colorado's summer sky. Occasionally you'll find albino forms. Get down on your belly to smell their sweet, spicy fragrance.

If you look closely, you may notice two different sizes of flowers in a population of forget-me-nots. The flowers of some plants are larger and hermaphroditic, having both male pollen-bearing parts and female seed-bearing parts. Other plants have flowers nearly half the size, but have only female parts. This type of reproductive diversity is called *gynodioecy*, meaning "two different types of females." Botanists believe that the energy saved by not producing pollen in the female flowers allows those plants to produce larger seeds and more vigorous seedlings. But the populations continue to produce hermaphrodites, which can self-pollinate, and, therefore, still produce seed when pollinators are limited.

Eritrichum is Greek for "woolly hairs," describing the texture of the leaves. *Nanum* means dwarf. The older species name, *aretioides*, depicts the habitat, which is often an alpine arete, a rocky ridge or mountain crest on high peaks throughout the northern hemisphere.

Stickseed Forget-Me-Not *Hackelia floribunda*

These plants are best remembered by their annoying seeds that stick to your socks, shoelaces and anything else you are wearing when you walk through them. This species is a tall slender plant, common in meadows and along roadsides. The pale blue flowers have bright yellow centers, but are not very abundant, contrary to the species name. The genus is named after P. Hackel (1850-1926), a German botanist who is credited with writing the *Flora of Bohemia*.

There are various legends associated with forget-me-nots. Perhaps best known is the German tale about a man who was led to a cave full of treasures by following a trail of blue flowers. As he entered the cave, a woman appeared and whispered, "Forget not the best!" Rather than heed her words, he hoarded gold and jewels found in the cave, leaving the beautiful flowers behind. As he ran down the trail, rocks fell from the mountain and killed him.

A Persian folktale tells how an angel and her human lover planted the flowers so that they could enter the Kingdom of Paradise together as immortals.

Yet another tells of two lovers enjoying a summer afternoon by a river. The gentleman picked a bouquet of blue flowers for his sweetheart and as he went to give them to her, he tripped and fell in the water. As he floated away, he tossed the bouquet to his lover and shouted, "Forget me not!"

Circumpolar Distribution

Many Rocky Mountain plant species have a circumpolar distribution, which is a fancy way of saying that they can be found in mountain ranges all around the northern hemisphere. Whether you are traveling in the Cascades, the Rockies, the Himalayas or the Alps, you may recognize about five dozen genera, or plant groups, that are the same in all of these regions, especially at higher elevations. Among them are the windflowers (*Anemone* spp.), columbines (*Aquilegia* spp.), forget-me-nots (*Hackelia* spp.), gentians (*Gentiana* spp.) and primroses (*Primula* spp.). Plants that share Eurasian distribution are also most likely to have folklore, legends, and medicinal history passed on to our culture. Pictured here in the Himalayan mountains of Pakistan is a species of fireweed, *Chamerion cylindricum*, very similar to our common species, *C. angustifolium* (p. 133).

Ballhead Waterleaf *Hydrophyllum capitatum*

Look for ballhead waterleaf blooming early in the summer season, nestled in the shelter of big sagebrush or hidden beneath the lush tall bluebells and meadow rue in an aspen forest. The clusters of lavender flowers are protected by the deeply lobed leaves. The long stamens make the flowers look soft and fuzzy, inspiring quaint names such as "woolen breeches" and "pussy foot." The flowers attract and are pollinated by bumblebee queens in the spring.

Fendler's Waterleaf *Hydrophyllum fendleri*

Fendler's waterleaf is common in the shaded understory of aspen forests and wet meadows. The flowers of Fendler's waterleaf are pale lavender or white and bloom on stems that rise above the leaves, while the flower clusters of ballhead waterleaf are below the leaves. Otherwise, the plant looks like a larger version of their cousins, but bloom later in the summer than ballhead waterleaf. This species is also popular with bumblebees.

Hydrophyllum fendleri is named in honor of Augustus Fendler, a 19th century plant collector who accompanied botanists George Engelmann and Asa Gray on their western expeditions in the late 1800s.

Bluebells *Mertensia* spp.

Two species of bluebells are common near Crested Butte. In early summer, look for dwarf bluebells growing in wet areas among the sagebrush or near aspen groves. By the time these have gone to seed, tall bluebells are blooming in the aspen understory, along streams and in wet mountain meadows. The genus is named in honor German botanist, F. K. Mertens (1764-1831).

Tall Bluebells *Mertensia ciliata*

Tall bluebells have soft hairless leaves, usually glistening with dew, that swish around your waist when walking along narrow mountain trails. Also known as chiming bells or languid ladies, the leaves make good potherbs or salad greens and have a slightly fishy taste.

Dwarf Bluebells *Mertensia fusiformis*

DAVID INOUYE

Dwarf bluebells are more typical of other borages, having leaves covered with stiff hairs. This species is distinguished from other short bluebells by the spindle shaped or "fusiform" root, like a carrot tapered at both ends. The plants rarely grow to more than ten inches high.

Silver Scorpionweed *Phacelia hastata*

Phacelia is a large genus comprising over one hundred species found throughout North America. There are sixteen documented in Colorado. They are named for the flowering stems that are arranged in coiled "fascicles," or clusters. Collectively, the genus is commonly called scorpionweed because of the curled flowering stem. Many phacelias are adapted to specific soil types. One of Colorado's endangered plant species is *P. formosula*, which grows only in the sandy soils of the Coalmont formation in North Park, Colorado.

Scorpionweeds are excellent colonizers of disturbed areas. Perhaps the finest example of this is on the coal tailings near Peanut Lake. One of the few plant species thriving in these sterile soils is silver scorpionweed, which has cream-colored or pale lavender flowers and grayish green leaves. This plant is found growing on rocky soils from lower elevation sagebrush to above treeline.

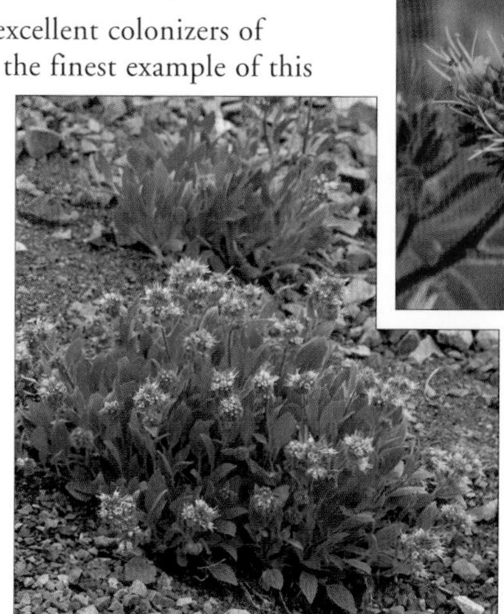

Purple Fringe *Phacelia sericea*

The showiest and most common local member of the genus *Phacelia* is purple fringe, which grows on rocky slopes high on the alpine tundra or on gravelly meadows and roadsides near spruce-fir and lodgepole pine forests. The flowers look fringed because of the long, yellow stamens that stick out of the deep purple corollas. The plants are usually buzzing with bumblebees and other insects that are attracted by their pungent fragrance. Long, soft hairs cover the leaves, giving the plant another common name, silky phacelia. *Sericea* means "silky."

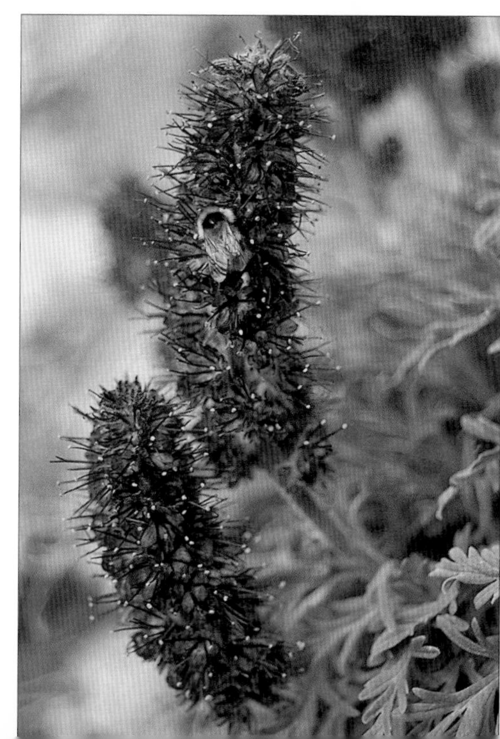

Mustard Family BRASSICACEAE

Over two thousand years ago, ancient Greeks, Romans and Egyptians mixed crushed seeds from these plants with unfermented wine, called must, to make a spicy paste. Today, mustard, as well as horseradish, broccoli, brussels sprouts, cabbage, cauliflower, radishes, canola oil and watercress are part of the harvest brought to the dining table from this family of plants.

Whether you are in the back alleys of town, riding through a hay meadow or basking on the summit of a high peak, you are never very far from a mustard. These plants include some of the most noxious introduced weeds, as well as several radically endemic species confined to only a few protected hollows on certain mountains in Colorado. Mustards are well adapted to growing in disturbed areas and on soils of particular mineral composition. This explains the ability of some to rapidly invade agricultural lands and roadsides, as well as the restriction of others to habitats so rare that the species are federally endangered.

One easy way to identify a mustard is to look for parts in fours. Four petals and four sepals are one of the signatures of the Mustard Family and the origin of one of the old family names, Cruciferae. The four petals make a cross or crucifix. Not all four-petaled flowers are mustards, however (see Bedstraw, p. 177 and Evening Primrose families, p. 132). Check for six stamens and a superior ovary (seed pod above the petals) to make sure it is a mustard. The seed pods are also distinctive and often critical for species identification, ranging from tiny, flat, heart-shaped pods to long, thin pods or short, puffy "bladder" pods.

There are over 3200 mustard species worldwide. In the Crested Butte area, there are nearly forty, including at least half a dozen introduced weeds and three very rare species.

HEARTLEAF BITTERCRESS *Cardamine cordifolia*

Heartleaf bittercress flourishes on old beaver dams and along cold streams in the high mountains. The spicy tasting leaves are edible and a plentiful trailside snack. Cress is an Old English word for plants in the Mustard Family, especially those used as salad greens. The generic name comes from the Greek word *kardamon*, which was used for many members of the family. *Cordifolia* means "heart-shaped leaf."

JANNETTE RUNGE

DAVID INOUYE

Golden Draba *Draba aurea*

This small, perennial, yellow-flowered mustard is one of the first plants to bloom following snowmelt and is common on gravelly or rocky soils throughout the Rocky Mountains. By the end of June, golden draba has gone to seed. This is one of twenty-eight species of *Draba* found in Colorado, eighteen of which are known in Gunnison County. Six species in this group are alpine endemics, restricted to various mountain ranges in the region, and are considered rare.

Drabas are also known as "whitlow-grass." A "whitlow" is an infected hangnail or ingrown nail. Though there are no specific references, it is likely that the name derived from the use of these plants to reduce such inflammations. *Draba* means acrid, referring to the sharp taste of the plants, which are high in ascorbic acid or vitamin C.

Wallflower *Erysimum capitatum*

Like many mountain plants, wallflower changes form depending on the elevation, growing as a tall, slender plant up to three feet high at lower elevations and hugging the ground on the alpine tundra. Wherever it grows, it is easy to recognize in bloom, having many large (~half-inch diameter) flowers clustered at the top of the stem, long, narrow leaves and long, thin seed pods. The flower color can range from pale yellow at lower elevations, to orange and lavender in some alpine populations.

The genus, *Erysimum*, is derived from the Greek word *eryomai*, meaning "to help or save," because of the medicinal uses of this and other mustards in plasters as relief from congestion and to treat stiff, sore muscles. *Capitatum* means "forming a head," referring to the cluster of flowers. Wallflowers are hardly inconspicuous or unassuming, but are known to grow next to walls.

Dame's Rocket *Hesperis matronalis* Non-native Species

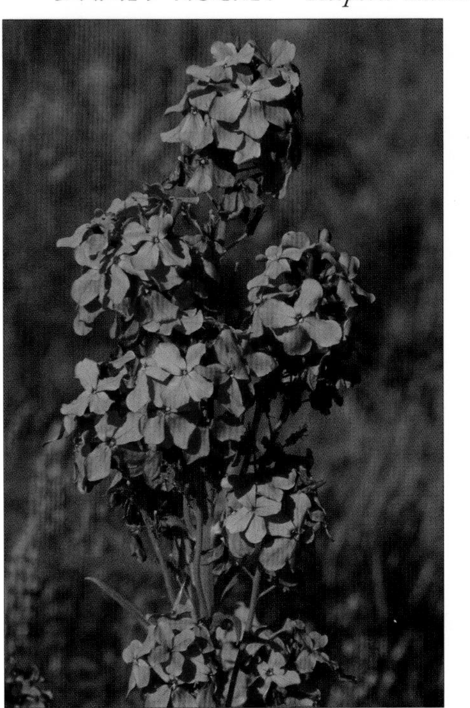

Hot-pink flowers of dame's rocket are a common ingredient in "wildflower" seed mixes, although it was imported from Europe as an ornamental. The plants can sometimes be found around old mining settlements and in nearby wildlands where they have escaped from gardens.

The Latin name means "lady of the evening," with *hesperis* referring to the sweet scent of the flowers, which is strongest at dusk. However, dame's rocket is listed as a noxious weed in Colorado and much of the U.S. because of its ability to proliferate and invade wildland habitats. When choosing seed mixes or shopping for potted plants, try to use native plants when possible and avoid any non-native species that may be invasive. Fireweed (p. 132-33) is an excellent native alternative to dame's rocket for adding brilliant fuschia to your garden, and is available in many garden centers.

Candytuft *Noccaea montanum (Thlaspi montanum)*

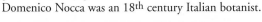

Another ubiquitous mustard, candytuft is common throughout western North America in a wide variety of habitats, from plains to tundra. Although small and inconspicuous, the clusters of white flowers are noticeable because they are one of the first spring wildflowers wherever they grow. They may grow from just a few inches to over a foot tall. The seedpods are heart-shaped. Domenico Nocca was an 18th century Italian botanist.

WENDY BROWN

DAVID INOUYE

Smelowskia *Smelowskia calycina*

Smelowskia is one of the most common and hearty alpine mustards in the Rockies, growing in large clumps and mats on steep scree fields and exposed talus slopes. Clusters of fragrant, white and pink-tinged flowers add a soft touch to the rocky tundra environment throughout the summer. The short, dark seedpods and deeply lobed grayish-green leaves are also very distinctive. The same species is also found on the Asian continent, where it was studied by a Russian botanist, T. Smelovskii. *Calycina* refers to the calyx, or sepals, of the flowers.

"Fungus Flowers"

In early spring you may find what looks like a small, showy yellow flower among the sagebrush. Look more closely and you will see that these flowers are really the rust covered leaves of rockcress (*Arabis* spp.). Rockcress is normally a tall, slender type of wild mustard with white or lavender flowers. Rocky Mountain Biological Laboratory researcher Dr. Barbara Roy has found that the bright yellow rust, a kind of fungus, mimics flowers both with its color and by causing the host plant to alter the growth of its leaves so that they are clustered like petals. The rust also exudes a sweet fluid that flies feed on. Pollinating flies that normally visit true yellow flowers are fooled and attracted to the floral mimics, thereby facilitating reproduction of the rust, which then produces spores that disperse by wind to infect other plants.

DAVID INOUYE

DAVID INOUYE

Cactus Family CACTACEAE

Usually when we think of cacti, we visualize a hot, sandy desert in southern Arizona, or the red rock country of Utah. Though you won't find towering saguaro or giant barrel cactus near here, there are some beautiful cacti growing in the cold, high country of the southern Rockies. Cacti are endemic to the western hemisphere, but have been introduced to continents and islands all over the globe, where they often become invasive non-natives.

Most cacti have sweet edible fruit, although the fruits may be a little too small to bother collecting from the well-armored plants. The protective spines are actually modified leaves on a cactus, while the fleshy green parts are the water-storing and photosynthesizing stems.

Cacti are typically tolerant of disturbance, so they will thrive where other native plants have a tough time getting re-established or are continually being eaten. In parts of sagebrush country where land is regularly grazed, cacti are often abundant, since cattle generally leave the prickly plants alone. The ball nipple cactus thrives on the railroad grade in Lost Canyon near Almont, an area of extreme disturbance that is now restored to natural conditions.

Despite their ability to endure extremes of hot and dry environments, as well as disturbance, cacti are some of the most threatened plant species due to collection by rock garden enthusiasts. There is even a thriving black market for cacti in some parts of the southwest. In Arizona, collection of cacti in the wild is considered illegal. Colorado has no such laws, except as applied to federally threatened or endangered species. It is always best to enjoy them in their natural habitat, unless you are rescuing them from the bulldozers.

PRICKLY PEAR *Opuntia polyacantha*

Bright yellow flowers of prickly pear bloom in mid-summer, an elegant contrast to the spiny, sprawling stems that grow low to the ground among sagebrush. This is the most common of three species of prickly pear in the Gunnison Basin. In the East River valley, you can find these cacti in the Almont Triangle (see p. 200). *Opuntia* is a huge genus, with over two hundred species, ranging from small stemmed, ground hugging plants to tree-like forms towering over ten feet high and pads over a foot in diameter. The stems are jointed, with flattish, oval pads that can easily grow into a new plant if separated from the parent. The fruits and pads are edible, though with this species the effort is greater than the reward. Another species in southwest Colorado is potato cactus (*O. fragilis*), which has smaller, more spherical joints, like little potatoes.

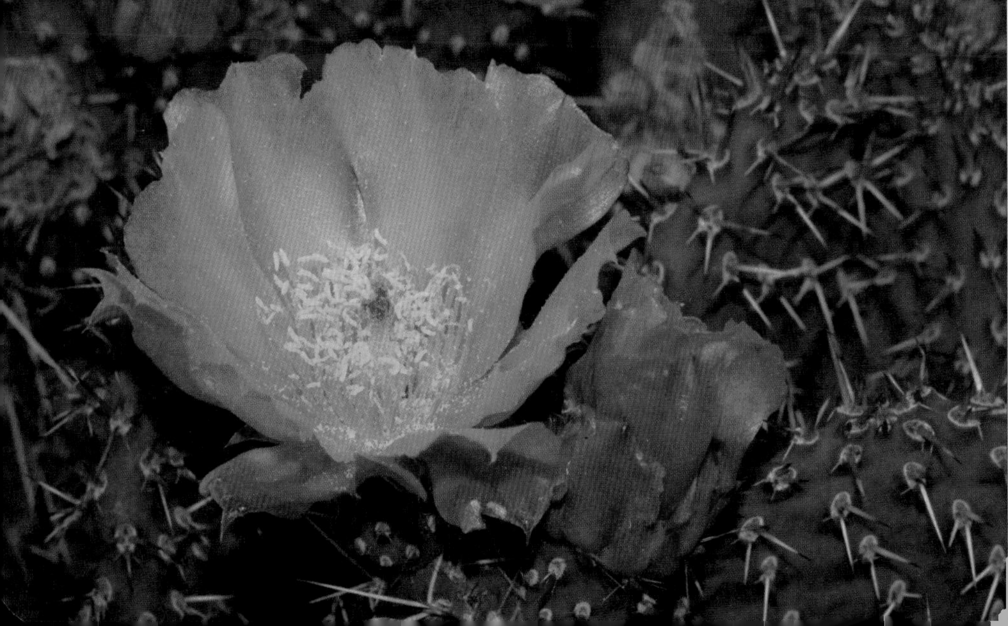

Mountain Ball Cactus *Pediocactus simpsonii*

The pale pink, waxy flowers of mountain ball cactus have a soft rose-like scent. These softball-sized and shaped cacti can be found growing on sunny, exposed areas among sagebrush. Locally, they are common along the Upper Loop Trail, in Crested Butte South and throughout the Jack's Cabin area, where they bloom in early summer. Mountain ball cactus is Colorado's highest growing cactus species and can be found all the way up to 10,000 feet. The genus, *Pediocactus,* is derived from the Greek word *pedion*, meaning "flatland," because they are most common on the plains. Our species is named after J.H. Simpson, an army engineer and friend of western botanist, George Engelmann, who had a special interest in cacti. These cacti often grow in clusters and can reproduce vegetatively by branching off new little balls, as well as reproducing by seed. In the late summer and winter, the succulent balls wither and recede into the ground, barely detectable until spring, when they revive and swell up to six inches in diameter.

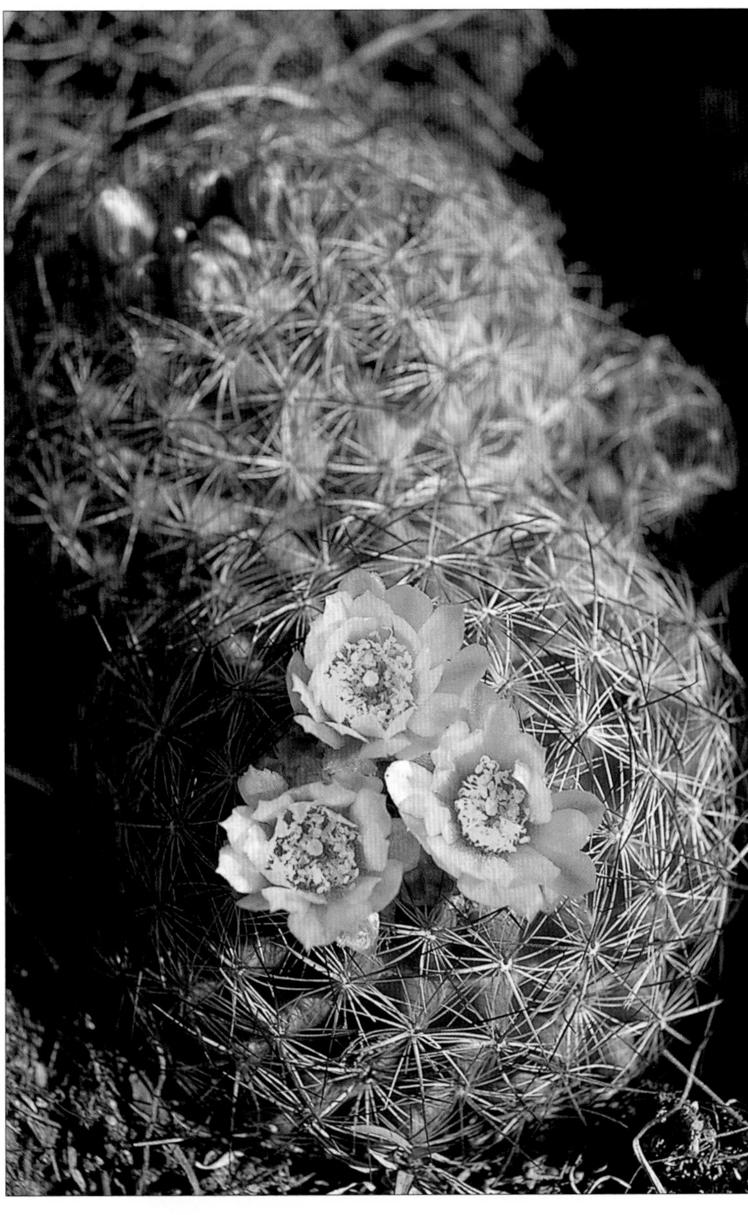

Bellflower Family CAMPANULACEAE

Many plants in this family are used in rock gardens and are available commercially at landscaping centers. Most commonly used are the annual lobelias, which are cultivated as garden border plants. A native species of lobelia, the cardinal flower, can be found growing near desert springs in western Colorado, but does not grow in the high mountains. However, three species of harebell are very common throughout the Elk Mountains.

The flowers in this family share the characteristics of a three-parted stigma and *inferior* ovary, meaning that the seed-bearing part of the plant is found below the point on the flowering stem where the petals and sepals are attached. Lobelias and harebells look very different though, as lobelias are bilaterally symmetrical and harebells are, as goes the name, bell-shaped.

HAREBELL *Campanula* spp.

Harebells are found around the world in the northern hemisphere, with over three hundred species recognized. These delicate, lavender-colored flowers are best known as the bluebells of Scotland. Another name, witch's thimble, comes from a Scottish superstition that witches commonly transform themselves into hares. They are also called lady's thimble, although the same superstition does not apply to refined women. The lovely flowers are regarded as a symbol of constancy and kindness, more fitting to a lady. The association with hares probably comes from the quaint British custom of naming plants after small furry animals, the bell being just the right size for a Beatrix Potter character to ring her children in for dinner.

Campanula is Latin for "little bell," an appropriate description for all of the species. The three species found in our mountains all look very similar. Joseph Barrell, author of *Flora of the Gunnison Basin* (1969), describes their differences most succinctly: "Parry's harebell directs its solitary blossoms toward the sky;" the blossoms of our common harebell are "anything but solitary, and are usually nodding;" the alpine harebell "blooms solitarily, and its low, sinuous stems barely get off the ground in its alpine habitat."

> *"...these hardy bells, swaying with exquisite grace on tremulous, hair-like stems are fitted to withstand the fiercest mountain blasts, however frail they appear."*
>
> – Neltje Blanchan

PARRY'S HAREBELL *Campanula parryi*

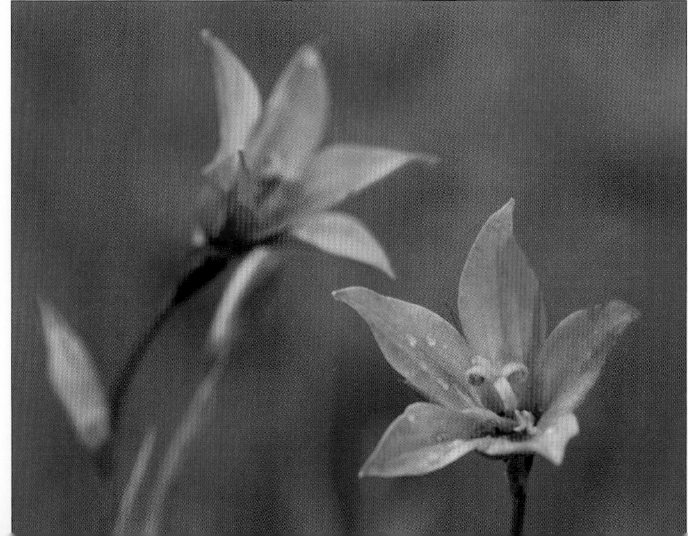

Common Harebell *Campanula rotundifolia*

Unlike the official species name (*rotundifolia* = "round-leaved") used for the common harebell, all of the native harebells usually have long linear leaves. All of them bloom from mid- to late summer. The common and Parry's harebell grow on drier soils in open meadows from sagebrush to subalpine elevations.

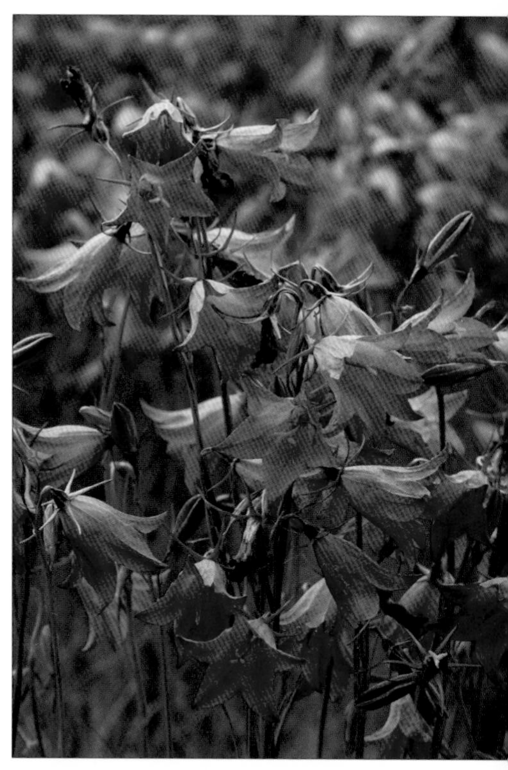

The most renowned harebell is commonly known as rapunzel (*Campanula rapunculoides*), which is a European native sold commercially as an ornamental and culinary herb. This is the plant craved by the pregnant mother in versions of the centuries old fairy tale, Rapunzel. Also known as "rampion" and creeping harebell, the roots and leaves of this plant are sweet and nutritious. Creeping harebell is listed in the *Colorado Flora* as an adventive, meaning that it is a non-native that tends to escape horticultural situations and can be invasive.

Navajo wisdom says that if a woman eats harebells during her pregnancy, she will give birth to a girl, an interesting corollary to the old European legend. A poultice of the root is also said to be effective for healing bruises, making it useful for new mothers after giving birth.

Alpine Harebell *Campanula uniflora*

Hemp Family CANNABACEAE

The Hemp Family is very small, but global in distribution. Perhaps one of the best known plants in the world, *Cannabis sativa*, is in this family and has been used for millennia as a narcotic and as a source of fiber. Botanically, hemp is closely related to mulberries (Moraceae) and nettles (Urticaceae, p. 195), two families that, like hemp, have inconspicuous unisexual flowers arranged in catkins.

WILD HOPS *Humulus lupulus*

Wild hops are vines and are found growing all over some of the old alley shacks around mountain towns. In the wild, hops climb shrubs and trees in canyons and along watercourses in the lower mountains and foothills. The flowers resemble pale green pine cones and are called strobules.

In the brewing industry, it's the European hops, *Humulus lupulus*, which besides being a lot of fun to say, are cultivated for the preservative effect, foaming quality and bitter flavor they lend to ales and stouts. Our native hops, *Humulus lupulus* var. *americanus*, are equally effective for all of these purposes.

Like their relative, *Cannabis sativa*, wild hops have a narcotic effect when smoked, though milder. More commonly, hops strobules have been used to stuff pillows and brew in teas for their sedative effect, promoting the relief of tension and anxiety, just as the fermented brew will do.

Caper Family CAPPARACEAE

Members of this family are most common in tropical and subtropical climates around the world. Best known is *Capparis spinosa*, a spiny shrub native to the Mediterranean region, which is the source of the pickled green pea-like delicacy we know as capers. Some species are also popular as garden ornamentals, especially *Cleome spinosa*, or spider flower. *Caper* is the Latin word for goat; some say the family is so named because the plants smell similar to the animal. The four-petaled flowers and long seedpods may lead casual observers to confuse them with members of the Mustard Family, with which capers are closely related.

ROCKY MOUNTAIN BEEPLANT *Cleome serrulata*

Despite its goaty smell, beeplant has been considered a vital food plant for many North American Indian tribes throughout its distribution, which includes most of the western states. Also known as stinkweed, the entire plant is made edible by steaming or boiling thoroughly to remove the bitter taste. The seeds are also nutritious and have been credited with supporting the survival of many tribes through periods of drought and famine. The plant is so highly valued that it is named along with corn, beans and squash in ceremonial chants of Pueblo tribes in New Mexico. Today, some native peoples still include beeplant in their diet as part of stews. Another widespread use of the boiled leaves is as a black paint for pottery and basketry.

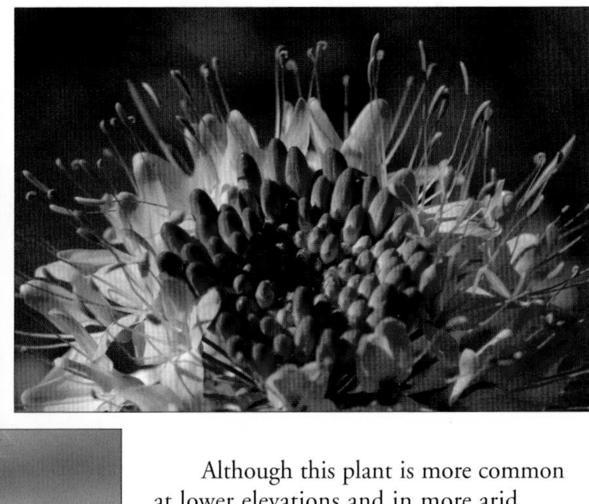

Although this plant is more common at lower elevations and in more arid conditions, it has recently appeared as high as Cement Creek, seven miles south of Crested Butte at 8,500 feet elevation. Beeplant is an annual and tolerant of disturbance, so it thrives along roadsides and other poor soil conditions. This would be an interesting plant to monitor to see if it increases its distribution up the East River Valley over the next decade. Beeplant would also be a beautiful addition to native gardens. Look for the bright pink flower heads atop three to five-foot branched stems in late summer, followed by long dangling seedpods.

Honeysuckle Family CAPRIFOLIACEAE

Plants in this family share characteristics of opposite leaves and branches and pairs of tubular flowers. I always remember this when using the acronym for shrubs and trees having opposite branches: MADCap, or maple, ash, dogwood and Caprifoliaceae. The Latin name, like the family Capparaceae, is somehow related to goats. However, in this case, most plants in this family are sweet-smelling. Some suggest that the name may come from someone's observation that goats (*capra*) enjoy feasting on the leaves (*folia*) of honeysuckles.

TWINFLOWER *Linnaea borealis*

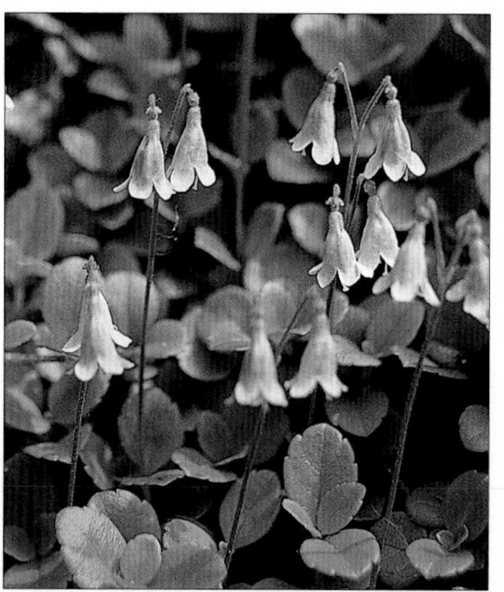

Twinflower is one of the most famous plants in the field of taxonomy, named in honor of the Swedish father of systematic botany, Carolus Linnaeus. Reputed to be his favorite plant, twinflower grows in northern forests around the globe. This woody-stemmed, creeping evergreen is atypical of the family, which includes mostly larger deciduous shrubs. When in bloom, the pairs of pinkish or white bell-shaped flowers are unmistakeable, scattered on the floor of coniferous forests. A close look will reward you with a light vanilla fragrance. Without flowers, the low spreading shrub with roundish dark-green leaves could be mistaken for kinnikinnik or mountain lover. Look for the opposite leaves, which are mostly smooth-edged, unlike the opposite finely serrated leaves of mountain lover or alternating, smooth-edged leaves of kinnikinnik.

TWINBERRY *Lonicera involucrata (Distegia involucrata)*

Ripe pairs of plump, succulent, dark-purple berries on these shrubs look irresistible, and are considered to be edible, but they are best left for the birds. The fruit is extremely bitter, although beautifully displayed beneath the bright red involucre, or envelope of leafy bracts, for which this species is named. The long (~ one inch), yellow, bell-shaped flowers produce abundant nectar, attracting hummingbirds and long-tongued bumblebees as pollinators. Twinberry is common along mountain streams and in moist soils all the way up to treeline. The genus commemorates Adam Lonitzer, a 16th century German herbalist.

Elderberry *Sambucus racemosa (S. microbotrys)*

The straight, dry, pithy stems of elderberry bushes have probably been used since prehistoric times to make music and fire. A *sambuce* was a Greek musical instrument, or bark whistle, which could be made by boring out the center of an elderberry branch. Elder comes from the Old English word *ellen*, meaning "fire kindler."

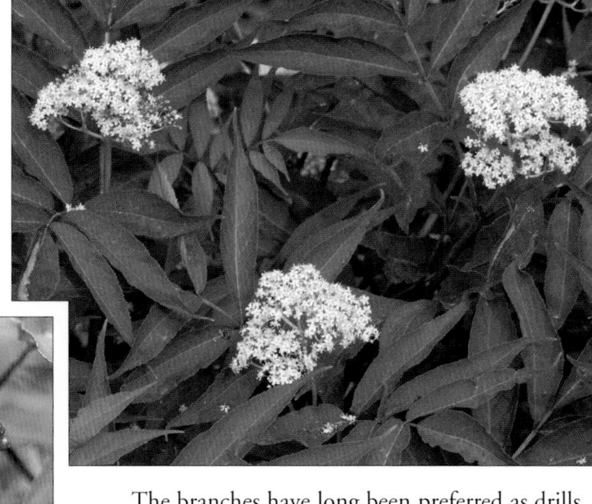

The branches have long been preferred as drills for the method of "rubbing sticks together" to make fire. The drill is twirled rapidly on another piece of wood called a hearth. The friction causes the drill and part of the hearth to turn into sawdust, forming an ember that can be used to start a fire.

These lush shrubs are found all over the mountains from aspen forests to alpine talus slopes, and are easy to recognize by their clusters of tiny cream-colored flowers and large compound leaves. Elderberries are also common ornamentals, although for some reason an anemic looking yellow-leaved variety has become popular among landscapers. In the fall, bunches of bright red berries attract birds and other wildlife.

Unfortunately, the red berries most commonly found around Crested Butte are somewhat toxic to humans. In other parts of the Rocky Mountains, an edible, blue-berried species (*Sambucus cerulea*) grows wild. The common European species, *Sambucus niger*, is cultivated to make juice, wine, jam and syrups. These concoctions are primarily used medicinally, although the fresh flowers of any of the species can be dipped in batter and fried to make elderberry fritters. Tinctures and teas made from the bark, leaves, flowers and berries have all been used as treatments for colds, fever and rheumatism. Elderberry is also noted as an emetic and mild diuretic.

Snowberry *Symphoricarpos oreophilus (S. rotundifolius)*

Snowberries are fairly unique in having shiny white berries, rather than bright reds or purples that announce their presence to foraging wildlife. Like others in the family, they are edible, but not always especially tasty. The Latin name, *Symphoricarpos oreophilus*, means "pairs of berries, mountain-loving"; *rotundifolius* means "round leaves." All of these terms make up a succinct description of this low-growing shrub. Snowberries are most commonly found in big sagebrush communities and aspen forests.

Pink Family CARYOPHYLLACEAE

Carnations are the best known members of the Pink Family, which includes a slew of other ornamentals such as sweet William, baby's breath, bouncing Bet, snow-in-summer and chickweed. Many have been introduced to North America from Europe specifically for gardening and have since become "naturalized," meaning that they have become widespread throughout the country in natural habitats, old fields and roadsides, as well as in well-tended landscapes. At least one, bouncing Bet (*Saponaria officinalis*), is listed as a noxious weed throughout the country because of its tendency to escape gardens and take over entire fields of native wildflowers.

At least a dozen indigenous species of pinks grow in the Elk Mountains, in addition to an equal number of exotic garden pinks that have escaped or have intentionally been planted as part of "wildflower seed" mixes in revegetation projects. Natives and non-natives alike tend to be good colonizers of disturbed, barren or gravelly sites.

The family name, Caryophyllaceae, means "hard leaf" in Latin, referring to the thick, stiff leaves of many species. Some taxonomists divide the group into two families based on characteristics of the sepals and petals, dividing out the Chickweed Family (Alsinaceae).

SNOWBALL SANDWORT *Arenaria congesta (Eremogene congesta)*

This sandwort thrives in a broad elevation range, from dry soils among sagebrush to exposed areas above treeline. They sometimes grow into large mats of thin pointy leaves, but are usually small clumps scattered on rocky soils. Clusters of small, white flowers at the top of slender stems look like little snowballs. The Latin name, *Arenaria congesta,* translates to "of sand, congested," describing the habitat and flowers. Some taxonomists have separated this genus into more than five groups and place this species in the genus *Eremogene,* meaning "desert flower," alluding to their preference for dry microhabitats. In the fall, look for the bundle of seed capsules, which look like tiny goblets, tossing dozens of black seeds to the wind.

MOUSE-EAR CHICKWEED *Cerastium arvense (C. strictum)*

Chickweed is one of the most widespread perennials around the globe. Clumps of chickweed will quickly colonize disturbed areas, such as roadsides, grazed meadows, and areas that have been developed for housing. This is the native equivalent of snow-in-summer (*Cerastium tomentosum*), a native of Eurasia which is cultivated for horticulture and a common element of gardens in mountain towns of Colorado. The native species is taller and perennial, whereas snow-in-summer is a mat-forming annual with very hairy leaves.

Moss Campion *Silene acaulis*

Mounds of moss campion are common on the alpine tundra, anchored by a deep taproot on dry, windy ridges and gravelly fields. Tightly packed cushions of leaves help the plant to conserve moisture and heat, as well as to trap bits of soil that will eventually build up around the mound to support more growth. Each plant may live over a hundred years, with large cushions growing to over three feet in diameter! Over its long life, a moss campion may become a "nursery" plant for other alpine species, providing the shelter, moisture and soil for seeds to germinate and grow. The magenta-pink flowers are usually crowded towards the warmer south-facing side of the cushion, acting as a sort of compass for cloud-shrouded mountaineers.

Moss campion is one of the many glacial relicts found on alpine peaks around the northern hemisphere. As glaciers advanced in the Pleistocene Era (~10,000 years ago), arctic species migrated south ahead of the ice. When glaciers receded, these species remained on high mountains that served as refuges similar in climate to their original arctic habitat during times of peak glaciation.

About 500 species of *Silene* are found around the world and are named after *Silenus*, foster father of the Greek god of wine, Dionysus, and the gods' attendant satyrs. A patch of bright-colored campions might inspire you to merriment and lechery for which these deities are known. Campion is derived from the Latin word *campus*, meaning "field," which is the habitat for many of the species. Plants in this genus are also commonly known as catchflies because many have sticky glands on their stems and leaves that act as a kind of flypaper, trapping harmful insects which might sneak up and steal nectar.

True Mosses

Mosses are primitive non-flowering plants and lack a vascular system to transport water and nutrients. Thus, they have no true roots or stems and the "leaves" have no veins. Mosses also reproduce with spores rather than seeds. You may think that all mosses look alike, but bryologists, scientists who study mosses, have identified over 30,000 moss species around the world growing in every type of habitat imaginable, from aquatic environments to the driest deserts. In Colorado, one of the most threatened habitat types are peat bogs, where sphagnum moss is harvested for gardening.

Staff Tree Family CELASTRACEAE

This is a family of mostly tropical and sub-tropical trees, shrubs and vines. Perhaps the most economically important member of this family is *Catha edulis*, commonly known as khat, a shrub native to the Middle East. Vast plantations of the shrub are cultivated, especially in the Arabian country of Yemen, where about 80% of adults in the country chew the fresh leaves. The plant contains a chemical called cathinone, which has a strong stimulant and sometimes hallucinogenic effect, though it is reputed to be non-addictive. Use of the plant is recorded in ancient Egyptian texts.

A popular ornamental plant in this family is a vine called bittersweet (*Celastrus scandens*), which is used as an ornamental in flower arrangements because of its bright orange seed pods. The wood of the spindle-tree (*Euonymus* spp.) was once used to make spinning distaffs, a tool used to hold fibers being spun into thread or yarn, giving the family its common name.

MOUNTAIN LOVER *Paxistima myrsinites*

Mountain lover is the only plant in the Staff Tree Family native to the Rocky Mountains. The low-growing shrubs (one to two feet high) are evergreen and very common in the shaded understory of aspen and coniferous forests. At first glance you might confuse it with kinnikinnik (p. 92), which often grows side-by-side with mountain lover. With a second look, it's easy to tell the difference between the two: mountain lover has opposite leaves with tiny teeth on the edges; kinnikinnik has alternating smooth-edged leaves. The flowers of mountain lover are tiny (~1/8" diam.) with four salmon-red petals; kinnikinnik has larger pink and white bell-shaped flowers. Both shrubs bloom early in the summer.

Mountain lover is distinguished as one of the Tertiary relicts of the Rocky Mountains, having survived as a species through twenty million years of geologic activity. The Latin name, *Paxistima myrsinites*, translates to "myrtle-like plant with thick stigmas." The flowers of mountain lover have unusually large stigmas, the female, pollen-receiving organ. Myrtles are also low-growing evergreen shrubs, mostly native to Australia and South America, and are related to the eucalyptus tree.

Dogwood Family Cornaceae

The dogwoods are a small family of more than a hundred species of woody plants found mostly in temperate climates around the world. In North America, different species of flowering dogwood trees are common on both the east and west coasts, and the tree is claimed by both Virginia and North Carolina (*Cornus floridus*) as well as B.C., Canada (*Cornus nuttallii*) as the state flower. In Atlanta, Georgia, a Dogwood Festival celebrates the spectacular trees each spring.

The name dogwood probably originated from the Old English term *dagge*, meaning any sharp, pointed instrument. The sturdy wood of the trees has been used for daggers, as well as printing blocks, knitting needles, toothpicks, cogwheels and fine instruments for cleaning watches.

Red Osier Dogwood *Cornus sericea*

The bright red stems of dogwood shrubs add color to the winter landscape along shaded streams and rivers among alder and willow. They can reproduce easily, as do willows, by laying roots from spreading stems so that they may form extensive thickets, and will grow up to ten feet tall. The large green leaves are oval and pointed at the tip, and arranged in pairs on the stems. In contrast with the large, showy blossoms of dogwood trees common in other parts of the country, those of this shrub are found in small clusters of tiny white flowers, each with four petals. In the fall, the leaves turn beautiful shades of red, orange and yellow, showing off the smooth white berries.

The stems, leaves and berries are important food for many species of wildlife. For humans, the shrub makes a beautiful ornamental in landscapes, and is especially good for attracting wildlife. The strong, straight and pliable stems are valued for basketry. The term "osier" means "willow," or any flexible stem used for basket weaving.

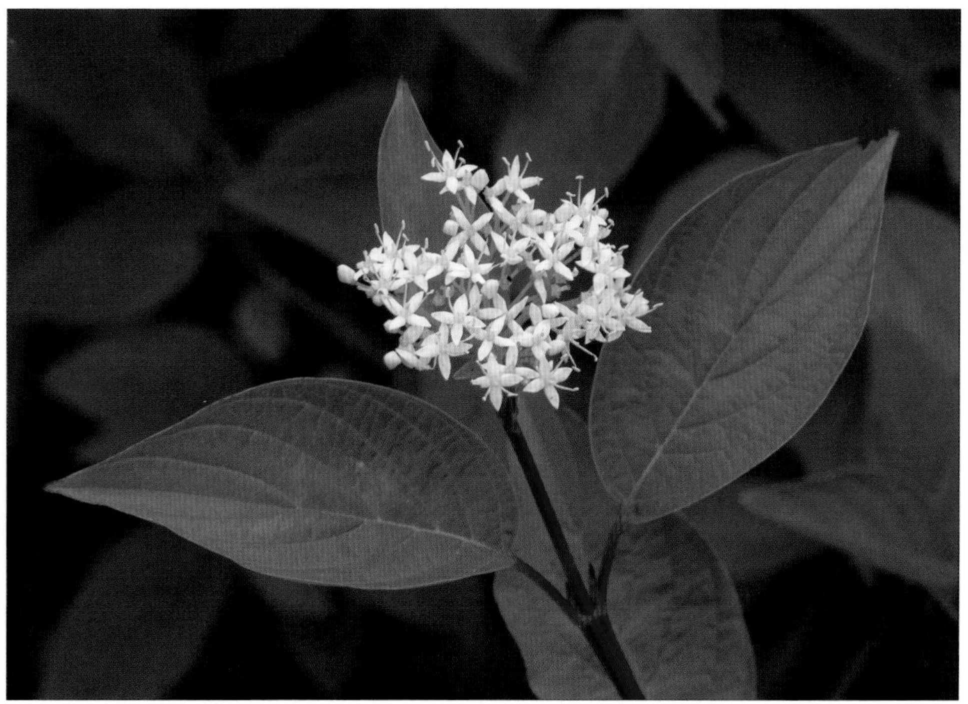

Stonecrop Family CRASSULACEAE

Stonecrops are a small family of about 900 species found all over the world, being especially diverse and abundant in South Africa. Most are succulent, having thick stems and leaves that store water and are capable of enduring long droughts. So resilient are these species that botanists have observed pressed collections to continue growing even after several months!

Many exotic stonecrops are widely marketed for rock gardens and houseplants, including various species of jade plants (*Crassula* spp.) and hens-and-chickens (*Sempervivum tectorum*). The family name, Crassulaceae, comes from the Latin word *crassus*, meaning "thick," for the succulent leaves. As a group, they are also known as orpine, because many have golden-yellow flowers. Orpine is derived from the Latin word *aurum*, which also ties linguistically to the east, or dawn, for the color of the morning sky. Many grow in dry, rocky habitats, hence the name stonecrop, and are useful as potherbs.

Flower Essences

An English physician named Edward Bach began experimenting with flower essences in 1928, using them to heal illnesses on an "energetic level." His ideas suggest that each type of flower has its own particular energy, which may be used to release tension in our own energy fields, and to "vibrate with the consciousness" contained in flowers. An essence of stonecrop is said to "awaken and enhance illumination, bringing a moment of grace to those in the midst of struggle or despondency."

King's Crown *Sedum integrifolium (Rhodiola integrifolia)*

King's crown is found in habitats similar to queen's crown, but always a little bit drier. In fact, you can often find them growing within a few feet of each other. The two plants look so much alike, you might wonder why they are sometimes placed in separate genera. Differences in sexuality distinguish the two. King's crown can be dioecious, having separate male and female plants, or it can be monoecious, having male and female flowers on the same plant. Queen's crown has "perfect" flowers with both stamens (male) and pistils (female). The flowers of king's crown are a velvety maroon color, or *Rhodiola*, another color of rose. The roots have a faint fragrance of rose, hence another common name, roseroot. *Integrifolia* means that the leaves are smooth-edged.

Thorough research has been done on the chemical and medicinal properties of *Rhodiola rosea,* a closely related species common in the mountains of northern Europe and Asia. The roots of this plant have been used for centuries as a remedy for physical and mental fatigue.

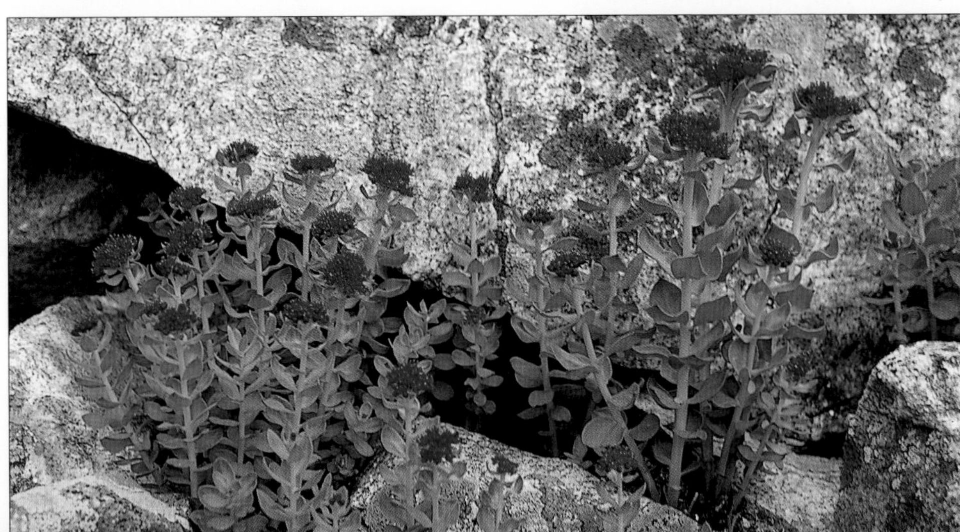

Yellow Stonecrop *Sedum lanceolatum*

Yellow stonecrop is common wherever there is dry gravelly soil and plenty of sun, from the sagebrush hills to alpine summits. Over a third of the Stonecrop Family are sedums, characterized by their plump, tubular leaves. These are one of the first spring wildflowers to bloom in the sagebrush, with bright yellow star-like blossoms and sprawling, reddish-green stems and leaves. The Latin word *sedum*, means "to sit," because they "sit" close to the ground or rocks on which they grow. This species has "lanceolate" leaves, meaning they are long, narrow and come to a point. The succulent stems and leaves are valued as survival food, though large amounts can be toxic.

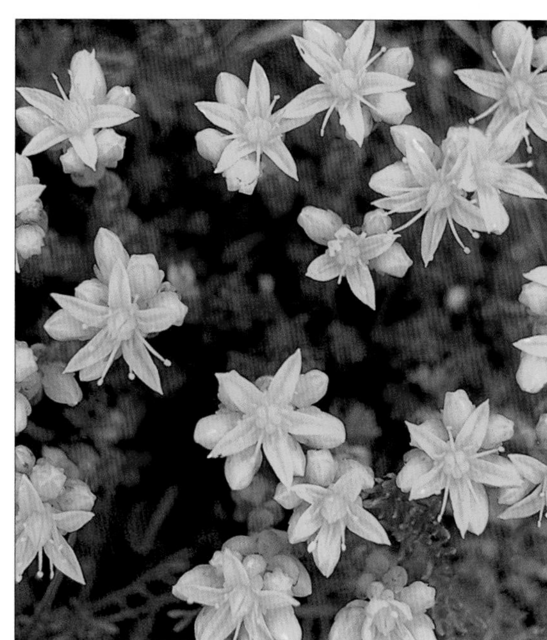

Queen's Crown *Sedum rhodanthum (Clementsia rhodantha)*

Also known as rose crown, the pale pink flowers of queen's crown crowd at the top of the succulent stems, resembling a head of clover. They bloom late in the summer along subalpine streams and marshes and like plenty of sun. The alternate Latin name honors Frederic E. Clements (1874-1945), an American plant ecologist who was well-known as the main author of the climax theory of plant succession. This theory suggests that every ecosystem has an "ultimate" suite of vegetation if left undisturbed long enough. *Rhodanthum* means "rose-colored flower."

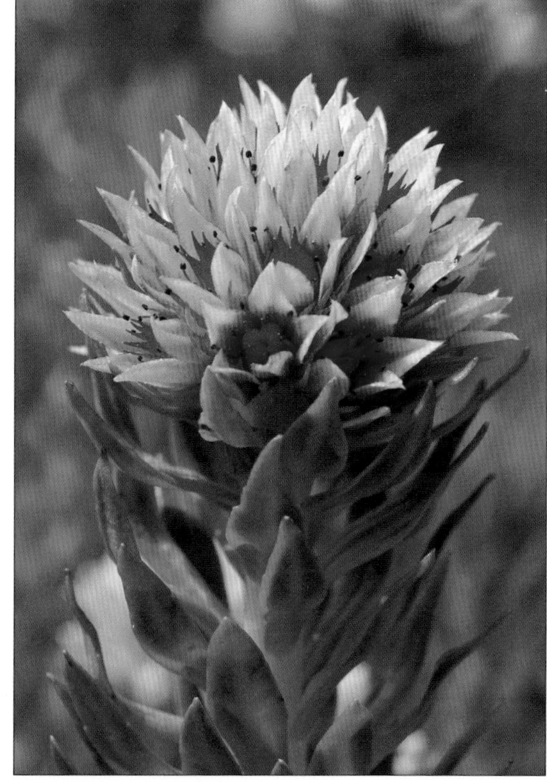

Sedge Family CYPERACEAE

Like the grasses (Poaceae) and rushes (Juncaceae), sedges tend to be passed over as mere greenery, and have reputations for being tough to identify beyond their status as a sedge. However, sedges are important indicators of the overall health of ecosystems, especially in wetlands, where they are most abundant. The tiny flowers of these species are wind-pollinated, as are grasses.

One famous sedge is papyrus (*Cyperus papyrus*), from which Egyptians made paper for several thousand years. Another sedge that has played an important role in civilization is the giant reed (*Scirpus totora*), which is used in South America to make rafts and islands for building houses and may even have been used to navigate the oceans as far as Polynesia. Other species are used for thatching roofs and in basketry.

SEDGE *Carex* spp.

There are over a thousand species of *Carex* found worldwide, composing nearly a third of the entire family. Many of them are native to arctic and alpine regions, while others are dominant components of wetlands throughout the world. In the southern Rockies there are over six dozen species of sedge. It is true that these are probably the most difficult wildflowers to identify; a dissecting scope and a large amount of patience are necessary to decipher many of them to their species. Even if you are not equipped with either of these tools, it is worthwhile to take the time to observe the aesthetic beauty of these cryptic flowers and appreciate the ecological importance of sedges.

WATER SEDGE *Carex aquatilis*

One of the most common sedges in North America is water sedge, which grows extensively in marshy areas.

Sedges are important food for many species of wildlife, including elk, muskrats, bears and ducks. The shoots and rootstocks are edible to humans as well; the tubers of a Chinese sedge, *Eleocharis dulcis*, are cultivated and harvested to make water chestnuts.

Some species of sedge form the dominant vegetation in certain habitats. For example, beaked sedge (*C. utriculata*) is common around montane and subalpine ponds. Alpine sedge (*Kobresia bellardi*) forms a turf on tundra in snow free areas, covering acres of ground on the high peaks.

The scientific name, *Carex*, is derived from the Greek word *keirein*, meaning "to cut." Many sedges have saw-toothed leaf margins. This is also the meaning of sedge, derived from the Old English word *segge*, which means "saw." Some species are commonly known as sawgrass.

Elk Sedge *Carex geyeri*

Elk sedge is one of the most common sedges in the Rocky Mountains, and is a dominant plant in the understory of montane and subalpine forests. This is one of the first plants to reappear each spring, and is important forage for wildlife. This sedge spreads by rhizomes, and grows to about eight inches tall. Just a few male and female flowers emerge from the tips of the stems. This species is protogynous, meaning that the female flowers mature first, followed by the male flowers. In the photo to the right, the female stigmas have emerged.

DAVID INOUYE

Cotton Sedge *Eriophorum polystachion (E. angustifolium)*

Fluffy white heads of cotton sedge dangle from stems in marshy areas in the mountains. Also known as bog wool, because of its puffs of bright white seed hairs, cotton sedge grows in marshes, fens and near the borders of high alpine lakes. A close relative, *Eriophorum chamissonis* (*C. altaicum*), is one of the rare plants found growing in the Elk Mountains and is easily distinguished because its seed head sits on top, rather than dangling from the stem. The same species grows in the Altai mountains of Asia. *Eriophorum* means "wool-bearing."

Heather Family ERICACEAE

The first thing that comes to mind when I think of the Heather Family is the misty hills of Scotland where the immortal souls in the mythical village of Brigadoon celebrate life. Unfortunately, these were considered wastelands to mere mortals. The rural folk and peasants who lived among the heather were known as heathens, or "heath dwellers," uncivilized and irreligious pagans from the country. Conversely, the Latin name, Ericaceae, is derived from the Scandinavian word for "honor." This name was probably given to commemorate Leif Ericsson and his father, Eric the Red, both Norwegian explorers and adventurers (and probably heathens, too). Their country of origin and much of the northern lands they explored are covered with heather.

Heathers are usually low-growing evergreen shrubs that often create a thick understory whether found in shady forests, windswept hills or vast bogs. But the family also includes large, showy-flowered shrubs like azaleas and rhododendrons, and some interesting saprophytic (gaining nourishment from decaying plants) plants like pinedrops. All prefer acidic soils, so are are fairly common in coniferous forests. Some taxonomists divide the heathers into blueberry (Vacciniaceae), pinedrops (Monotropaceae) and wintergreen (Pyrolaceae) families.

KINNIKINNIK *Arctostaphylos uva-ursi*

Besides being fun to say, kinnikinnik is one of the most common evergreen shrubs in the Rockies and grows in mountain forests around the world. Also known as bearberry, the bright green, glossy leaves and smooth red branches drape over the ground as an understory plant from the ponderosa pine foothills to the upper montane lodgepole pine forests. The pale pink, bell-shaped flowers are typical of other flowers in the family, described by William Weber, author of *Colorado Flora* as "beautiful creations, like porcelain Easter eggs into which one peers to see exotic scenes."

In the Sierra Nevada, there are over forty species of *Arctostaphylos*, which are collectively known as manzanita, a Spanish word for "little apple." The bright red berries look just like miniature apples, but are seedy and mealy, unlike their juicy namesakes of the Rose Family. The Latin name for this species, *Arctostaphylos uva-ursi*, translates to "bear grapes, grapes of bear," echoing the redundancy of the common name. Birds, rodents and deer, as well as bears, forage for the abundant fruit.

Kinnikinnik is the Native American word for a mixture of dried herbs used for smoking, with leaves from this plant often being the main ingredient. Kinnikinnik is also sold commercially as an herbal remedy to treat bladder and kidney infections, and is often referred to in this context as uva-ursi.

Wood Nymph *Moneses uniflora*

Finding these elfin flowers in the woods is a treat. The perfect flowers, also known as "shy maiden," nod demurely in the shade of mossy forests and reward close observers with a scent reminiscent of lily-of-the-valley.

One-sided Wintergreen *Orthilia secunda*

The low, spreading one-sided wintergreen is easily distinguished from other wintergreens by its greenish white flowers which all hang from one side of the stem. The lush leafy stems may spread to form small patches up to more than a foot in diameter.

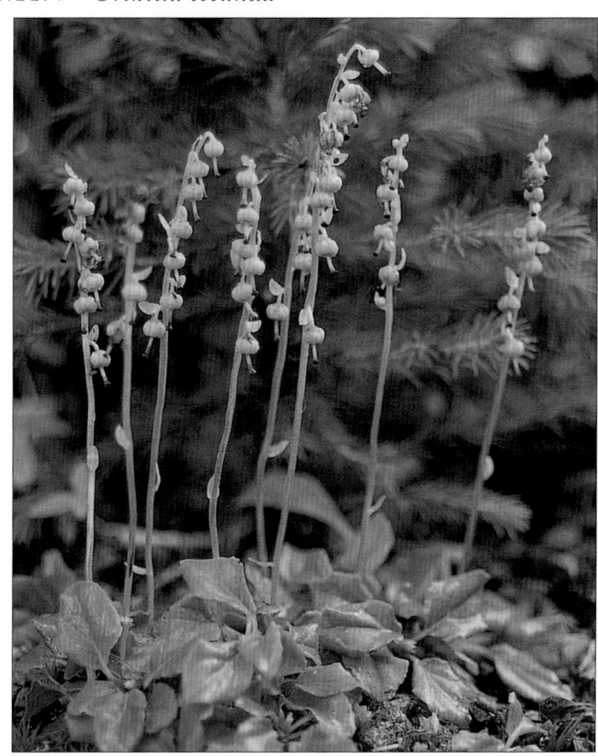

SHINLEAF WINTERGREEN *Pyrola asarifolia (P. rotundifolia)*

Poke around in the shady understory of a coniferous forest and you will find several species of wintergreen. The wintergreens have rosettes of waxy, dark green basal leaves from which arise single stalks of nodding pink, white or greenish flowers. As their names imply, the leaves remain green beneath the snow. Wintergreen flavoring comes naturally from creeping wintergreen (*Gaultheria humifusa*), a low evergreen shrub that is also found in spruce-fir forests around here. The Latin name, *Pyrola*, means "little pear tree," alluding to the resemblance of wintergreen leaves with leaves of the pear. In the spring and fall, look for the dried reddish-brown flowering stalks with up to a dozen seed pods lined up along their stems, just like a row of tiny Chinese lanterns.

DWARF BLUEBERRY *Vaccinium myrtillus*

The dwarf blueberry is a low, spreading evergreen shrub, and is sometimes the dominant understory in spruce-fir and lodgepole pine forests. Our blueberries do not produce the succulent fruits found in the Northeastern and Northwestern U.S., but none-the-less, provide important forage for wildlife. Look beneath the leaves and you may find small, pink urn-shaped flowers, miniatures of those found on kinnikinnik. Also known as huckleberry, whortleberry and bilberry, a tea made of leaves from these plants has been used in Europe for centuries as a treatment for diabetes. The brew is an effective kidney tonic and helps to stabilize blood sugar levels.

Pea Family FABACEAE

The Pea or Legume Family is second only to grasses in economic importance to humans. Many of our staple foods, including lentils, peanuts, peas and beans are in this family, plus alfalfa, which is grown for animal feed and sweet clover, one of honeybee's favorite source of nectar. The word *legume* is derived from French and Latin words meaning "anything that can be gathered." However, despite their overwhelming importance as food, many plants in this family, including the seeds, are extremely poisonous. Over 12,000 species have been identified around the world, making it the third largest plant family, behind orchids and sunflowers.

Peas are especially important ecologically because of their role in the nitrogen cycle. Specialized bacteria called *Rhizobium* grow on the roots of legumes and are able to convert atmospheric nitrogen to a form of nitrogen that is available to plants, which is then converted to plant proteins. Legumes enrich poor soils due to this symbiotic relationship, hence the common practice of crop rotation with legumes used in agriculture. The plants are also a rich source of nitrogen in the form of protein to wildlife and insects that eat them. Each plant species co-exists with a certain species of *Rhizobium*; the plant benefits by getting nitrogen and the bacteria receive carbohydrates from the plant. Members of this family also share the characteristics of compound leaves and the trademark pea flower.

Gratitude to Plants, the sun-facing light-changing leaf
and fine root hairs; standing still through wind
and rain; their dance is in the flowing spiral grain
in our minds so be it.

from "Prayer for the Great Family"
– Gary Snyder

Drummond's Milkvetch *Astragalus drummondii*

With nearly 1,600 species worldwide and over a hundred species in the Rocky Mountains alone, *Astragalus* is the largest genus in the Pea Family and in the Western U.S. Because you usually need both flowers and seedpods to identify each species, they are also one of the most frustrating groups to learn. Over two dozen grow in the Gunnison Basin, but because they are more commonly found in desert sagebrush environments, only half a dozen are found in the higher elevations of the East River Valley.

The milkvetches have the ability to colonize unstable habitats and to grow in dry climates and poor soils, leading to rapid evolution of the genus. Many are adapted to very specific soil conditions, a trait that is common in many rare plant populations. In Colorado, two dozen species of *Astragalus* are listed rare, threatened or endangered; four of these occur in the Gunnison Basin.

Astragalus is Greek for "ankle bone." The genus is also known as rattleweed, a name used long ago for some plants in the Pea Family because of the sound made when you shake a ripe seed pod. *Astragalus* can also mean "vertebra." Another interpretation is that the root nodules containing *Rhizobium* give the appearance of a row of tiny backbones.

Milkvetch is a name coming from the idea that using any of these plants for fodder would increase milk production in goats. Vetch comes from an old-world term meaning "weak," because they are often trailing, climbing or otherwise weak-stemmed plants.

Many plants in this genus are selenophytes, meaning they can concentrate selenium from the soil into their tissues. The mineral, which is toxic in large amounts, is returned to the soil in soluble form that can be absorbed by other plants that animals eat. Alkaloids and nitrotoxins produced by many milkvetches are also poisonous, causing severe nervous disorders and deformities in range animals. Because of these toxic effects, the plants are sometimes called "locoweed" or "crazyweed." The true locoweeds of the genus *Oxytropis* are also extremely poisonous and are often confused with milkvetches in appearance (see locoweed, p. 100, for a description of differences).

One common species growing in big sagebrush communities is Drummond's milkvetch, a tall (12-18" high), robust, hairy-leaved plant with cream-colored flowers. Unlike most vetches, this species is not poisonous.

CHAINPOD *Hedysarum boreale*

Robust clumps of chainpod show up in a wide variety of habitats, from sagebrush to subalpine, but generally in sunny locations with well-drained soils. Also known as sweet vetch, the bright pink flowers are distinctive in the way they hang to one side on the slender stems, which grow to two feet tall. But the long, flattened pod is what inspires the common name, as it is constricted between the seeds, thus resembling links of a chain. The thick taproots are sweet and edible. This hearty perennial would be a beautiful addition to native gardens.

PEAVINE *Lathyrus lanszwertii* var. *leucanthus (L. leucanthus)*

Perhaps the most appealing feature of this plant is its reputation as an aphrodisiac, which inspired the Latin name, *Lathyrus*, meaning "very passionate." *Leucanthus* means "white-flowered." The creamy white flowers turn pale orange as they age, adding softness to the aspen understory or sagebrush where they grow. Bright pink nectar guides aid in seducing pollinators to visit in exchange for a sip of nectar.

DAVID INOUYE

Lupine *Lupinus* spp.

Early in the summer, lupines cast a soft purple-blue haze over entire hillsides in mountain meadows and among sagebrush. Also known as bluebonnets, old maid's bonnets or wolfbean, there are over two hundred species of lupine, mostly in the western hemisphere. Fifty species are found in the Rocky Mountains.

All of Colorado's native lupines are easily recognized by their blue or purple spike of pea-shaped flowers and palmately compound leaves, meaning that each leaf has many leaflets which are like fingers coming from one central point or palm. Most are large and shrub-like, although the dwarf lupine is only about four inches high.

DAVID INOUYE

Besides being beautiful, lupine flowers are fun to play with. You can easily observe the special "trigger" adaptation for pollination in lupines by pressing on the pointed keel, or lower petal, of the flower. This simulates a bee or other pollinator buzzing in for nectar. Bright yellow pollen squirts out of the tip of the keel, which would normally be brushed on the insect's belly and transferred to the next flower it visits.

Another interesting adaptation is the way lupines fold their leaves at night and unfold them during the day. This maximizes capture of sunlight energy during the day and minimizes water and heat loss during the night. Lupines also track the sun with their leaves.

Lupines are named after *lupus*, the wolf, because they were once thought to rob, or wolf, the soil of nutrients. This erroneous belief derived from the fact that lupines, like most members of the Pea Family, are able to thrive on poor soil, due to their symbiotic relationship with nitrogen-fixing bacteria. The analogy to the wolf makes more sense in light of the fact that these plants are extremely toxic to sheep. In some areas of the west, lupine poisoning is the number one cause of death for sheep on the open range. It is interesting that people have been exterminating wolves for decades and not the plants, though I certainly would not advocate lupine slaughter either. Many native birds and animals, such as bears, elk and rodents, are immune to the lupine alkaloids and use the seeds, pods and roots for forage.

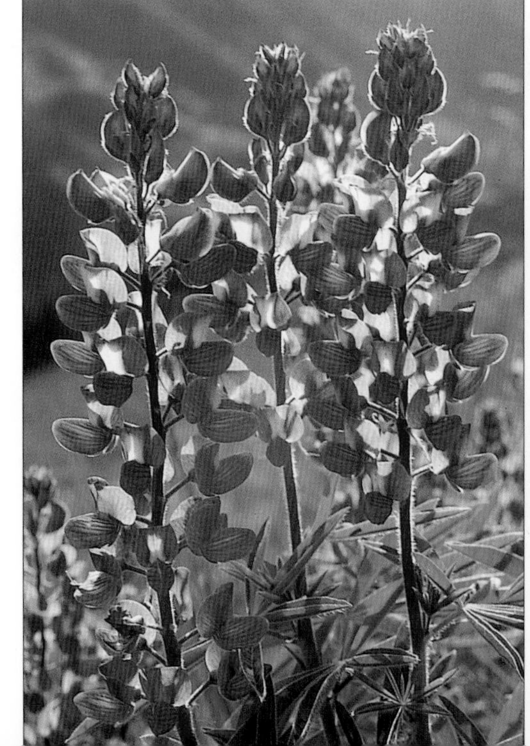

In addition to the alkaloids produced by the plants as deterrents to fungi and insects, some lupines can absorb toxic amounts of selenium from the soils, which creates other deleterious effects in animals that eat them. Although the bean-like seeds look tasty and are even suggested as wild edibles in some books, it is best to leave them for the wild critters whose digestive systems are known to handle them well.

Silvery Lupine *Lupinus argenteus (L. caudatus)*

In the mountain meadows of the Gothic area, silvery lupine is said to be the most common wildflower. This is an extremely diverse species, with at least ten varieties recognized in Colorado. The tall spikes of flowers range from pale blue to deep purple, and white or pink albinos are not uncommon. When a flower has been pollinated, the upper petal, or banner, changes from white to purple, signaling to bees that it has been pollinated and no longer supplying nectar.

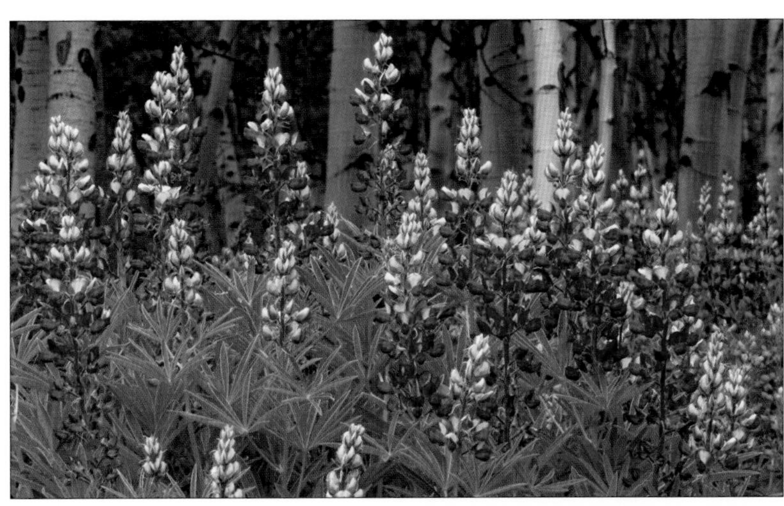

Dwarf Lupine *Lupinus lepidus (L. caespitosus)*

The dwarf lupine is easy to miss, since the flowering stems grow no higher than the leaves, and the entire plant normally grows to about eight inches tall. This species is common among sagebrush and blooms in early summer.

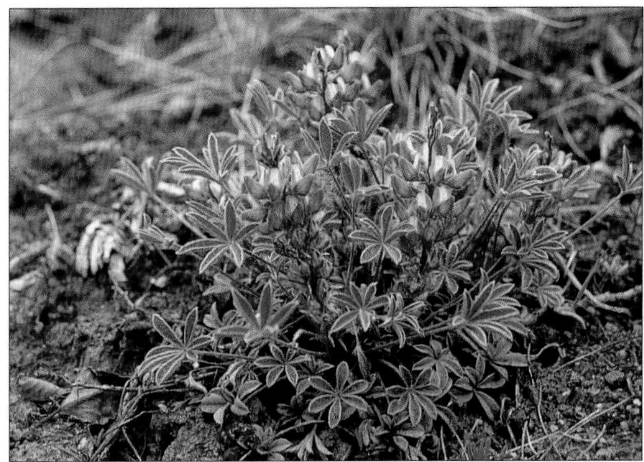

Legend of the Bluebonnet

One of the most charming flower legends is the story of a Comanche girl who had lost all of her family to drought and famine. The only thing she had left to comfort her was a doll that had been made by her mother, decorated with bright blue jay feathers. When the shaman asked what the remaining tribal members could do to redeem themselves and end the suffering, the spirits requested that the tribes most prized possession be offered to the gods. Hearing this, the young girl gave her doll to the fire late one evening and scattered the ashes to the four winds. In the morning, nourishing rains returned to the land and the hills were covered with cheerful blossoms of bluebonnet. The bluebonnet is thus regarded as a symbol of forgiveness and selflessness.

Lambert's Locoweed *Oxytropis lambertii*

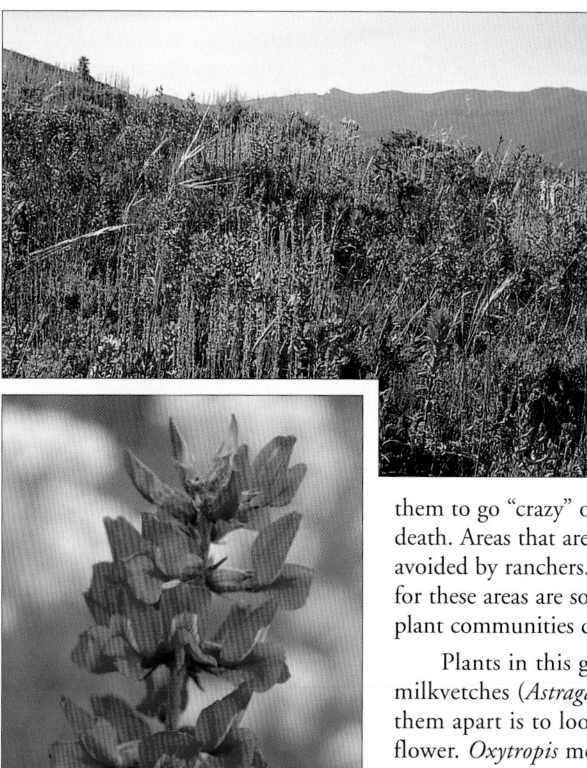

One of the most spectacular floral displays is the bright magenta Lambert's locoweed when in full bloom mid-summer among the sagebrush. Lambert's locoweed is known as one of the most poisonous plants in the Western U.S. Fortunately, this is also one of the easiest plants to recognize. The plant's toxicity is related to its ability to take up the heavy metal barium from the soil. Livestock can become addicted to locoweed, causing them to go "crazy" or "loco," which usually results in death. Areas that are abundant in locoweed are strictly avoided by ranchers. This is a benefit to wildflower lovers, for these areas are some of the most beautiful and diverse plant communities due to less impact from grazing.

Plants in this genus are often confused with milkvetches (*Astragalus* spp.). The easiest way to tell them apart is to look at the lower petal or keel of the flower. *Oxytropis* means "sharp keel," because this petal is pointed. In milkvetches, the keel is blunt or rounded. Another clue to tell the two groups apart is that locoweeds usually have only basal leaves, while milkvetches have branched, leafy stems.

This species is named in honor of A.B. Lambert (1761-1842), who was a well-known British botanist.

Alpine Locoweed *Oxytropis podocarpus*

Clusters of lavender-colored flowers precede the fat seedpods of this beautiful alpine locoweed. This loco grows in broad ground-hugging mats on exposed rocky slopes of high peaks and ridges. Truly extreme botanists will appreciate and distinguish between the many shapes, colors, and degrees of hairiness on seedpods in the pea family.

Clovers *Trifolium* spp.

There are over 300 species of clover worldwide, and about forty found in the Rocky Mountains. The common name is derived from German and English words that mean "to stick," probably relating to the fact that clovers are the most important plants around the world for honey production. Most clovers are very fragrant and prolific nectar producers.

Whiproot Clover *Trifolium dasyphyllum*

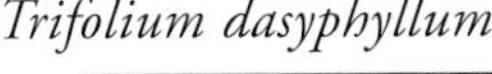

Whiproot clover is a common alpine and subalpine species, and spreads by rhizomes to create mats several feet in diameter. The flowers have both white and pink petals that grow in loose clusters at the end of long stems.

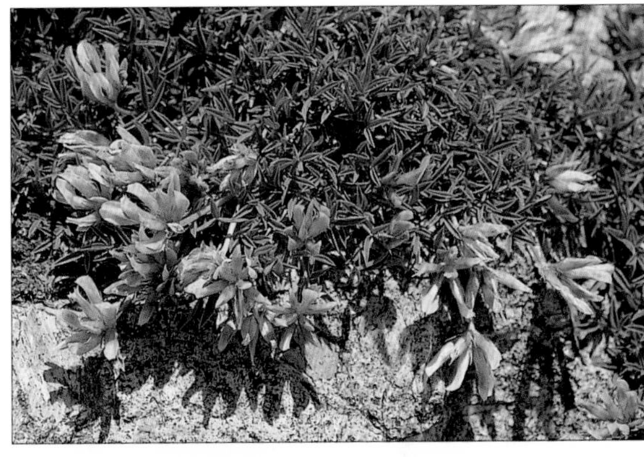

Dwarf Alpine Clover *Trifolium nanum*

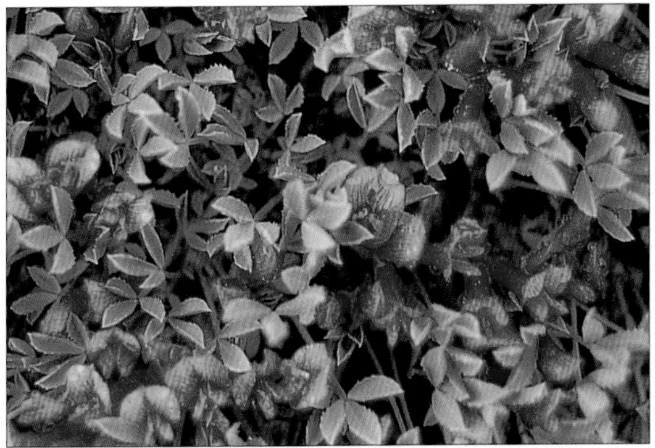

Tight, ground-hugging mats of dwarf alpine clover produce small clusters of one to three flowers. These are often part of mosaics of cushion plants that include several species such as alpine forget-me-not, alpine phlox, and moss campion.

Parry's Clover *Trifolium parryi*

The large bright pink heads of Parry's clover brighten the alpine tundra landscape, where it most commonly grows in rocky soils around snowmelt basins.

Charles Parry was a 19th century Colorado botanist and explorer who specialized in alpine plants and has over eighty species named after him. Joseph Hooker, the eminent 19th century British botanist, deemed Parry the "King of Colorado Botany," because he so broadly collected and documented Colorado's mountain flora.

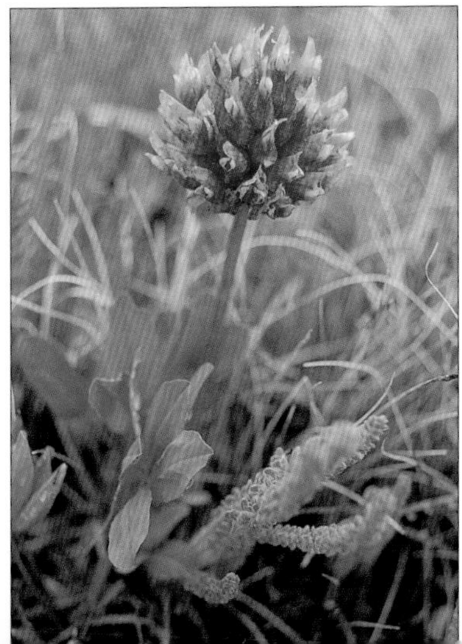

Red Clover *Trifolium pratense* Non-native Species

Red clover is one of several species of clover imported from Europe, and is now naturalized throughout North America. The dried flowers and leaves are valued for nutritional and medicinal teas.

Since ancient times, clover was believed to bring good luck in all aspects of life. Not only four-leaved mutants, but common three-leaved clovers are believed to bestow their possessors with prosperity, as well as endow them with the ability to detect witches, sorcerers and good fairies. A dream about clover foretells a happy marriage, long life and wealth or the promise that one will "live in clover." Although these beliefs are originally pagan, Christians adopted the clover leaf as a symbol of the Trinity, which is often the basis of design for churches and cathedrals.

Sweet Clover Non-native Species

The tall, lanky stems of sweet clover grow abundantly on roadsides and other disturbed areas across the continent. Although these are not "true clovers," they share the characteristics of three leaflets that is most common in the clover genus. Both a yellow species, *Melilotus officinalis*, and a white species, *Melilotus albus*, grow together throughout Colorado. Sweet clover was imported from Europe long ago as a source of nectar for honeybees and is still cultivated in fields for this purpose. *Melilotus* means "honey flower."

White Dutch Clover *Trifolium repens* Non-native Species

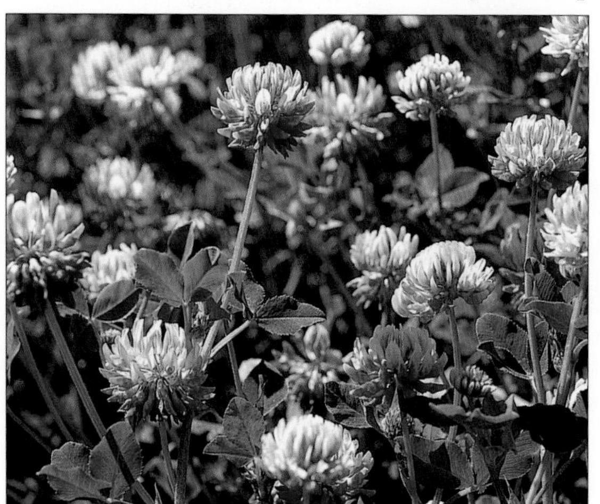

This is one of the most common species used as forage for livestock, and is widespread in pastures and lawns throughout North America. Although clover is important as a source of nitrogen and protein, ranchers avoid growing too much in their pastures because animals develop "the bloats" and an extreme sensitivity to sunlight if they eat too much of it.

In undisturbed landscapes, longstem clover (*T. longipes*) is the most common tall white native clover species found throughout the mountains, and looks similar to white Dutch clover.

American Vetch *Vicia americana*

The American vetch is common throughout North America, climbing nearby plants wherever its seeds sprout. In the southern Rockies it is especially common among the sagebrush, creating a beautiful blend of soft green and purple. Vetch comes from the Latin word for "weak," describing the spindley stems of these plants. However, the long, coiled tendrils at the ends of their leaves allow them to climb anything. The Latin name, *Vicia*, means "to bind or twist."

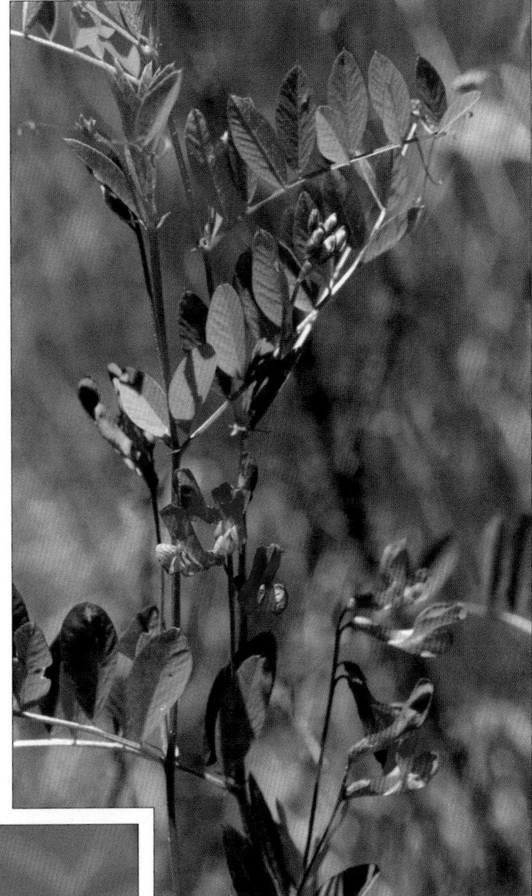

American vetch is sometimes confused with peavine (*Lathyrus* spp.), which is not as good at climbing, but grow in identical habitats, often side-by-side or even twined together with vetches. One way to tell the difference between the two is to inspect the flower's style, or female organ. In vetches, the style is hairy all around; peavines have hairs only on the upper side of the flat style. If flowers are absent, look on the under side of the leaf; peavine leaves have parallel veins, while American vetch leaves have a mid-rib with spreading side-veins forming a "V" for vetch!

The foliage and seeds of American vetch are important forage for many birds and other wildlife. Some contain compounds producing toxic levels of cyanide when digested, so it's best to leave them for the critters. Conversely, the European fava bean (*V. faba*) is one of many vetches cultivated for food.

Fumitory Family FUMARIACEAE

The name fumitory comes from the Latin *fumus terre*, meaning "smoke of the earth." Supposedly, the leaves and roots of some species smell like smoke. I've also heard that the soft, wispy, gray-green leaves of many fumitories helped to earn the name. Bleeding hearts (*Dicentra* spp.), an ornamental plant found in many mountain gardens, are probably the best known members of this family. Some botanists include this group with poppies (Papaveraceae). However, they look nothing like poppies except upon careful inspection of the flower parts. Superficially, the flowers and seedpods bear a much closer resemblance to members of the Pea Family, with which they are often confused. Seeds of these plants have small white bumps called eliasomes, which are specialized food meant to attract ants. The ants gather the seeds, remove the eliasomes for food, and thus provide the service of distributing the seeds.

FLORAL LARCENY

Some birds and insects that seek nectar as a food source commit the "crime" of "floral larceny" by taking nectar without providing the service of pollination. One way this is done is by "nectar robbing," in which insects or birds cut a hole in the back of the flower and steal nectar without passing over the pollen bearing parts. In another strategy, "nectar thieves" take nectar from the front of the flower, but because they lack the behavior or the right "fit" to collect pollen in the process, do not exchange pollen with other plants. These behaviors influence evolution of plant species in ways that are just beginning to be understood.

GOLDEN SMOKE *Corydalis aurea*

One of the first plants to bloom in early summer and lasting late into August, low-growing (6-12 inches high) golden smoke is common in gravelly soils among sagebrush and on disturbed roadsides. Clusters of pale yellow flowers inspired their other common name, "scrambled eggs."

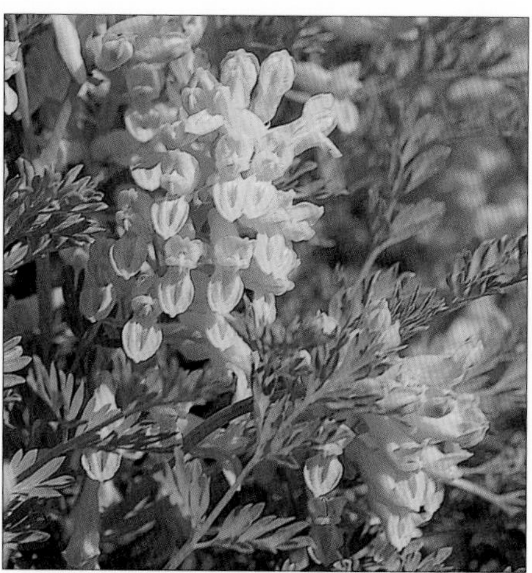

CORYDALIS *Corydalis caseana*

Corydalis grows in dense stands up to five feet tall, with velvety soft, fern-like leaves and hollow juicy stems. The pink and white flowers smell sweet like lilacs. Each flower has a long spur or crest on the back, giving it the Greek name *Corydalis*, which means "crested lark." If you look closely at the spur, you may notice a small cut or hole, made by a species of bumblebee that "robs" nectar from the flowers.

Many plants have evolved seed dispersal systems using hydrostatic pressure. Touch a corydalis pod and I guarantee you'll be surprised. These green, bean-shaped pods are spring-loaded! If you lightly touch them when they are just ripe, they will explode, the sides curling back as glossy black seeds scatter everywhere.

In California, a subspecies is sometimes called fitweed because of reports that it is toxic to livestock, causing "fits" or twitches in victims. Fortunately, none of our local ranchers have reported any such problems with corydalis, perhaps because something in the plant's chemistry causes animals to avoid eating it. Paradoxically, a tincture made from plants in this genus is recommended as a mild sedative by some herbalists. The plant chemicals responsible for this effect are very similar to morphine and codeine, products of the Poppy Family to which corydalis is closely related.

Corydalis is endemic to this region of Colorado. Although local populations are quite healthy, this is one of the only areas that these unusual plants can be found in the state. The species is very common in the Pacific Northwest. Around the world, there are over three hundred species of *Corydalis*. The Rocky Mountain species, *C. caseana*, was named in honor of botanist E.L. Case, who is credited with first documenting the plant.

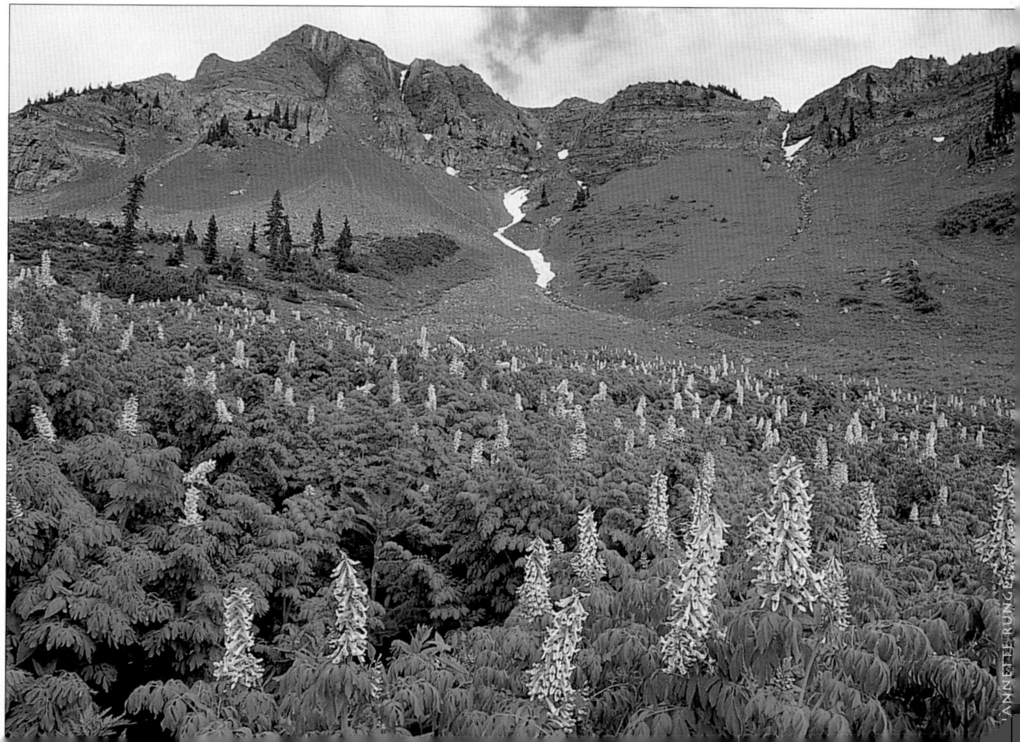

©ANNETTE RUNGE

Gentian Family GENTIANACEAE

There are about three hundred species of gentians in the world, mostly occurring in cooler mountainous regions. Fourteen different species grow in the Elk Mountains, ranging from the monument plant, which grows to nine feet tall, to the late-blooming arctic gentian, which may only grow to six inches high on the alpine tundra.

Gentians are regarded as harbingers of autumn, being some of the latest bloomers of the summer season. For many species, August is the earliest one can expect to find most of them in bloom, but they will last through to the first hard frosts in October. Most gentian flowers are also responsive to light, opening only in bright sunshine and closing at the passing of a cloud or at dusk. If you are patient, you can watch them close beneath the shade of a hat or your hand. This reaction helps protect the delicate reproductive organs from being damaged by frost or stormy weather.

Plants of this family are named after Gentius, King of Illyria, who ruled part of ancient Rome around 200 B.C. He is credited with the discovery of the medicinal virtues of gentians, thereby curing a mysterious fever that had stricken his army. Much older Egyptian records tell of medicinal uses of gentians as well, which include treatment of malaria (the mysterious fever in Illyria?) and rheumatism.

A Hungarian legend from the 11th century tells us that the king, St. Ladilas, discovered gentians while looking for a cure for the plague. He shot an arrow into the sky and prayed that it would fall upon the plant that would cure his people. The arrow landed on a gentian.

Today, a sip of gentian elixir is a common after-dinner drink and an effective cure for indigestion. The bitters of "bitters and tonic" is an extract of a European species of gentian root.

DAVID INOUYE

Monument Plant *Frasera speciosa*

The monument plant or green gentian is found in mountain meadows, most often as a huge rosette of smooth leaves, each leaf up to two feet long. Rocky Mountain Biological Laboratory researcher, David Inouye, has found that these plants will live for up to sixty years as rosettes of leaves, storing up energy to bloom and make seed. When they're eventually stimulated to bloom, all that energy is used up to grow a flowering stalk that may tower up to nine feet high, bearing hundreds of four-petaled flowers. After its orgiastic season of flowering, the plant dies, leaving thousands of seeds to carry on its genetic legacy, should they survive. This kind of life history is commonly called "big bang" reproduction or "death by reproductive exhaustion." These types of plants are known scientifically as "monocarpic perennials," i.e. they live for many years, but produce flowers, fruit and seed only once. Mass blooms seem to occur about every two to seven years, creating a forest of monument plants in our meadows. Other years, you may have a hard time finding any in bloom. Monument plants also provide a feast of nectar for dozens of species of insects. The genus *Frasera* is named in honor of early American botanist, John Fraser (1750-1811). *Speciosa* means "showy" or "handsome."

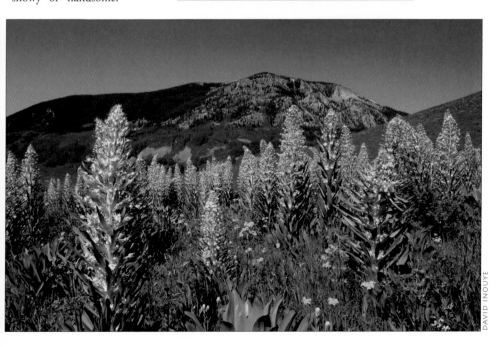

DAVID INOUYE

DAVID INOUYE

Explorer's Gentian *Gentiana affinis (Pneumonanthe affinis)*

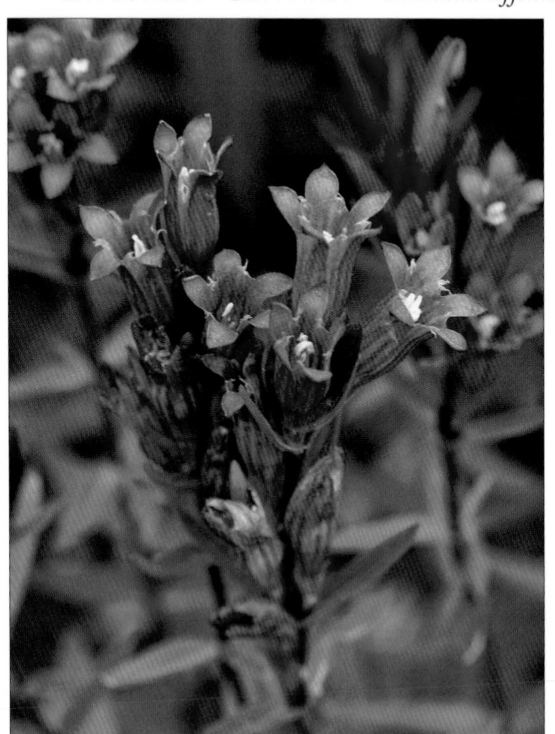

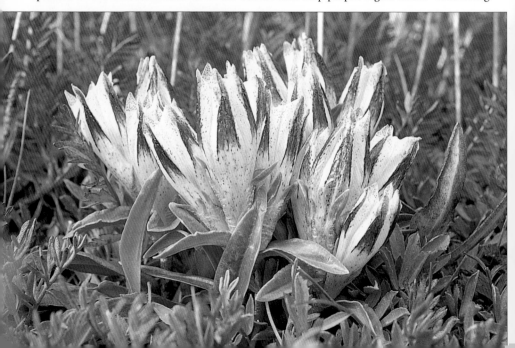

This is a smaller and more slender version of the bottle gentian (p. 109) that prefers marshy meadows. The stems are deep maroon, contrasting with the smooth, bright-green leaves. Like its cousins, explorer's gentian tends to bloom late in the growing season.

> *"Living is not enough.*
> *One must have sunshine,*
> *Freedom, and a little flower."*
>
> – Hans Christian Anderson

Arctic Gentian *Gentiana algida (Gentianodes algida)*

These are one of the latest summer bloomers, found only in grassy meadows of the alpine tundra. They rarely grow to more than six inches high, but are very noticeable because of their large (more than two inches long) tubular flowers. The neatly pleated, cream-colored petals are speckled on the inside and streaked on the outside with deep purple. *Algida* means "cold-loving."

Bottle Gentian *Gentiana parryi (Pneumonanthe parryi)*

Bottle gentians are one of the showiest fall wildflowers. The alternate Latin name, *Pneumonanthe*, refers to the tubular corolla, which resembles a miniature, inflated lung (*Pneumo*="lung"; *anthe*="flower"). The inside of the flower is electric blue and is large enough for the bumblebee pollinators to crawl into. The bottle gentian is common in mountain meadows and near open streamsides.They are only found open on bright sunny days.

Little Gentian *Gentianella amarella (G. acuta)*

DAVID INOUYE

Also known as rose gentian or northern gentian, the pale lavender flowers of this annual gentian are often overlooked among the tall grasses and other plants in the high mountain meadows where they grow. If you do find one, look inside and you will see a fringe lining the tubular corolla, unique among the local gentians. *Amarella* means "bitter," referring to the taste of the root associated with many gentians. According to the wisdom of *Bach Flower Remedy's* (see p. 88), the essence of this plant will help a person "to have more faith in themselves and others, benefitting those easily discouraged and prone to despondency and depression."

Siberian Gentian *Gentianella prostrata (Chondrophylla prostrata)*

DAVID INOUYE

Sometimes called moss gentian, this is the tiniest of native gentians, usually not more than two inches tall. The bright blue flowers are like little beacons of light nestled in the short grass of the alpine tundra. The petals are united into a pleated, eight-point star. These flowers are very responsive to changes in light, closing within a minute or so if shadowed by a cloud or a hand. Siberian gentians are native to the alpine tundra in mountain ranges all over the world, both northern and southern hemispheres.

Fringed Gentian *Gentianopsis detonsa (G. thermalis)*

Fringed gentian was first described by botanists exploring in Yellowstone, so it was originally associated with warm springs, hence the alternate species name, *Gentianopsis thermalis.* Fortunately, warm springs are not a strict habitat requirement. These gentians are abundant in wet subalpine meadows and near streams, warm or not. Another close relative, *Gentianopsis barbellata,* is found in subalpine meadows and is distinguished by having longer flower petals, but fewer flowering stems per plant. There are several species of these annual plants found in the eastern U.S. as well, where William Cullen Bryant was inspired to write a poem about them.

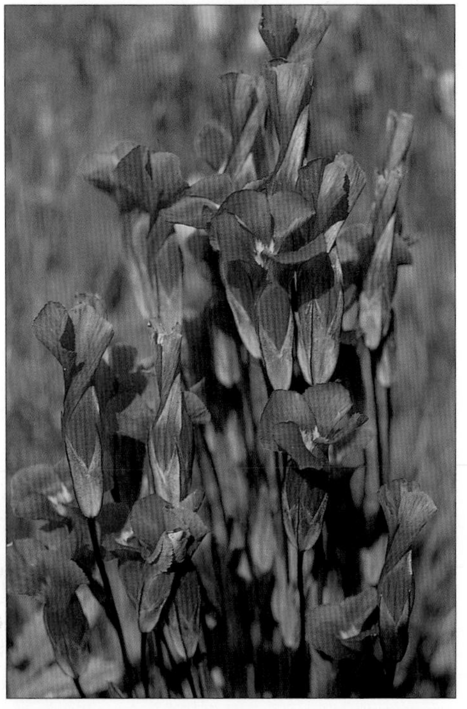

To the Fringed Gentian

Thou blossom bright with autumn dew
And colored with the heaven's own blue,
That openest when the quiet light
Succeeds the keen and frosty night.

Thou comest not when violets lean
O'er wandering brooks and springs unseen,
Or columbines, in purple dressed,
Nod o'er the ground-bird's hidden nest.

Thou waitest late and com'st alone
When woods are bare and birds are flown,
And frosts and shortening days portend
The aged year is near his end.

Then doth thy sweet and quiet eye
Look through its fringes to the sky,
Blue, blue, as if that sky let fall
A flower from its cerulean wall.

I would that thus, when I shall see
The hour of death draw near to me,
Hope, blossoming within my heart,
May look to heaven as I depart.

– William Cullen Bryant

Star Gentian *Swertia perennis*

Named after Emanuel Sweert, a 16th century Dutch herbalist, the star gentian is one of few in this family that tolerates some shade. They commonly bloom in late summer, growing in marshy areas and mossy streambanks of the subalpine. The five-petaled, star-shaped flowers are a deep, dusky purple. *Perennis* means that they are perennial.

DAVID INOUYE

Geranium Family GERANIACEAE

Members of this family all share the characteristic of a long, pointy fruit, reminiscent of a crane's beak. *Geranos* means crane in Greek. Potted geraniums are cultivated from a tropical genus, *Pelargonium*, native to South Africa. Sweet-smelling oil can be extracted from fragrant geranium (*P. odorantissimum*) and is commonly used in aromatherapy for its calming effect. Common storksbill, *Erodium cicutarium*, is a European geranium that has become naturalized throughout much of North America, having been imported for its medicinal properties as an astringent, useful for healing wounds.

GERANIUM *Geranium* spp.

One of my favorite seedpods is the delicate ovarian chandelier of wild geranium. The thick beak-like fruit is the hardened style of what was a showy white or pink five-petaled flower. The style is the stalk that displays the pollen-receiving stigma and is the path through which the pollen nucleus moves to fertilize the ovules, which develop into seeds. Attached to the base of the style are five single-seeded ovaries. As the fruit dries, the style splits and the ovaries curl up towards the tip of the style. This creates a carousel of mini-catapults that fling and disperse the seeds.

WHITE GERANIUM *Geranium richardsonii*

White or Richardson's geranium can be found growing in the shade of aspen groves or spruce-fir forests. Sir John Richardson (1787-1865) was a Scottish botanist and zoologist who served on Captain John Franklin's arctic expedition.

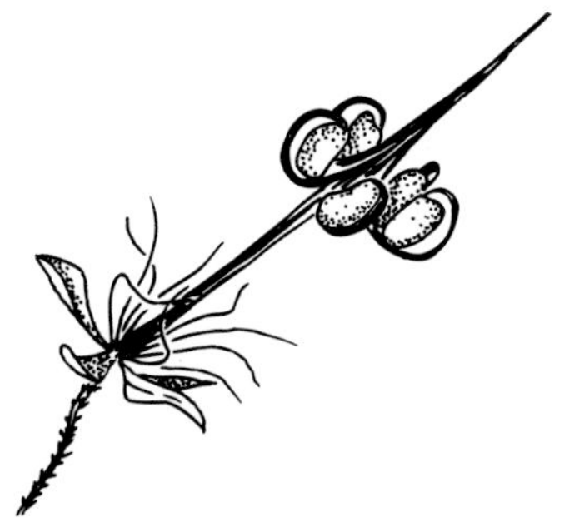

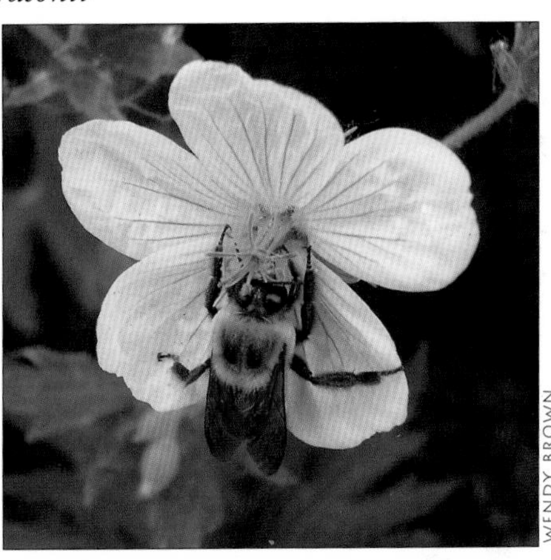

WENDY BROWN

PINK GERANIUM *Geranium viscosissimum*

Pink or sticky geranium prefers open, sunny sagebrush country and mountain meadows. *Viscous* means "sticky," for the glands that cover the leaves and stems.

Both wild geraniums bloom throughout the summer. The lobed leaves look similar to larkspur or monkshood when the flowers are absent. Be careful not to confuse the two if you are collecting roots or leaves as herbal remedies. Larkspur and monkshood are extremely poisonous, but geraniums have astringent properties that are useful for reducing inflammations of everything from sore throats to ulcers and hemorrhoids. The leaves are also important food for wildlife.

Currant Family GROSSULARIACEAE

The Currant Family is comprised of a single genus (*Ribes*) of berry-producing shrubs known as currants and gooseberries. The two types of shrubs are usually distinguished by the presence or absence of spines and prickles: currants are spineless, while gooseberries are prickly and "goose" you if you grab a branch unknowingly! Over 125 species of wild currants and gooseberries are found on the planet.

Currants were originally the name for a special type of seedless grape grown in the city of Corinth, Greece. The French called these culinary fruits *raisins de Corauntz* or "raisins of Corinth." Because of their similarity, the sweet, juicy *Ribes* fruit and the shrubs producing them became known as currants. Gooseberries have nothing to do with geese, the word being a twist of the French term *gros berie*, or "large berry." This is also the origin of the family's Latin name, Grossulariaceae.

Currants are also well-known in the northwestern U.S. as the alternate host of white pine blister rust. This powdery fungus attacks and kills any of the species of five-needled or "white" pines, which are important timber species. Any species of *Ribe*s is necessary to support part of the fungus' life cycle. In the 1930s, a massive campaign was launched under the auspices of the Civilian Conservation Corps (CCC) to destroy any currants or gooseberries that grew among white pine forests.

Ribes is an Arabic term for "acid-tasting," describing the flavor of the fat berries produced by these plants. Some are very sweet, but some are so bitter they should be left for wildlife as forage in late summer and fall. Many are cultivated for their fruit or as ornamentals, since they are equally beautiful in flower. Native Americans used the berries as an ingredient for pemmican, a mixture of dried, shredded buffalo meat, fat and dried fruit.

WAX CURRANT *Ribes cereum*

Squaw or wax currant is fairly common and is usually found at lower elevations than the mountain gooseberry, although it will grow in rocky areas from sagebrush to tundra. *Cereum* means "waxy," for the texture of the leaves. These spineless shrubs are robust, sometimes growing to over five feet tall. The white or pink tubular flowers are very fragrant and develop into large red berries that are good for making jam, jelly or pie.

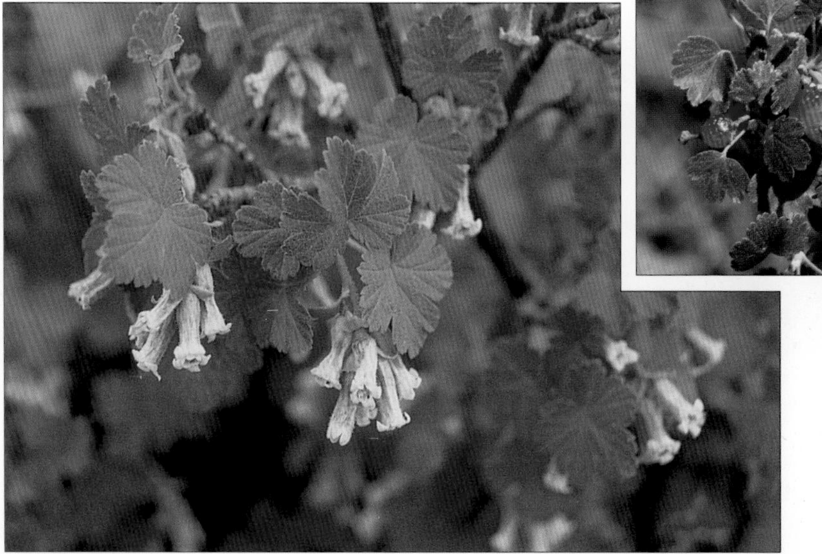

Mountain Gooseberry *Ribes montigenum*

The most common *Ribes* in the Elk Mountains is mountain gooseberry. The species name means "of the mountains," and indeed, it grows all over the mountains on rocky montane and subalpine slopes. They are usually low-growing shrubs, one to three feet high and become covered with beautiful salmon pink, saucer-shaped flowers in mid-summer. The ripe red berries are somewhat bitter.

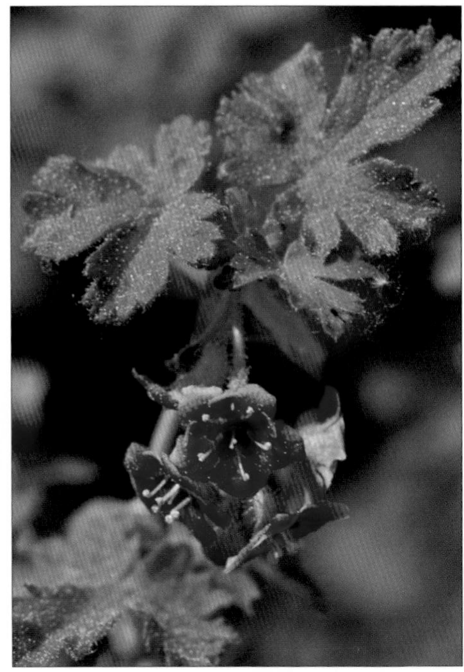

"I choose to live...
so that which came to me as seed
goes to the next as blossom
and that which came to me as blossom,
goes on as fruit."

– Dawna Markova

Wolf's Currant *Ribes wolfii*

Large maple-like leaves, clusters of shallow saucer-shaped white flowers, and dark purple or black berries are distinctive characters of Wolf's currant. Also known as western currant, this is a common shrub in the understory of subalpine forests, streamsides and occasionally on the alpine tundra. This species is named after a 19th century plant collector named John Wolf, not for wild dogs that once roamed our mountains.

Joseph Barrell, author of *Flora of the Gunnison Basin,* notes the Currant Family as one of the more interesting groups in the region: "To a collector interested in the ecologic and geographic distribution of plants, the eight species of the genus *Ribes* in the Gunnison Basin are a delight to study. They are as strongly marked ecologically and geographically as they are morphologically, and in observing their behavior in a large natural area such as the Gunnison Basin, one senses his closeness to the great drama of moving plant populations that has produced the world of plant life that we know today."

Iris Family IRIDACEAE

Every gardener is familiar with this family, which includes over forty species used as ornamentals, including gladiolas, freesia and crocus, as well as iris. Saffron-yellow dye and spice comes from the stigmas, or female parts, of *Crocus sativus*. Flower parts come in threes, and leaves are long, flat and grass-like.

Thou art the Iris, fair among the fairest,
Who, armed with golden rod
And winged with the celestial azure, bearest
The message of some God.

– Henry Wadsworth Longfellow, *Iris*

WILD IRIS *Iris missouriensis*

Early in summer, wet meadows are drenched in the blue of wild iris, especially in areas that have been grazed heavily. Wild iris is poisonous, so it is avoided by livestock, thereby outcompeting grasses. The plants spread rapidly by underground stems, or rhizomes, as well as by seed.

Although the plant is sometimes described as a "violent emetic and cathartic," the dried root has been used medicinally for various treatments, including blood cleansing, as a poultice for sores, a treatment for syphilis and, in small doses, as a laxative. On the other hand, Native Americans are said to have used it to poison their arrows.

These plants are named after the Greek goddess of rainbows and messenger of the gods, Iris. More recently, the flowers were named after French King Louis VII, who adopted the iris as his emblem, dubbing the flowers *fleur-de-lis* ("Flower of Louis"). The three-parted flowers were said to symbolize royal qualities of wisdom, faith and courage.

In North America, the wild iris is also known as blue flag, because their leaves resemble rushes or reeds, known as *flagge* in Old English. Our species was named by Thomas Nuttall, a 19th century botanist who collected specimens along the Missouri River in Montana during the 1830s.

Blue-eyed Grass *Sisyrinchium montanum*

Also known as eyebright, blue star and grass widow, these pretty little blue or purple flowers often get lost in the grasses and rushes of wet meadows and marshes because their long narrow leaves blend right in. Each flower blooms for only one day, but the plant may produce fresh flowers for several weeks. The genus, *Sisyrinchium*, means "pig snout" in Greek, inspired by the observation that swine enjoy grubbing for the roots of blue-eyed grass.

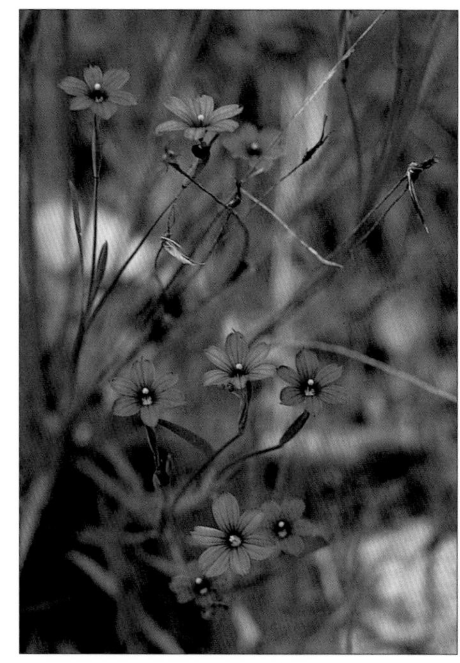

I'll Paint What I See

"A flower is relatively small.
Everyone has many associations
with a flower, the idea of flowers.
You put out your hand to touch the flower, lean forward to smell it,
maybe touch it with your lips almost without thinking,
or give it to someone to please them.
Still, in a way, nobody sees a flower,
really. It is so small,
we haven't time, and to see
takes time, like to have a friend
takes time. If I could paint the
flower exactly as I see it,
no one would see what I see
because I would paint it small
like the flower is small.
So, I said to myself,
I'll paint what I see,
what the flower is to me,
but I'll paint it big and
they will be surprised into
taking time to look at it.
I will make even busy
New Yorkers take time
to see what I see of flowers."

– Georgia O'Keefe

Rush Family JUNCACEAE

The rushes are far less prolific than the closely related sedges (p. 90), with only about three hundred species worldwide, about a dozen of which are found in the Elk Mountains. Unlike the sedges, which occupy a variety of habitats, these plants are restricted to marshy areas.

A simple rhyme helps to distinguish between the grasses, sedges and rushes: "Sedges have edges, rushes are round, and grasses hang out in joints." This ditty is all about stems. The shape of most sedge stems is triangular in cross-section; rushes are round with a pithy center; grass stems are round also, but have nodes, or joints on the stems.

RUSH *Juncus* spp.

Also known as wiregrass, because of their thin, stiff stems, rushes have been used by cultures all over the world to weave baskets and make cordage. Both the common and scientific names, rush and *Juncus*, are derived from Old English and Latin words that refer to these uses (in Old English, *rusche* means "to braid or twist"; *Juncus* means "binder").

Look closely at the miniature flowers. They are like tiny lily flowers, with three sepals and three petals, but with feathery stigmas (female parts) to catch the wind-blown pollen.

Rushes are common plants in wet hay meadows and welcome to the rancher as an element of winter feed. Many wildlife species feed on rushes as well. One of our most common local species is *Juncus arcticus* var. *balticus*, or Baltic rush. Dark green patches are easily spotted in hay meadows.

Mint Family Lamiaceae

Many of the mints are standard herbs on kitchen shelves; sage, thyme, marjoram, basil, oregano, rosemary and savory all belong to this family. Dozens of species are cultivated and used for medicinal purposes as well as for cooking, being effective as a treatment for just about everything from congestion and nausea, to headaches and sore muscles. Oils of citronella, lavender and patchouli are also derived from different mint species. Most are low-growing herbs and shrubs, but a few are tropical trees, such as teak and chaste tree. The family is most diverse in the Mediterranean region where the use of many of these cooking herbs has been elevated to a fine art.

All of these plants share the characteristic of square stems, although not all plants with square stems are mints (see the Madder Family, Rubiaceae, p. 177). In combination with opposite leaves and tubular flowers, a square-stemmed plant is probably a mint. Crush a leaf and smell it; most species have at least a faintly "minty" fragrance.

The fragrant biochemicals serve a purpose for the plant, as well as for humans. Like many plant chemicals, they protect the plant from disease and herbivory. Likewise, mint oils are common ingredients in insect repellants.

Labiatae and Lamiaceae are alternately used as Latin names for the Mint Family. Both refer to the shape of the flowers that have a "gaping mouth," or lamia and "lip-like" petals, or labia.

"Give and Take...
For to the bee a flower is a fountain if life
And to the flower a bee is a messenger of love
And to both, bee and flower,
the giving and the receiving is a need and an ecstasy."

– Kahlil Gibran

Giant Hyssop *Agastache urticifolia*

This native plant resembles two other mint species, the blue-flowered hyssop (*Hyssopus officinalis*), a native of the Mediterranean region, and the Bible hyssop, (*Origanum syriacum*), which has been used for ritual cleansing and as a culinary herb for centuries in the Middle East. They are tall plants, sometimes over three feet high, and are abundant in dry mountain meadows. The flowering spikes are crowded with pinkish-white flowers, which are usually buzzing with bees and other pollinating insects. *Agastache* translates to "lots of grain," because the flowers look somewhat like fat grasses. Giant hyssop has leaves that resemble those of nettles (*Urtica* spp., p. 195), a tall green, stinging plant that is often growing nearby. You won't have much trouble telling the two apart; nettles will sting you and hyssop, when rubbed or crushed, has a musty, minty fragrance similar to oregano.

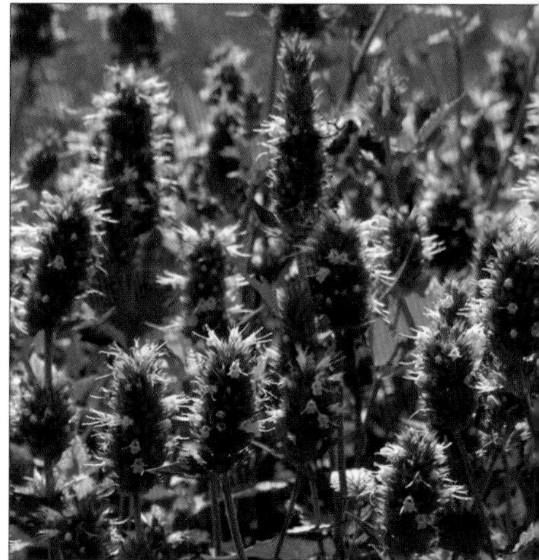

Wild Mint *Mentha arvensis*

The intoxicating aroma of wild mint is often detected before you see the plants. According to Greek mythology, this is a blessing bestowed by Hades, ruler of the underworld, whose mistress was a nymph named Minthe (aka Menthe). Persephone, the jealous wife of Hades, cast a spell on Minthe, turning her into a lowly plant. Hades softened the curse by willing that the more his lover was trampled upon, the sweeter she would smell.

Sniff around for wild mint in marshy areas, hayfields, along streams and irrigation ditches. These plants are common around the northern hemisphere; depending on the local habitat, mints will grow from six to twelve inches tall. The plants spread rapidly by rhizomes and stem fragments easily root in moist soils. Flower clusters at the leaf nodes range from pale blue to deep lavender. Peppermint (*M. piperita*) and spearmint (*M. spicata*) are two other well-known members of this genus. Both of these European natives have escaped cultivation and grow wild near settlements.

Mints have been used by many cultures as a stimulant and digestive aid. The Latin word, *mens*, refers to the mind, or thought. Garlands of mint were used by the Romans and Greeks as a brain tonic, to stimulate clear thoughts, concentration and inspirations. Mint tea is popular in Arabia, where the plant is regarded as a symbol of friendship and love. Mints are also the source of menthol, which is used to relieve aches, pains and stiffness in muscles and joints, as well as to relieve congestion.

Little Bee Balm *Monardella odoratissima*

One of the sweetest and most complex fragrances in all our mountain flora is in the leaves of little bee balm. Patches of semi-shrubby bee balm are found in dry, rocky areas in high mountain meadows. Although this species is locally common, it is considered a rare plant in Colorado, since it is uncommon throughout the region. The small pink flowers form a cluster on top of short, six to eight-inch high stems. Some other common names are coyote mint, wild bergamot, cloverhead mint and mountain oregano. The genus is named in honor of Nicolas Monardes, a 16th century Spanish botanist.

A larger and more common relative of little bee balm is *Monarda fistulosa*, which is common in the foothills and plains of Colorado, and is also sold commercially as an ornamental and medicinal herb. Bee balm tea is effective for reducing fevers and curing tummy aches. Like its close relative, pennyroyal (*Hedeoma* spp.), these plants have been used for centuries to stimulate labor in an overdue pregnancy. Unfortunately, many women using it for this purpose have made themselves very sick; herbs, like other medicines, should always be used with caution. However, you can safely rub leaves on your skin as a mosquito repellent, or use as a poultice to relieve bee stings.

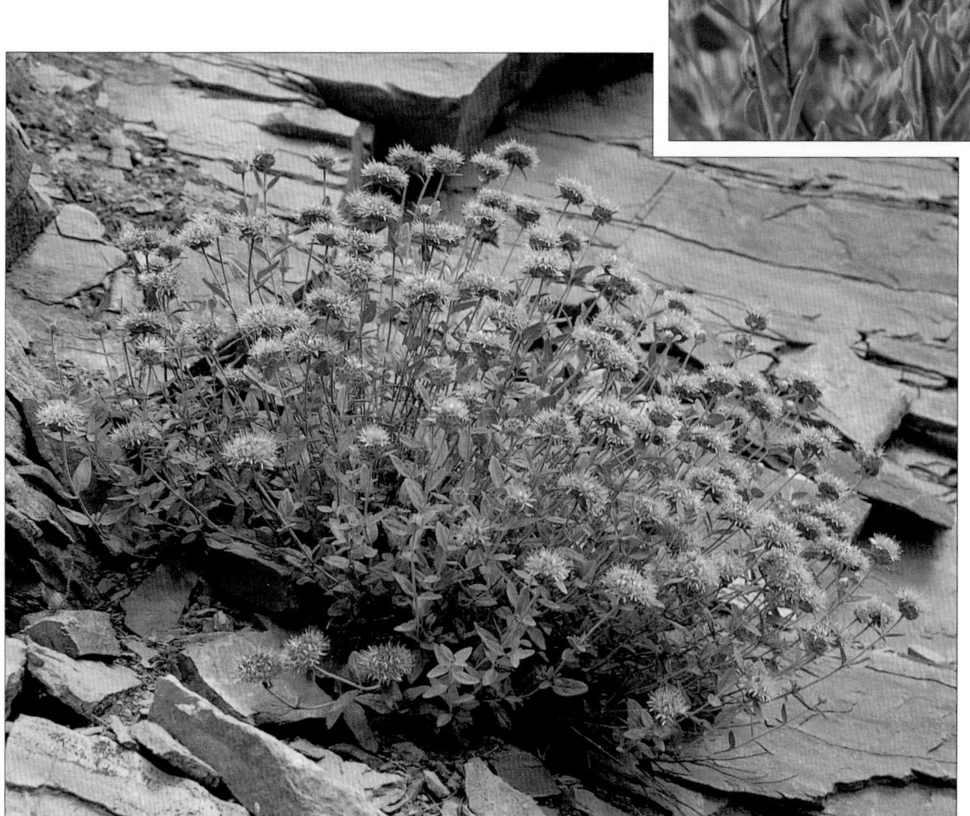

Lily Family LILIACEAE

A symbol of purity, innocence, harmony and perfection, lilies have been the inspiration of poets and artists for thousands of years.

The Greeks regarded the lily as the symbol of Artemis, goddess of nature and the moon. According to legend, two drops of milk fell from the mouth of Hercules while he was nursing at the breast of his mother, Hera, queen of gods and wife of Zeus. One drop spread across the sky and became the Milky Way. The other fell to earth and bloomed as a white lily.

In Christian legend, a white lily is dedicated to the Virgin Mary in honour of her purity and grace. Renaissance art depicts lilies in the Annunciation, when Mary was told by the Archangel Gabriel that she would be the mother of Christ, as well as in the empty tomb of Jesus three days after he died. Lilies are are often used in Easter ceremonies as a symbol of the Resurrection.

The Lilies are a huge family, especially diverse in the Himalayas, and include many ornamentals such as tulips and day lilies. Because of their delicate and stunning beauty, many lilies are vulnerable to destruction by wildflower fanciers. One native species, the wood lily (*Lilium philadelphicum*) is now considered rare in Colorado, mostly due to overcollection.

Many members of this family are extremely poisonous; when in doubt of identification, don't try it! There are also some very edible species in this group, so you may be tempted to experiment.

Some taxonomists divide this group into over twenty families; others maintain one large extended family. All are easily recognized by having flower parts in threes: 3 petals, 3 sepals (or 6 tepals), 6 stamens and a 3-lobed stigma.

WILD ONION *Allium brandegeei*

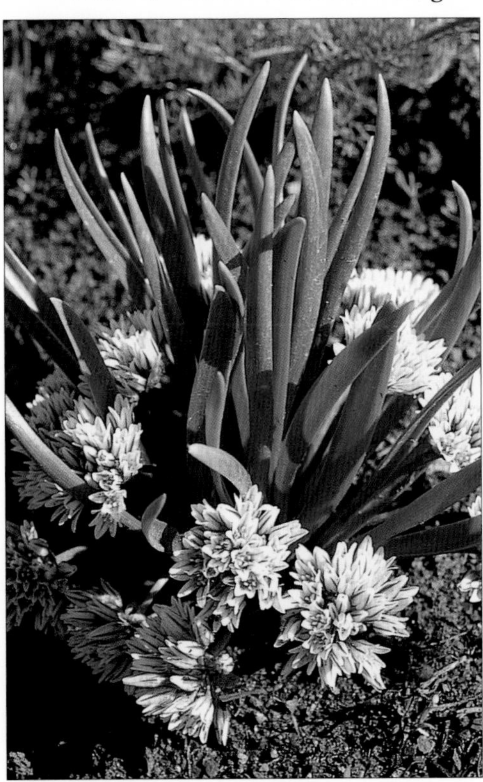

Onions, garlic, leeks, chives and shallots are all related to the wild onion. Vast colonies of this low-growing onion can be found blooming in early summer in sunny areas with dry, rocky soils, especially in association with big sagebrush. Wildlife, large and small, from bears to pocket gophers, enjoy their pungent bulbs as much as humans do.

A squeeze and sniff of the leaves will tell you it's an onion, but the deep-rooted bulb is tough to dig up if you don't have long, strong claws. There are three other species of wild onion in the southern Rockies (*A. cernuum, A. geyeri, A. rubrum*). Brandegee's is by far the most common and easy to recognize by its peppermint-striped flowers that are clustered close to the ground below the leaves.

Mary Katherine and Townshend Brandegee were a husband and wife pair of botanists for whom over 120 plant species are named. Townshend worked with the Hayden Survey, a team which explored this area in the late 1800s. Mary Katherine was a physician, botanist, and first woman curator of the California Academy of Sciences herbarium.

Mariposa Lily *Calochortus gunnisonii*

There are three species of mariposa lily in Colorado, but only one in Gunnison County, which is named after the founding father, Captain J.W. Gunnison. The flowers are most often associated with sagebrush, but are sometimes found in mountain meadows or near aspen groves. The genus has nearly five dozen species, over thirty of which are endemic to California. Many of them are extremely rare or endangered, partly because of restricted habitats, and partly due to over-enthusiastic collecting for the garden trade.

Also known as star tulip and butterfly tulip, each perfect flower blooms at the top of a slender stem, with three smooth, white petals and three narrow, green sepals. Gaze into the center of a mariposa lily and you'll find a perfectly symmetrical mandala, with patterns of fringed yellow glands, circles and spots of purple and green, plus six lavender anthers and a three-parted stigma. *Mariposa* means "butterfly" in Spanish, an appropriate name for the delicate flowers that look like fluttering wings. The scientific name, *Calochortus*, means "beautiful grass" in Greek, alluding to the slender stem and leaves.

Native Americans harvested the sweet bulbs of the mariposa lily for food. They can be eaten raw, boiled like tiny potatoes or dried and ground into flour to make flat breads and cakes. Known as *sego* to the Shoshone and Ute Indians, another species, *Calochortus nuttallii*, became the state flower of Utah, where Mormon pioneers were taught by local tribes of their nutritional value and were thereby saved from starvation during locust plagues in the 1840s. Wildlife, ranging from bears and bighorn sheep to small rodents, also harvest the bulbs as well as the succulent green seedpods.

"There is material enough in a single flower for the ornament of a score of cathedrals."

– John Ruskin

Glacier Lily *Erythronium grandiflorum*

DAVID INOUYE

One spring flower display that shouldn't be missed is fields and forests of glacier lilies. These are some of the first flowers to bloom as the snow melts, and are often found together with spring beauties and buttercups by the thousands in aspen forests and high meadows. Glacier lilies are also known as frost lilies, avalanche lilies or snow lilies, relating to their habit of emerging near the edge of melting snowbanks.

Erythronium means "red flower," probably referring to the anthers, which are often red or bright orange, but are usually yellow. In the Eastern U.S., related species have spotted leaves and have thus been dubbed as trout lily or fawn lily. This species has no spots, so is better named for their snow-loving character.

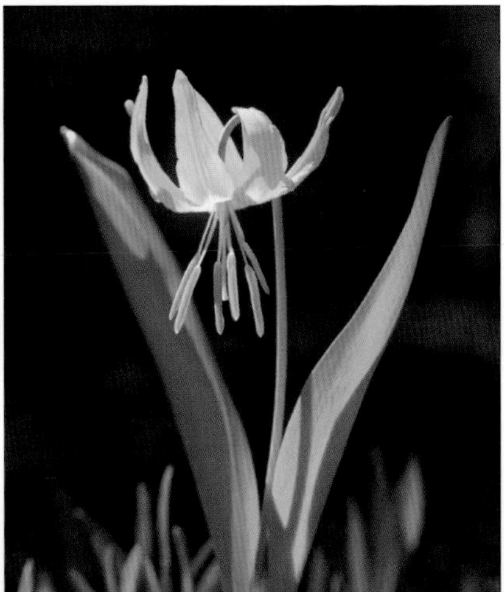

The entire plant is edible and important forage for wildlife. Bears will dig up large areas of meadow to find the bulbs, which are a favorite food. Glacier lilies also produce abundant nectar, attracting many different pollinators, including hummingbirds.

STARFLOWER *Maianthemum stellatum (Smilacina stellata)*

Patches of dainty starflowers grow in the cool shade and rich soils of spruce, Douglas-fir and aspen forests. Both starflower and a larger relative (*M. racemosum*) are sometimes called false Solomon's seal, because they resemble the true Solomon's seal (*Polygonatum* spp.) of the Eastern U.S. Both have six-petaled, star-shaped flowers and round scars on their rhizomes that resemble the Star of David, or Solomon's seal; Solomon was the son of David and third king of Israel. However, starflower differs by having clusters of flowers at the ends of the stems rather than dangling from the leaf nodes as with Solomon's seal. Starflower is more closely related to the sweet-smelling lily-of-the-valley (*Convallaria majalis*). In the fall, look for the round green and purple striped berries. The berries are edible and the leaves make good potherbs. A tea made from the rhizome is a good expectorant and treatment for mild headaches.

DAVID INOUYE

"One could not pluck a flower without troubling a star."
– Francis Thompson

TWISTED STALK *Streptopus amplexifolius (S. fassettii)*

Lush colonies of twisted stalk are usually found in the understory of spruce/fir forest wherever the ground is wet. Like starflower, they are sometimes confused with Solomon's seal (*Polygonatum* spp.), a group of Eastern U.S. species that look nearly identical, except that the stem does not zig-zag like the twisted stalk. Both have greenish-white, bell-shaped flowers that dangle in pairs from the leaf nodes. The leaves of twisted stalk also clasp or surround the stem, unlike those of Solomon's seal. The Latin name, *Streptopus amplexifolius*, literally means "twisted stalk with clasping leaves." Look for these plants in the fall, when their bright red, edible berries shine like ornaments in the soft light of the forest.

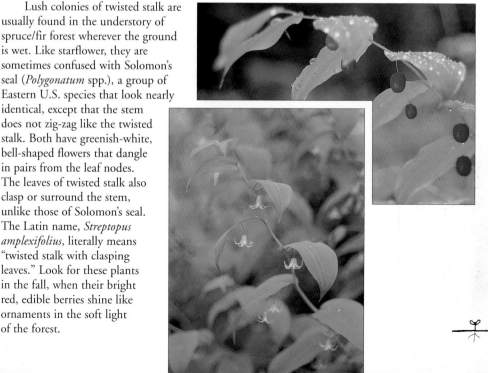

Corn Lily *Veratrum californicum (V. tenuipetalum)*

DAVID INOUYE

Perhaps the most notable botanical phenomenon in Crested Butte is the annual display of corn lilies marching down Elk Avenue on the heads and tails of Rocky Mountain Biological Laboratory students in the Fourth of July parade. The large pleated leaves of corn lily have been traditional parade fashion for over twenty years.

Fifteen species of corn lily are found in the northern hemisphere. Our local species is also common in the Sierra Nevada and coastal ranges of California; *Veratrum* means "very black roots" in Latin. Dense stands can be found in wet montane and subalpine meadows.

Corn lily grows at a rate of two inches per day and flowering plants reach up to seven feet tall, not unlike its namesake. The flowers have six tepals, a clue to its membership in the Lily Family. The hundreds of greenish-white blossoms on top of the leafy stalk form a densely branched cluster that looks much like the tassels on corn from a distance. Other common names are false hellebore (because it resembles hellebore, a European member of the Buttercup Family) and skunk cabbage (because its early growth looks like the large, broad basal leaves of skunk cabbage). This latter name should really be false skunk cabbage, because the true skunk cabbage is a completely different plant that is not native to Colorado.

All parts of the plant are extremely poisonous to livestock. If a female eats too much corn lily while pregnant, severe birth defects may occur in offspring. The cyclops effect in lambs is one monstrous result. The taste of corn lily is bitter so it is rarely eaten by cattle or wildlife; thus, large populations of corn lily can be indicators of overgrazing, where everything but the poisonous plants are eaten.

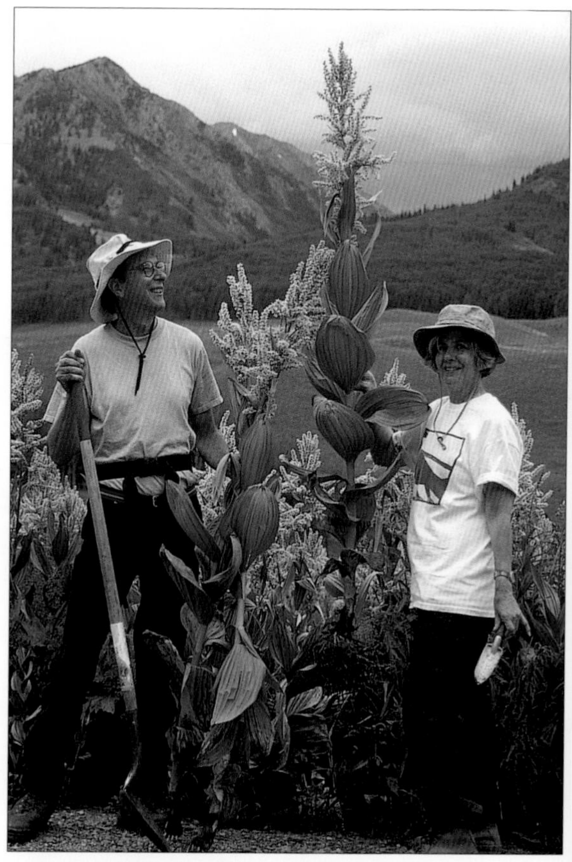

Larry Frolik and Cissie White doing research on corn lilies at Rocky Mountain Biological Lab through the Earthwatch educational program.

True Skunk Cabbage

Although commonly referred to as skunk cabbage in local lore, *Veratrum* spp. bears only scant resemblance to the true skunk cabbage, a member of the Arum Family (Araceae) and characterized by an unusual flowering stalk called a spadix. The phallic looking spadix is sheathed by a bright yellow or green leaf-like appendage called a spathe. Skunk cabbage is so named because it has a distinctive foul odor, which attracts its primary pollinators, flies. The huge basal leaves can grow up to five feet long, but the flowering stalk tops out at about one foot. Western or yellow skunk cabbage (*Lysichiton americanum*) can be found in marshes and wet woods along the coast from Alaska to northern California and east to western Montana. Another species, *Symplocarpus foetidus*, grows in the northeastern U.S.

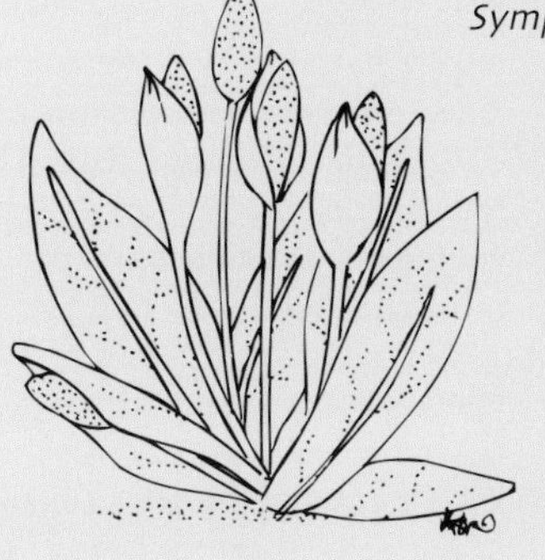

Despite its disgusting aroma, skunk cabbage is edible (unlike corn lily) and is important food for wildlife, especially black bears. However, calcium oxalate crystals found in all parts of the plant cause a burning or stinging sensation in the mouth when eaten raw, so Native Americans learned to cook the young green leaves to remove the oxalate before eating. The root is roasted and ground into flour. This is similar to the preparation of taro, a close relative of skunk cabbage and a staple food in Polynesia.

RMBL researcher David Inouye has been studying the life history of these plants since 1984. His observations have revealed that corn lilies may live for over twenty years and form clones, meaning that several stalks belong to a single plant. The clones may be hundreds of years old, or even more, rivaling the ages of aspen clones. Colonies bloom in mass every two to seven years, perhaps in response to moisture and temperature conditions over a series of seasons.

DAVID INOUYE

DAVID INOUYE

Death Camas *Zigadenus elegans (Anticlea elegans)*

Death camas is appropriately named, being one of the more deadly plants in our area. One way to recognize the flowers is by the heart-shaped green or yellow glands at the base of the white petals. *Zigadenus* means "yoke gland," describing these nectaries. *Anticlea* was the name of the mother of Ulysses (Odysseus), the king in Homer's Odyssey. The elegant beauty of these flowers is a deceiving cover for what is a dangerously poisonous plant. The bulbs of death camas are easily confused with edible bulbs of other members of the Lily Family, such as onion, mariposa lily and blue camas, especially before the flowering stalks appear. Also known as wand lily, large colonies of these plants can be found in moist mountain meadows all the way to treeline.

Rare Plants

At least one of every eight plant species, or over 12% of the known species of plants in the world, is under threat of extinction, according to a comprehensive worldwide assessment of plant endangerment. Among the plants most at risk, the survey found, are 14% of Rose species, 32% of Lilies, 32% of Irises and 29% of Palms.

Flax Family LINACEAE

Flax fibers have been used by people around the world for thousands of years to create ropes, nets and cloth called linen. The common name is derived from the German word *flachs*, meaning "to ply or braid." *Linum* is an ancient word, used for millenia to describe these blue-flowered plants that produce such durable stem fibers. Fragments of cloth found in the Mediterranean from biblical times are made of linen. The Shroud of Turin, a sacred cloth that may have been Christ's burial covering, was made of linen. Today, linen remains one of the most durable fibers found in nature, and a favorite in high fashion circles.

Common flax, *L. usitatissimum* (meaning "useful"), is the commercial source of linen fiber and linseed oil. Linseed oil is an important ingredient of paints, varnishes, inks and linoleum. Linoleic acid is abundant in flax seeds, and is an essential unsaturated fatty acid in animal diets. In the Middle East, Europe and Canada, common flax is grown by the hundreds of acres, to produce all of these products that are now part of most modern households, whether it be used as wood sealant or an ingredient in your salad dressing. For more interesting information on flax, check out this amazing website: www.saskflax.com

BLUE FLAX *Linum lewisii (Adenolinum lewissii)*

Blue flax looks very similar to the cultivated annual variety, but is a perennial plant. The delicate azure-blue flowers are abundant in mountain meadows and sagebrush swales. Each five-petaled flower blooms for a day and then sheds its petals in the slightest breeze. A single plant will bloom for several weeks throughout mid-summer and then develop dozens of tiny bowl-shaped pods, which scatter the seeds to the wind. Like the cultivar, blue flax fibers can be used to make cordage and the seeds are a source of oils. Look for the slender stems in late fall and winter, bearing dozens of beautiful bowl-shaped seedpods. This species is named in honor of Captain Meriwether Lewis of the Lewis and Clark expedition and is the only native flax found in the Elk Mountains. A common look-alike is *L. perenne*, which is a European variety often used in wildflower seed mixes.

JANNETTE RUNGE

Mallow Family MALVACEAE

We can all thank the Mallow Family for our underwear, since this is where cotton fiber comes from. Remains of cotton textiles have been found at Mayan archeological sites in Mexico dating back to 3500 B.C. Four of thirty-nine species of cotton worldwide have been domesticated for use in the textile industry, with Mexican cotton (*Gossypium hirsutum*) being the primary species used today. The Mallow Family thus has played a significant role in politics and culture of the United States, being tied to the slave industry and the consequent Civil War.

Some gourmands are grateful for okra (*Hibiscus esculentus*), an edible member of the family, and most would agree that gardens are enriched by the colorful blossoms of hollyhocks and hibiscus. Hibiscus flowers are the unofficial emblem of the surfer culture, and likely to be found on a t-shirt or flip-flops in many American households. Of the more than three hundred species of *Hibiscus* found around the world, only four are considered native to Hawaii. One of these is Pua Aloalo (*H. brackenridgei*), the Hawaiian state flower, and is endangered, as is much of Hawaii's native flora.

CHECKER MALLOW *Sidalcea candida*

At first glance, checker mallow is easily mistaken for a wild geranium; both have five petals and palmately lobed leaves. Look a bit closer and you'll see that the multiple stamens of checker mallow are bundled together in a tiny fountain at the center of the flower and the leaves are much more deeply lobed. If you find the fruit, you'll see that the mallow produces a round capsule with multiple seeds, which gives many plants in the family the common name "cheeseweed," since it resembles the old-style wheels of cheese.

As with our native geraniums, there are both white and pink species of checker mallows; the pink mallow is *Sidalcea neomexicana*. Both prefer moist habitats and are most common in sunny locations in marshy areas or along streams from 7,000 up to 11,000 feet. You are most likely to see these plants blooming in late summer.

DAVID INOUYE

Copper Mallow *Sphaeralcea coccinea*

In contrast to their cousins, the checker mallow, these plants are most common in drier soils among sagebrush, and are a reminder that the area is influenced by the Great Basin desert, which protrudes into the Gunnison Valley. *Sphaeralcea* is bright orange and thrives in sunny, open areas, a welcome sight in an often drab landscape and earning it another common name, cowboy's delight. Other Great Basin species, such as yucca, prickley pear cactus and crimson paintbrush are likely to be found nearby. Near Crested Butte, Jack's Cabin cutoff and the hills to the west of Almont campground are excellent places to explore and look for plants of the high desert.

The root of this plant has also been used as a remedy to soothe sore throats and hemorrhoids, as it shares the mucilaginous properties that make marsh mallow useful as a gelatin and give okra its slimy texture.

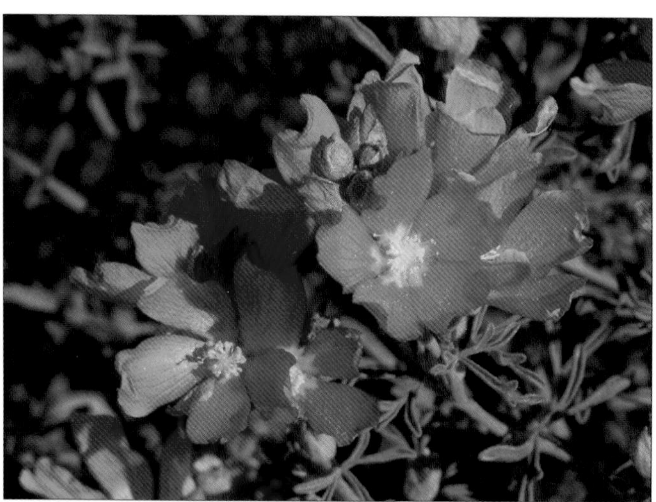

Marsh Mallow

As for the marsh mallow and its role in creating S'mores, it is true that the original concept of the puffy sugar treat used sap extracted from the roots of a plant native to Europe and the Middle East, *Althea officinalis.* From ancient Egyptian times until the mid-1800s, the beautiful pink-flowered wetland species served the purpose of thickening the honey-based confection. Today, most marshmallows use gelatin, a product of animal bones, to hold their shape, and honey has been replaced by corn syrup for sweetener.

Water Lily Family NYMPHACEAE

The most famous of the water lilies is the sacred lotus (*Nelumbo nucifera*) of Hindu and Buddhist faiths, symbol of divine purity and truth. Lotus flowers are cultivated for food in India, as well as worshipped. The roots, stems, flowers and seeds are edible and besides being nutritious, are alleged to induce a languid, dreamy state when eaten. Meditating in the lotus position may have the same effect. Many florists use the large, woody seedpods in flower arrangements.

One of the many wonders of the plant world is the giant Amazon water lily (*Victoria amazonica*), which has floating leaves over six feet in diameter and is capable of holding the weight of a small child!

The Water Lily Family is named after the water nymph and Greek goddess of springs, Nymphe. In medieval Germany, water lilies were believed to be maidens disguised as flowers to avoid the advances of lecherous men. Chaste women carried water lilies as an antidote to love potions. Contrarily, modern herbalists regard water lilies as the "Kama Sutra among flower essences," and may prescribe an essence of water lily to help someone release their sexual inhibitions.

"More than anything, I must have flowers, always."
– Claude Monet

Yellow Pond Lily *Nuphar polysepala (N. lutea)*

Also known as spatterdock, pond lily, wokas and nack-rose, this is the only species native to the Western U.S., and is related to four other species found floating on ponds in the Eastern U.S. According to Scandinavian folklore, there are trolls called "nacks" who sit at the bottom of lakes and ponds fishing for people. The long rubbery stem of the water lily is the line and a flower is the troll's lure.

Seeds of the water lily have been used as food by Native Americans, roasted and eaten like popcorn, or ground into flour. The rootstocks are also edible. Water lilies bloom on subalpine ponds and lakes from mid- to late-summer.

Evening Primrose Family ONAGRACEAE

The sweet smell of evening primroses (*Oenothera* spp.) reminded early botanists of the scent of European primroses. However, primroses and evening primroses are very different families, with smell perhaps the only common feature. Flowers in this family share the characteristic of an inferior ovary. Here, inferior does not mean "worse," but rather "below," meaning that the seed-bearing part of the flower is formed below the petals, stamens and pistils. All have four petals, four sepals and a four-parted stigma. The quadruple flower pattern is sometimes confused with plants in the mustard family that also have four-petaled flowers. Checking the ovary or seedpod is the easiest way to distinguish between the two families, because mustards have superior ovaries, meaning their seed pods grow above the rest of the flower.

Many of this family bloom at dusk and are pollinated by night-flying insects, especially hawk moths (p. 47). Fuschias are also in this family and are popular ornamentals native to the Andes.

FIREWEED *Chamerion angustifolium (C. danielsii; Epilobium angustifolium)*

Fireweed is named for its bright color and for its ecological role as a pioneer in burned areas. But wildfire is only one kind of disturbance that sets the stage for fireweed to flourish. Landslides, avalanches, bulldozers and even pocket gophers also create the open soil that this plant prefers. Reproducing by both seed and underground rhizomes, fireweed will quickly stabilize the soil and eventually give way to other plants in the successional milieu.

Also known as great willowherb, because of leaves and fluffy seeds that resemble those of the riparian shrubs, fireweed is found on roadsides, meadows and sunny forest edges from the foothills to tundra. Other common names are cottonweed and blooming Sally.

Livestock, elk, deer and bears, as well as bees, will feast on fireweed. Young shoots and leaves are fine forage for the wild gourmand as well, best lightly steamed or sautéed.

The genus, *Chamerion*, means "lowly oleander," because the leaves vaguely resemble oleander's. Many botanical references also cite the species as *Epilobium angustifolium*, which literally translates to "upon the pod, narrow-leaved." The flowers bloom from the bottom up on the tall leafy stem, so that blossoms and buds can be found above ripe seedpods near the end of the season. Another interpretation of the generic name is its reference to the inferior ovary of the flowers, a characteristic shared by all of the family. The fertilized ovary will grow from half an inch in flower to a four-inch long pod before it bursts and releases hundreds of windblown seeds, each with its own tiny parachute.

Closely related to fireweed are the willowherbs (*Epilobium* spp.), most of which look like miniature versions of the flamboyant fireweed, bearing white or pink blooms. Both fireweed and willowherb demonstrate a classic strategy that plants use to promote cross pollination. Known as *protandry* in botanical lingo, this simply means that the stamens release their pollen before the stigma is receptive. In the photo to the far right, the stigma is ripe in the middle of the spent stamens and ready to receive pollen from the neighbors, as delivered by nectar gathering insects. Above, male anthers release pollen. Other plants, such as pasque flowers and water lilies have a *protogynous* strategy in which the stigma matures first.

Ripe "male" anthers

JANNETTE RUNGE

Ripe "female" stigma

Dwarf Fireweed *Chamerion latifolia*

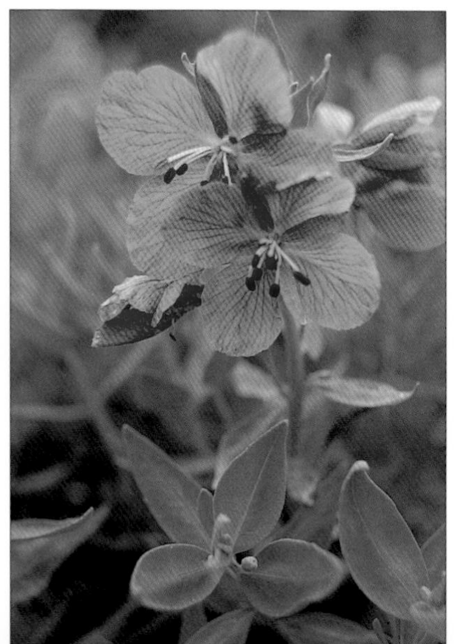

A smaller species of fireweed, *Chamerion latifolia*, is less common and occurs in small patches along streams and on talus slopes in the subalpine and alpine tundra. Also known as "river beauty," this species has broader petals, shorter leaves, and a stigma shorter than the anthers, whereas the taller fireweed has longer leaves and a long stigma. Both species are used as herbal remedies for many ailments, including hiccups, whooping cough, colitis and prostate problems. Tea made from dried leaves is used as a tonic and laxative. Poultices may be used to sooth abrasions.

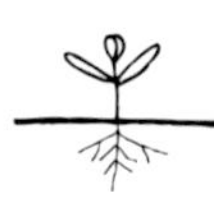

Stemless Evening Primrose *Oenothera caespitosa*

The huge (3-4" diameter) white, four-petaled flowers of stemless evening primrose are common on gravelly soils and roadsides. The flowers bloom in the evening and usually turn pink and shrivel by the following midday. If they are not pollinated by dawn, they stay open longer to attract day-time pollinators. This is one flower you should not pass without smelling; the lemony fragrance is intoxicating. This is surely what the Greek naturalist, Theophrastus (~300 B.C.), thought when he named the genus *Oenothera*, which means "wine scented." The specific name, *caespitosa*, means that the leaves and flowers grow in clumps, close to the ground. Another trademark of the evening primrose is the sticky, stringy, yellow pollen, which will probably get stuck on your nose when you sniff them.

Tall Yellow Evening Primrose *Oenothera elata*

These spectacular short-lived perennials grow along roadsides and irrigation ditches. Growing up to four feet tall, each stalk will produce several large (up to four inches in diameter) bright yellow flowers in the evening, which wilt to a pale orange by midday. *Elata* means tall. Like its cousin, the stemless evening primrose, they attract long-tongued moths as pollinators.

This is one of over a dozen species of *Oenothera* that are native to Colorado, and over 200 world-wide. Another North American species, *Oenothera biennis*, is cultivated for the oil extracted from seeds, which is reputed to relieve rheumatoid arthritis and many other maladies. The roots of evening primroses are edible and nutritious.

Orchid Family ORCHIDACEAE

There are around 20,000 species of orchids worldwide, making this the world's second largest plant family, next to the Sunflowers (see page 37). Orchids evoke a sense of exotic romance, owing partly to their proliferation in tropical regions of the world, as well as to their often potent fragrance and delicate beauty. The name orchid is derived from the Latin word *orchis*, which means testicle, because of the shape of many orchid roots. Because of this resemblance, orchids are believed to be aphrodisiacs and, if eaten by a pregnant woman, to promote the birth of a boy. Another derivation of the word orchid is from the Lithuanian *arzus*, which means lustful. Something to think about next time you pin on a corsage or drape a friend in leis!

In addition to having developed some fascinating pollinating mechanisms, all orchids have a symbiotic relationship with specialized fungi, which are necessary for the germination of their tiny dust-like seeds and the continued survival of the plant. Because terrestrial orchid species are dependent on a particular kind of mycorrhizal fungus which attaches to the roots of the plant, it is extremely difficult to successfully transplant or cultivate many wild orchids. Fortunately for lovers of chocolate, ice cream and other confections, methods were developed over 150 years ago to cultivate the vanilla orchid (*Vanilla planifolia*), source of the vanilla bean, which is the dried seed pod of this viney tropical orchid.

Most tropical orchids are epiphytic, growing on other plants, while temperate species are terrestrial. Although the local orchids are tiny and will not be found hanging from the trees, they are fascinating in form and easy to find if you know what to look for.

Fairy Slipper *Calypso bulbosa*

The jewel-like fairy slipper is one of a dozen species of wild orchids native to the Elk Mountains. These are the first of the mountain orchid species to bloom, beginning in mid-May, and are found in the diffuse light of coniferous forests, usually on north-facing aspects. This is the most colorful of Colorado's orchids with bright pink petals crowning the yellow, maroon and white "slipper." Each flower is solitary, on a short stem emerging from a single broad basal leaf. Like many orchids, the fairy slipper has a bulbous, or testicle-shaped root, inspiring its species name, *bulbosa*. The flowers rely on deceiving naïve bumblebee pollinators, for they make no nectar. Although the bees quickly discover that the flowers have no reward, in the learning process they may pollinate a flower or two. Orchids produce tiny seeds; a single pollination event will result in many thousands of seeds that can be dispersed by wind.

Another common name, calypso orchid, may be interpreted as a reference to the lid or hood (from the Greek word *kalyptra*, meaning covering or veil) that protects the reproductive organs of the flower. In Homer's epic poem, the Odyssey, Calypso is also the name of the sea nymph who detained the willing Odysseus on his return from Troy. Like the sea nymph, these orchids are captivatingly beautiful and prefer secluded haunts. They are sometimes also called Venus' orchid, after the Greek goddess of love andbeauty. Although calypso orchids are usually not very abundant where they grow, they can be found in northern temperate forests around the world.

Coralroot Orchid *Corallorhiza maculata*

In the shade of coniferous forests, you will find three kinds of coralroot orchids. An exception to the "testicled" roots of other species, coralroots have a branched mass of roots resembling, you guessed it, coral! Actually, the "roots" of these orchids are underground stems, or rhizomes. These plants have no green leaves and are saprophytic, meaning that they are dependent on fungi associated with decaying organic matter. The entire plant is pale pink or red. Spotted and striped coralroots (*C. maculata* and *C. striata*), named for the patterns on their pink and white flowers, can be found growing side-by-side in spruce-fir forests. The third species, *C. trifida*, is very pale green with plain white flowers.

Bog Orchid *Platenthera aquilonis (Limnorchis hyperborea)*

One native orchid that is easy to find is the northern green bog orchid, which has greenish-white flowers and grows in bogs or wetlands. If you see elephant heads blooming, chances are there are bog orchids near by. The plants grow to over a foot tall and the tiny flowers have a spur poking out the back. Get down on your knees and take a whiff of their sweet lusty fragrance. A closely related orchid, *Platenthera obtusata*, is pollinated by nectar-feeding mosquitoes, which can sometimes be spotted flying around with a little yellow dot (the pollen bundle) on their heads, proof that mosquitos are useful!

The bog orchids are one of the largest genera in the family, with over five hundred species worldwide. The genus, *Limnorchis*, means "orchid of wet places," as in limnology. The long, narrow lower petals of the flower inspired the alternate Latin name, *Habenaria*, which means "rein" or "narrow strap"; another common name is rein orchid. Bog orchid is found in northern latitudes around the world as far as the Arctic Circle; *hyperborea* means "beyond the north."

Lady's Tresses *Spiranthes romanzoffiana*

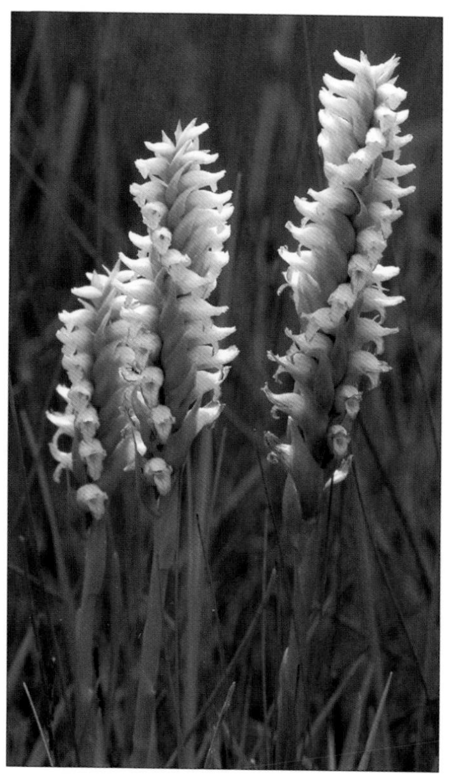

Of two dozen species of *Spiranthes* in the world, two are found in Colorado and one of those is rare (*S. diluvialis*). Romanzoff's lady's tresses is quite common, blooming late in summer in open sunny areas with wet soils throughout northern Eurasia as well as North America. The spirals of white flowers are unmistakable. Another common name is pearltwist. Count Nikolai Romanzoff was an early 19th century Russian nobleman and sponsor of several expeditions to the northwest coast of North America.

> *"The flower is the poetry of reproduction. It is an example of the eternal seductiveness of life."*
>
> – Jean Giraudoux

Mycorrhizae

Mycorrhizae, meaning "fungus roots," are a mutually beneficial symbiotic relationship in which a fungus grows into and around the roots of a plant. Eighty percent of the world's plants are known to have mycorrhizal associations. For many plants the relationship is a necessity; almost all orchids and conifers require mycorrhizae for healthy growth. Likewise, for many of the fungi, a mycorrhizal association is obligatory. The roots of the plant provide nourishment to the fungus, while the fungus aids the roots in absorbing water and minerals by forming a vast network of threads, or mycelium, that extend and reinforce the plant's root system. In addition to increased nutrient and water absorption, the fungus often increases the plant's resistance to root pathogens, soil toxins and temperature extremes. Next time you see a mushroom, think about this important partnership that its underground parts have with the plants growing around it!

Broomrape Family OROBANCHACEAE

Members of this family are partially or fully parasitic, meaning they derive their nutrition through the roots of other plants. Many lack the green chlorophyll necessary to produce their own food, so some plants are pale pink or white, giving them the common name, "ghost plant." *Orobanche* translates to "vetch strangler," because many plants in the Pea Family (Fabaceae), or vetches, are common ghost hosts. Yellow-flowering shrubs called broom, also in the Pea Family, are often victims of these parasitic plants, hence the name broomrape. An infestation of broomrapes can result in huge losses of leguminous crops.

Broomrapes are sometimes included in the Snapdragon Family (Scrophulariaceae) because their flowers are similar in form to snapdragons, the main difference being their parasitic habit. Likewise, Indian paintbrushes (p. 184-188) and louseworts (p. 190-191), which are traditionally placed in the Snapdragon Family, are now believed to be more closely related to broomrapes, partly because they are semi-parasitic. New technologies in DNA analysis are helping taxonomists gain a clearer understanding of the evolutionary relationships among these families and genera.

BROOMRAPE *Orobanche fasciculata (Aphyllon fasciculatum)*

This species of broomrape is parasitic on big sagebrush (*Artemisia tridentata*) and is fairly common in the lower elevations of the Elk Mountains where sagebrush is dominant. They are also sometimes called cancer root, because of their harmful effect on the host. Despite their lifestyle, these plants are fascinating and beautiful to look at and worth a search beneath the shrubs. The most common mountain species occurs in clumps, or *fascicles*. Look also for a one-flowered species, *O. uniflora*. Broomrapes have been used medicinally to treat a variety of ailments, serving as a laxative, sedative, aphrodisiac and tonic.

Grass-of-Parnassus Family PARNASSIACEAE

Parnassia is named after Mount Parnassus, an 8,000 foot peak in central Greece, sacred home of Apollo and the nine Muses of literature, art and science. These goddesses have fascinating names: Calliope, Clio, Enterpe, Melpomene, Terpsichore, Erato, Polyhymnia, Ouramia and Thalia. In ancient Greece, these were the spirits believed to inspire poets, dancers, writers and other artists, along with those who study heaven and earth. A museum is a place filled with work inspired by the Muses and a place for study.

This is a small family of only one genus and about fifty species that are found growing in wetlands around the northern hemisphere. Some botanists have included this group in the Saxifrage Family, which has historically been a confusing taxonomic group, and has most recently been divided into seven separate families, including the Currant Family (Grossulariaceae). Distinctive features of this herbaceous group of plants are the basal leaves and slender flowering stalks, which make them difficult to distinguish from grasses when not in bloom. Most species grow in wetland habitats, either in marshes, bogs or along streams. Special glands attached to the stamens are unique to this family.

FRINGED PARNASSIA *Parnassia fimbriata*

Look for the ruffled mounds of parnassia leaves along the mossy banks of streams on the tundra and in high spruce forests. The eight to twelve inch flowering stem has a single leaf about halfway up and grows from a ruffled mass of smooth-edged, kidney-shaped basal leaves. A single perfect five-petaled white flower blooms at the tip of each stem. The base of each petal is fringed and bears a gem-like yellow nectar gland.

MARSH PARNASSIA *Parnassia palustris (P. parviflora)*

The unfringed marsh parnassia occurs in the Elk Mountains in habitats similar to those where fringed parnassia grows, but usually more open and sunny locations. These plants have smaller flowers and no leaf on the stem. This species is circumboreal, meaning it is found on continents around the northern hemisphere.

Grass Family Poaceae

They may not look like wildflowers, but technically, grasses do have flowers. Since grasses are wind pollinated, the tiny blossoms lack showy petals or sweet nectars to attract pollinators. Instead, these plants put their energy into massive pollen and seed production. This is both a woe and a benefit to humans who may suffer from allergies and hayfever, but sustain themselves with grains.

Next to conifers used for wood production, grasses are the most economically important plant family. In fact, the rise of human civilization is often credited with the advent of agriculture, with wheat crops being the foundation of both. Add to this oats, rice, barley, corn, sorghum, hay and sugarcane, and you may wonder if the Greeks didn't have a Grass Goddess among their dozens of deities. Yes, in fact, Demeter is the Greek goddess of agriculture, grain and fertility. Her Roman counterpart is Ceres, whose name appears in our language as "cereal."

However, their dominance in the wild world exceeds its importance to *Homo sapiens*. Grasses rank fourth in the number of species around the world, behind orchids, sunflowers and legumes. Vast open spaces of prairies and savannahs are dominated by grasses, which support the teeming herds of wildlife that migrate (or once did) across these plains. Grassland ecosystems are supremely adapted to grazing and wildfire and, in many respects, are dependent on these natural disturbances for their continued health. Fire and foraging have the effects of promoting the recycling of nutrients within the ecosystem and of checking the encroachment of shrubs and trees. Grasses have a network of fine roots that are important in stabilizing soils following a fire. The presence, absence and abundance of grass species are indicators of the overall health of grassland and desert ecosystems, telling land managers if various uses, such as grazing and recreation, are too much, too little or just right.

The co-evolution of grasses with wildlife and fire is evident in the plants' growth and structure, as well. Grasses grow from the base of the leaves rather than from the tips, as do most other plants, so that they are able to recover rapidly after being nibbled, burnt or mowed. The leaves and stems break easily at the base, so that foraging animals can get a bite to eat without uprooting the entire plant.

There are over 1,500 species of grasses in North America, sixty of which grow in the Elk Mountain region. Mountain meadows are dominated by tall bunch grasses such as fescue (*Festuca* spp.), muhly (*Muhlenbergia* spp.) and brome grasses (*Bromus* spp.). Needle-and-thread grass (*Stipa* spp.) and onion grass (*Bromelica* spp.) are also common. Rather than go into descriptions of each, I encourage you to take the time to break away from the more colorful and commanding showy wildflowers and appreciate the beauty and grace of grasses with their less conspicuous flowers. Here are a few that are very easy to identify without having to know a lot of technical terms.

Brome Grass *Bromus inermis (Bromopsis inermis)* Non-native Species

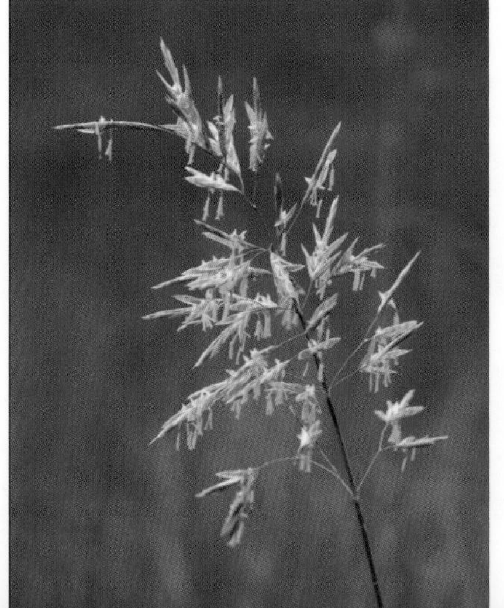

Brome grasses are easily recognized by their loose panicles of flowers and short awns, or bristles that extend from the tip of the flower. This is one of the many grasses that has been intentionally imported from Eurasia to "improve" rangeland forage; thirteen of the twenty-one species of brome in Colorado are non-native. Unfortunately, non-native grasses have become invasive throughout North America, crowding out native plant species and increasing risk of fire in some regions where fire has not historically been a natural part of the ecosystem. While smooth brome is considered somewhat palatable to livestock, other non-native bromes, such as cheat grass (*B. tectorum*) and red brome (*B. rubens*) are not, and have become a significant problem in rangeland management.

Thurber's Fescue *Festuca thurberi*

Thurber's fescue is a dominant grass in the high mountains, and young plants are primary forage for both wildlife and cattle. This is a huge bunchgrass, growing to three feet tall and equally wide, and is often the main species in the understory of aspen forests as well as subalpine meadows.

Junegrass *Koeleria macrantha*

Fluffy flowering spikes of junegrass are easy to spot in open areas from sagebrush to subalpine meadows. In flower, they spread out to release and catch pollen. In seed, the spikes become smooth and slender. Junegrass blooms early in the season and is one of the shorter bunchgrasses, usually growing no more than a foot tall.

This grass is widespread throughout North America except for the southeastern U.S. where it is considered rare. The species was named in honor of George L. Koeler, a German botanist in the late 1700s.

Timothy Grass *Phleum pratense* Non-native Species

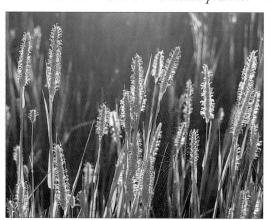

Timothy grass was introduced from Eurasia to be cultivated for hay. Since then, it has escaped and found itself at home in moist mountain meadows and prairies all over the continent. The tight cylindrical flower head looks like a miniature cattail. At higher elevations, this species is replaced by the smaller, purple-flowered alpine timothy (*P. alpinum*), which is native to arctic and alpine regions around the world. *Phleum* is Greek for "copious," describing the tight bundle of flowers. *Pratense* means "of meadows."

Phlox Family POLEMONIACEAE

Some of the showiest and most fragrant mountain wildflowers are in the Phlox Family. All have tubular corollas that flare out to five broad petals. The Latin name for this family, *Polemoniaceae,* is obscure, either honoring the second century B.C. Greek philosopher, Polemon, or alluding to some "polemic" event that coincided with its discovery. One author reports that the "discovery of its supposed properties occasioned a war between two kings." What properties, what war and what kings remains a secret.

Floral Scents

The business of pollination has evolved complex chemistry and behaviors in both plants and pollinators. The primary function of floral scents for the plant is to attract pollinators. Insects can detect very low levels of chemical compounds from great distances. Some floral scents mimic sexual pheromones of insects, especially well documented in many species of orchids. Other plants are reported to have a hallucinogenic or narcotic effect on insects, which contributes to floral fidelity in certain pollinators. This is very important if the pollen of a plant is to be transferred to another flower of the same species, thereby allowing seed production.

Collomia *Collomia linearis*

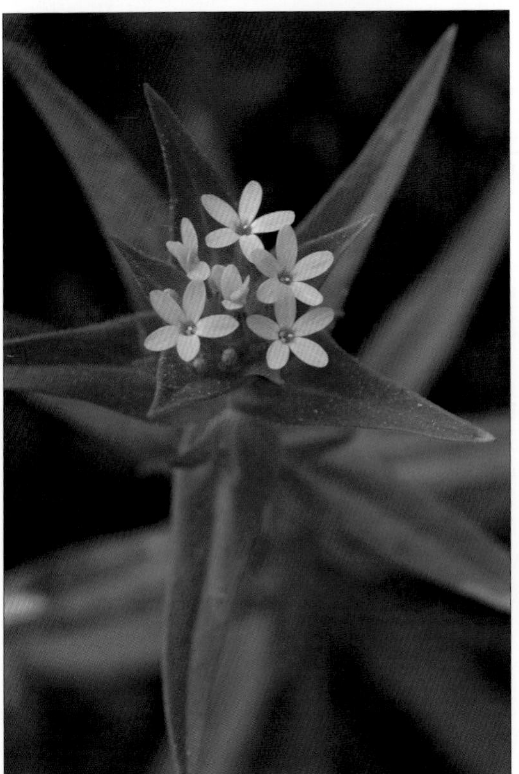

The tiny pink flowers of collomia may often be passed up, since it grows in the company of many more flamboyant species in mountain meadows. Collomia is an annual and plays a significant role as a native pioneer species in disturbed soils. Whether the disturbance is "natural," such as the churning of soils by pocket gophers, or human caused, collomia is often the first species to take root in sunny meadows. Depending on where it grows, the plant will grow to just a few inches or become a much-branched plant up to a foot tall. Look closely and you'll see the long tubular corolla characteristic of the family, giving it the common name "tiny trumpet." *Collomia* refers to the "kolla," or mucilaginous glue, that forms when the seeds are soaked in water; *linearis* describes the long narrow leaves.

Scarlet Gilia *Ipomopsis aggregata*
Pink Trumpets *Ipomopsis tenuituba*

The bright red tubular flowers of scarlet gilia are pollinated primarily by hummingbirds, as well as long-tongued moths and butterflies, that can reach down the narrow throat of the flower to slurp up nectar. This plant is a monocarpic perennial, producing only a rosette of leaves (center photo) for one to eight years, flowering when the plant has stored enough energy. After it flowers, the plant dies, leaving hundreds of seeds to carry on its legacy. Also known as skyrocket gilia and fairy trumpets, these flamboyant blooms can be seen throughout the summer from sagebrush flats to subalpine meadows. This is a large genus, with thirteen species found in Colorado. *I. aggregata* tends to grow in large colonies or clusters (aggregates) because the seeds fall close to the parent plants.

Gilia is named for Filippo Luigi Gilii, an 18th century Italian naturalist and clergyman who also served as director for the Vatican observatory.

Glandular hairs on the sepals and stems produce a skunky-smelling oil that helps to repel ants that may eat the flowers and seeds, similar to Jacob's ladder (*Polemonium* spp.), earning the genus another common name, skunkweed. This biochemistry is interesting when contrasted with aspen sunflowers (*Helianthella*), which secrete nectar to attract ants and is often found growing near *Ipomopsis*.

Thriving at slightly higher elevations, pink trumpets are very similar in overall morphology and habitat when compared to their cousin, scarlet gilia, preferring dry sunny sites in subalpine meadows. This species features pale pink flowers, narrower flower tubes (*tenuituba*) and is generally more hairy than the red species.

Both species of *Ipomopsis* are favorite subjects of pollination biologists at Rocky Mountain Biological Laboratory, where dozens of plants are raised in captivity for experimental use. Hybrid populations form in the wild where the two species meet, creating a wide range of flower colors, from white, to salmon, to bright red and lavender. Hummingbirds are attracted more to red species and night flying moths to light colored flowers. However, birds and moths are not so partial to color as they are to nectar. The effect of flower visitors on nectar supply has a greater influence on future visitors than flower color. Thus, moths tend to deplete nectar from more visible white flowers at night, thus leaving red flowers more full the next morning when hummers become active. Nectar-robbing bumblebees are also attracted to these plants (see p. 104).

Alpine Phlox *Phlox condensata*

Mounds of phlox look like leftover patches of snow along the roadsides in late spring. There are four species in the Elk Mountains, plus several others used in rock gardens. The most common is many-flowered phlox (below), which blooms among sagebrush in May and June. A smaller, mat-forming species, *Phlox condensata* (above), occurs on the alpine tundra. Both form carpets and cushions of thin, pointy, loosely packed leave covered with fragrant white or pinkish flowers. *Phlox* means "flame" in Greek, describing the brilliant pink blossoms of some species. Although the flowers look flat, these too have a long tubular corolla characteristic of the family.

Many-flowered Phlox *Phlox multiflora*

Leafy Jacob's Ladder *Polemonium foliosissimum*

Leafy ladders reaching towards sky-blue flowers inspired the common name, derived from the Bible, for this genus of plants. Like its cousins, sky pilot and scarlet gilia, Jacob's ladder is endowed with glands that produce a skunky odor acting as a repellent to nectar stealing insects. These plants grow in upper montane and subalpine meadows, growing up to three feet tall. Horticultural varieties have become popular in the gardening trade.

"And he (Jacob) dreamed, and behold a ladder set up on the earth, and the top of it reached to heaven: and behold the angels of God ascending and descending on it."

– Genesis 28:12

Showy Jacob's Ladder *Polemonium pulcherrimum* ssp. *delicatum*

JANNETTE RUNGE

Look for the pale blue flowers of showy Jacob's ladder in moist, shaded areas in spruce-fir forests, aptly named in Latin as very beautiful (*pulcherrimum*) and delicate. This species is lower growing that the leafy Jacob's ladder. At left, an Indian paintbrush grows among the flowers. Below, the ladder-like leaves are shown.

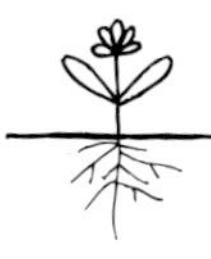

Sky Pilot *Polemonium viscosum*

Rocky talus and scree slopes are the home of sky pilot, a plant you may smell before you see. Although these plants are infamous for their pungent skunky odor, careful research demonstrates that the fragrance of populations varies with elevation and is sweeter the higher you go. The main pollinators of skunky smelling flowers are flies, while bumblebees are led to sky pilot by sweet scents. Close to treeline, the nectar robbing activity of ants can seriously diminish seed production, so the species has adapted by making its own stinky, sticky ant repellent (*viscosum* means "sticky"). The bumblebees will still pollinate, but the ants keep their distance. Sky pilot has pinnately compound leaves like Jacob's ladder, but they are more like a spiral staircase with leaflets all around the stem.

ANNETTE BUNGE

Buckwheat Family POLYGONACEAE

Many of the species in this family are well adapted to poor soil conditions and desert environments. However, the family also includes some aquatic and alpine plants. Probably the most well-known members are sheep sorrel (*Acetosella vulgaris*) and curly dock (*Rumex crispus*), both common roadside weeds and colonizers of disturbed ground throughout North America. Both were imported from Eurasia as nutritious, edible and valuable medicinal species.

Speaking of edibles, buckwheat or kasha (*Fagopyrum esculentum*), a staple of Russian cuisine and a hearty ingredient for pancakes, is the keynote species in this family. And whose mouth does not water at the thought of strawberry rhubarb pie? The fat leaf stems of rhubarb (*Rheum rhaponticum*), another member of the family, make this possible, and the "pie plant" is commonly found around old mining and farm settlements.

BUCKWHEAT *Eriogonum* spp.

With over three hundred species, found mostly in the dry desert and alpine habitats of western North America, the wild buckwheats are one of the most difficult groups of plants to identify. *Eriogonum* means "woolly joint" in Latin, noting the hairy stem nodes on many buckwheats. Many are considered rare or endangered, particularly because they are often endemic to specific soil types. Also, their habitats are often subjected to various human abuses of mining, excessive grazing, development and off-road vehicle recreation. There are four species in the Gunnison Basin, all but one of which are fairly common. Seeds of wild buckwheats are important forage for many wildlife species, including rodents, birds and ants.

COLORADO BUCKWHEAT *Eriogonum coloradense*

The Colorado buckwheat, pictured on page 19, is a dwarf alpine and subalpine species that only occurs in the high mountains of southwestern Colorado and is listed as threatened because of its narrow distribution. This is a low-growing, loosely branched shrub with woody stems, clusters of pinkish-white flowers, and long narrow leaves that are green on top and have thick woolly hairs on the undersides. Colorado buckwheat thrives on dry rocky slopes and ridges, and is most abundant in the Elk Mountains north of Crested Butte.

REDROOT BUCKWHEAT *Eriogonum racemosum*

The soft-pink, feathery flowering stalks of redroot buckwheat are common among sagebrush in the lower elevations. The stems may be branched, and the leaves are mostly basal. Both stems and leaves are covered with soft hairs.

Sulphur Buckwheat *Eriogonum umbellatum* var. *aureum*

There are at least six varieties of *E. umbellatum* in Colorado, two of which are common in the Gunnison Basin. Almost identical in form and habitat are creamy buckwheat (below) and sulphur buckwheat. This species has bright yellow flowers, which age to a blazing orange or red. Both form extensive mats of small leathery leaves, often with a thick felt of woolly hairs beneath. These characteristics are classic adaptations to frost, drought, wind and intense sun. The flowers bloom on short stalks that look like an inside-out umbrella; "umbrella plant" is another common name for many of the wild buckwheats.

Creamy Buckwheat *Eriogonum umbellatum* var. *majus (E. subalpinum)*

Creamy or subalpine buckwheat grows throughout the mountains in dry sandy soils from sagebrush to tundra, and has cream-colored clusters of flowers that turn rose-pink as they age. The tight mats of leaves can grow to several feet in diameter. This species is generally taller than the sulphur buckwheat described above.

Alpine Sorrel *Oxyria digyna*

Alpine sorrel can be found around the world, nestled in crevices of cliffs and talus on the alpine tundra. Both the Latin (*Oxyria*) and common names (sorrel) mean "sour," describing the mouth-puckering taste of the leaves which are loaded with ascorbic acid, or vitamin C. Hikers can quench their thirst, ward off scurvy and spice up a backcountry salad by adding this plant to their diet. The kidney-shaped leaves are easy to recognize, and the flowering stalk looks like a miniature of the weedy dock (*Rumex* sp.) found in wet and disturbed places in the lowlands.

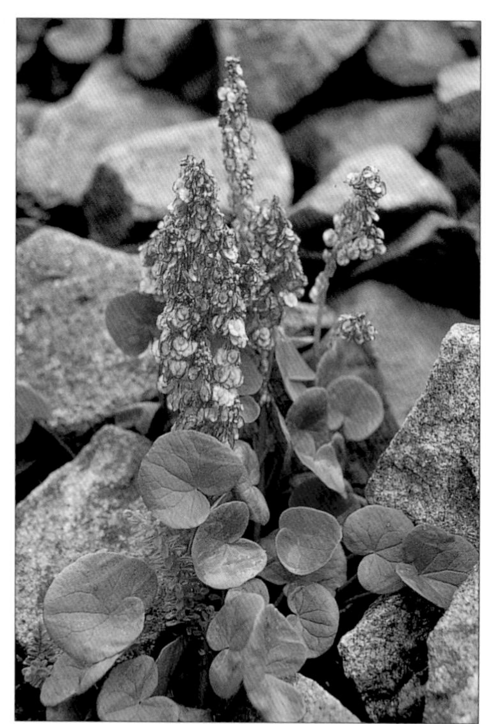

Water Smartweed *Polygonum amphibium (Persicaria amphibia)*

Mountain lakes are often rimmed with floating mats of water smartweed, which bloom with short spikes of pink or white flowers in mid-summer. This species is common in wetlands throughout North America and is an important source of food for waterfowl.

American Bistort *Polygonum bistortoides (Bistorta bistortoides)*

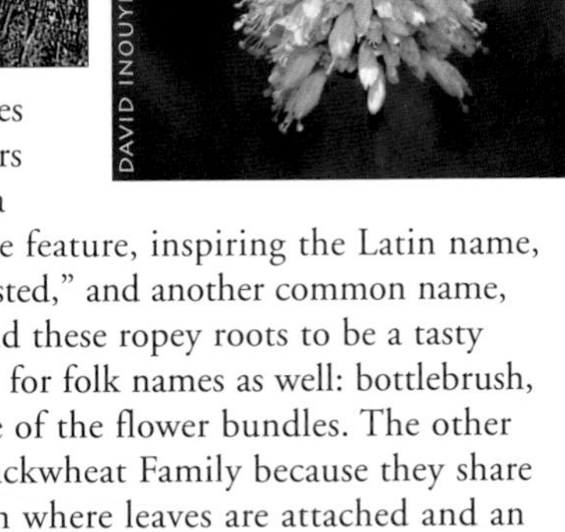
DAVID INOUYE

Late in summer, American bistort sometimes dominates the alpine landscape, waving its tight cluster of white flowers in the wind a foot above the rest of the low-growing tundra vegetation. The long, contorted root is another distinctive feature, inspiring the Latin name, *Bistorta bistortoides*, which means "twice twisted, twice twisted," and another common name, "snakeweed." Bears, elk and rodents, as well as people, find these ropey roots to be a tasty side dish. The flowers, stems and juice are notable features for folk names as well: bottlebrush, knotweed and smartweed. Bottlebrush refers to the shape of the flower bundles. The other two names are sometimes given to many plants in the Buckwheat Family because they share the characteristic of swollen nodes, or knots, on the stem where leaves are attached and an astringent, stinging juice that "smarts" when you get too much on your skin. The astringent quality of the juice or tea made from the plant makes a good medicine to help heal scrapes, sprains and sore throats.

Lichens

Another type of "plant" found just about everywhere is lichen. Actually, lichens are not true plants, but are mutually beneficial symbiotic relationships between fungi and algae. An easy way to remember how lichens work is in the story of "Alice Algae" and "Freddie Fungus," who got together and took a "lichen" to each other. Alice Algae, a good cook, because she is green and able to photosynthesize, provides the food in the relationship; Freddie Fungus provides the shelter and absorbs water and minerals. Lichens take on many forms, including crusty mats that grow on rocks and wispy "beard lichens" that grow on trees. There are over 17,000 species in the world, made of combinations of different species of fungus and algae. The name lichen is derieved from the German word, *leichein*, meaning "to lick," because they seem to lick the rocks and trees they grow on. Lichens are also famous for being the only plants able to survive at very high elevations, and are found at the summit of Denali and Mt. Everest.

Purslane Family PORTULACACEAE

The Purslanes are a small North American family of about two hundred species. They are mostly succulent plants known for their delicious edible leaves and roots. Many are used as ornamentals in rock gardens, especially rock rose (*Portulaca grandiflora*) which has many-petaled flowers similar to roses, available in a spectrum of western sunset colors. Bitterroot (*Lewisia rediviva*) is another well-known member of this family and namesake of the Bitterroot Mountains, Valley, and River of Montana, where the large pink-flowered plant is so abundant that it was dubbed the state flower.

The scientific name, Portulacaceae, is derived from the Latin word *porta*, meaning "door," referring to the door-like lid on the seed capsules of some species. Purslane is derived from the French word, *porcelaine*, since the smooth flower petals have the delicacy and sheen of fine china.

SPRING BEAUTY *Claytonia lanceolata*

Along with their co-habitants, the glacier lilies, spring beauties are among the first wildflowers to bloom each spring, sometimes emerging right through thin patches of snow. A pair of long, narrow (hence the name *lanceolata*, meaning "lance-shaped") leaves grow opposite each other on a slender, spindly stem, and a cluster of white and pink striped flowers emerges above the leaves. Look for spring beauties in big sagebrush communites, near aspen forests and on up to treeline through the summer. Many animals, including bears, pocket gophers and hungry hikers, seek out the round tubers for sustenance in spring. This species, as well as its cousin the alpine spring beauty (p. 152), commemorate John Clayton, who was a North American botanist in the early 1700s.

Alpine Spring Beauty *Claytonia megarhiza*

The robust alpine spring beauty is best known for its magnificent taproot, which grows up to six feet long and one to three inches in diameter, tunneling deep into the rocky alpine tundra. The roots and rosettes of broad, waxy, succulent leaves are edible and important forage for alpine critters like marmots, pikas and ground squirrels. They are one of the earliest plants to flower above treeline, blooming as soon as the snow melts, just like their lowland cousins.

Pygmy Bitterroot *Lewisia pygmaea (Oreobroma pygmaea)*

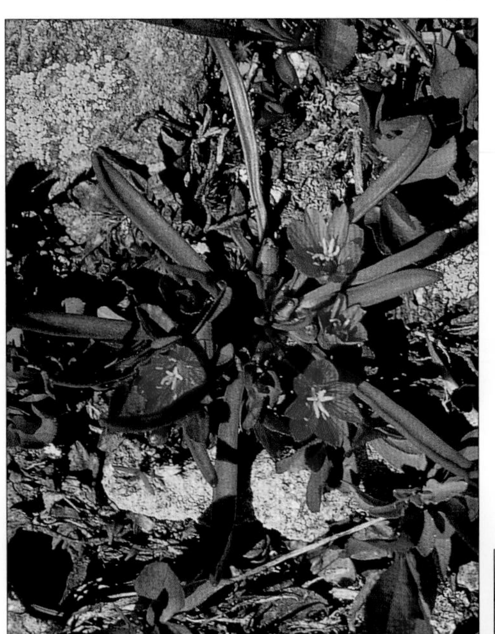

Captain Meriwether Lewis of the Lewis and Clark Expedition (1804-1806) was introduced to these and related species for their sweet, potato-like tuber, which was a staple of many Native American tribes that were encountered along his journey. Another name sometimes used for this genus is *Oreobroma*, which means "mountain food." The clusters of narrow, succulent leaves are usually lost among the short grasses and sedges where they grow. However, when they bloom, the five-petaled flowers, ranging from pale pink to deep magenta, are easy to spot, even though they only grow to about three or four inches high. Look for the flowers in early summer in moist places near sagebrush or follow their blooms through the summer to where they grow in moist, open areas up to treeline.

Primrose Family PRIMULACEAE

Some of the first spring blooms are primroses, inspiring the family name, which comes from the Latin word *primus* for "first." Primroses are one of many groups of primarily wetland plants known as cowslips, a name arising from the belief that a plant would grow wherever a cow left a patty, aka "cowslop." However, these lowly origins are balanced by the belief that primroses are a symbol of good luck, trust and friendship. To indulge in an afternoon stroll on a path lined with primroses is definitely worthwhile. No relation to the evening primroses (p. 132), these plants have five-petaled tubular flowers, mostly basal leaves and usually superior or half-inferior ovaries.

DWARF ROCK JASMINE *Androsace chamaejasme*
NORTHERN ROCK JASMINE *Androsace septentrionalis*

Rock jasmine is found growing in gravelly soils from sagebrush to alpine tundra. In the warm lowlands, they may grow to eight inches high, but are usually only a couple inches tall in the more severe environment of the tundra. Wherever you find them, you'll have to get down on your belly to observe these tiny flowers, which resemble those of jasmine (*Jasminum* spp.), tropical plants in the Olive Family used to scent tea, rice and incense. Fairy candelabra is another name inspired by these Lilliputian primroses. The Latin word, *septentrionalis*, means "plant of the north." *Chamaejasme* means "dwarf jasmine."

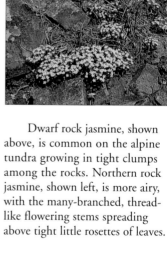

Dwarf rock jasmine, shown above, is common on the alpine tundra growing in tight clumps among the rocks. Northern rock jasmine, shown left, is more airy, with the many-branched, thread-like flowering stems spreading above tight little rosettes of leaves.

Shooting Stars *Dodecatheon pulchellum*

JANNETTE RUNGE

Shaded and sunny marshes and streamsides, from the lowest valley to the highest peak, are the places to look for shooting stars. The backswept, magenta-colored petals are reminiscent of cyclamens, another primrose that is native to the Mediterranean region and is often sold as a house plant.

Wild shooting stars grow in sprays of twelve or so blooms nodding from the top of a tall (6-16"), leafless stem. So beautiful are these flowers that they are said to require the protection of a dozen deities, hence the Latin name, *Dodecatheon*, which translates to "twelve gods." *Pulchellum* means "very pretty." These beautiful flowers make no nectar and are "buzz pollinated" by bumblebees who vibrate their wings while holding onto the flowers. This shakes the pollen out of the anthers, like shaking salt from a saltshaker. They harvest some of the pollen to feed their larvae, but pollinate the flowers in the process.

Albino Wildflowers

White variations of flowers that are normally other colors are common in many plant species. Usually the albino forms are somewhat rare, but occasionally these plants will reproduce well enough to create healthy populations. In the horticultural trades, albinism is sometimes a desirable trait because of its uniqueness. In nature, the success of the mutation depends on how it affects the plant's ability to produce seed. In cases where cross-pollination becomes infrequent between the albino and colored forms, extensive distinct populations can result and the new color variety may be considered to be a new species. This is the case for a rare species of penstemon found in Wyoming and northeastern Colorado, *Penstemon laricifolius* var. *exilifolius*, and white sweet clover (*Melilotus alba*) that is native to Eurasia, but now common throughout North America.

GALE PICKETT

Parry's Primrose *Primula parryi*

Shocking-pink Parry's primrose thrives along subalpine and alpine streams and marshes, near snowmelt basins and seeping cliffs. Because they are found so high, you usually don't find them blooming until mid-to-late summer. Pollinating flies are attracted by their skunky odor although bees are also frequent visitors. This is one of many plants named after Charles Parry, a 19th century botanist who collected extensively in the Colorado Rockies. *Primula* means "little first one," although this is one of the largest mountain primroses, up to eighteen inches high, with flowers up to an inch in diameter.

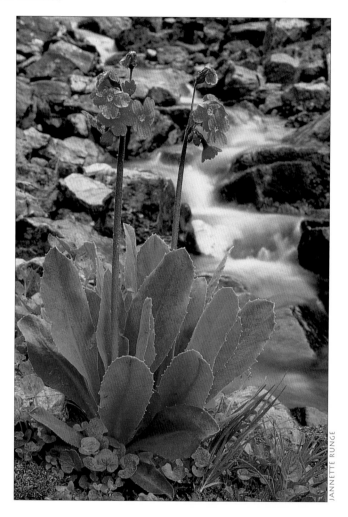

JANNETTE RUNGE

"Do not, as some ungracious pastors do, show me the steep and thorny way to heaven; whiles, like a puff'd and reckless libertine, Himself the primrose path of dalliance treads, and recks not his own rede."

– William Shakespeare, *Hamlet*

Buttercup Family RANUNCULACEAE

The Buttercup Family is a large group of over 1,800 species worldwide. Some of our showiest flowers are in this family, including larkspur, monkshood, columbine, anemones, as well as the shiny yellow flowers that give this family its name. Many of the plants in this family prefer growing in wet areas, hence the family's Latin name, *Ranunculaceae*, which means "of froggy places," from *rana* the frog.

Based on differences in fruit structure, some taxonomists divide this family in two so that columbines, larkspurs, marsh marigolds, monkshood and globe flower become part of the Hellebore Family (Helleboraceae). Both groups share the characteristic of many stamens, which is considered to be a primitive floral feature. Thus, members of this family are regarded as some of the earliest flowering plants to have evolved.

MONKSHOOD *Aconitum columbianum*

Many a man who is pure in heart
and says his prayer by night
May become a wolf when the Wolfsbane blooms
and the moon is shining bright"
– Gypsy woman, in *Frankenstein Meets the Wolf Man*

The deep-purple blooms of this plant accentuate the brooding character associated with its name. The "hood" is the upper petal, which conceals the nectaries clustered inside the flower. Usually found in wet meadows or near high mountain streams, monkshood blooms mid- to late-summer, depending on the elevation. Like their close relative and look alike, larkspur, these plants are extremely poisonous, but because they are not as abundant, they are less of a threat to livestock. The deadly alkaloids are sometimes used for medicinal purposes as cardiac and respiratory sedatives.

Aconite is an ancient Greek name meaning "poisonous." A hill called Aconitus is where, according to Greek legend, Hercules fought Cerberus, the three-headed dog who guards the gates of Hell. As they fought, Cerberus flung foam from his mouth across the countryside. Where the bits of spittle landed, monkshood grew, carrying with them the poisonous demeanor of the dog.

Monkshood was also an ingredient in a magic salve used to change someone into a werewolf during medieval times. Along with belladonna, opium and poison hemlock, monkshood was used to induce the delirious state of these legendary monsters. That is why the plant is sometimes called wolfsbane.

This species of monkshood was first collected along the Columbia River in the northwestern U.S., hence the name *A. columbianum*.

Windflower *Anemone multifida*

Though it is not very showy, windflower is a common and beautiful find on a mountain hike. They grow in many different habitats, from coniferous forest to alpine ridges. The blossoms range in color from deep rose to soft pink and the entire plant, including the multi-lobed leaves, is covered with long, soft hairs. In many ways, they look like miniature versions of the early-blooming pasque flower (p. 158), another member of this genus.

Most references to the windflower claim that the name *Anemone* comes from the Greek word *anemos*, meaning wind, as named by the ancient Greek botanist Theophrastus. The flowers are reputed to open at the command of warm spring breezes. Although I have never observed them responding to the wind, the flowers do open in bright sun and close when the sun sets or goes behind the clouds.

An alternative interpretation is that the generic name is a twisted form of *Na'man*, the Middle Eastern name for Adonis, the lover of Aphrodite, the Greek goddess of love and beauty. The crimson-flowered windflowers of the Middle East are said to have sprung from his blood when he was killed by a wild boar.

A few drops of tincture made from the whole plant is said to help treat extreme anxiety and PMS. However, the plant is also considered poisonous, so it is probably best avoided for internal uses. It is so toxic, in fact, that there is a European superstition that says that the wind blown over anemones is poisoned. Therefore, it is sometimes thought best to hold your breath and run past a field of these flowers.

Narcissus Anemone *Anemone narcissiflora (Anemostratum narcissiflorum)*

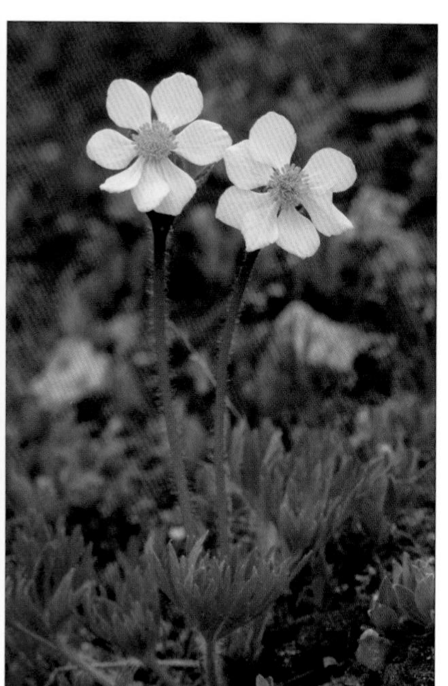

This white-flowered anemone grows in moist places in the subalpine and alpine tundra. They are easily confused with the globeflower (*Trollius albiflorus)*, which grows in similar habitats. Narcissus anemone is easily recognized by the hairy leaves and stems and bright white flowers, whereas the globeflower is not hairy and has very pale yellow flowers. The two plants also have very different fruits; globeflower produces many-seeded capsules called follicles, and Narcissus anemone matures into clusters of one-seeded achenes.

The Greek story of Narcissus is meant to warn about the consequences of excessive vanity. Narcissus was a handsome man whose beauty captivated the hearts of women and men who met him. One infatuated nymph, Echo, died of a broken heart when he ignored her. Nemesis, the god of revenge, put a spell on Narcissus so that he fell in love with his own image reflected in a pool of water. He was so mesmerized with his own beauty that he died of thirst, and then turned into a flower.

PASQUE FLOWER *Anemone patens (Pulsatilla patens)*

Also known as wild crocus, windflower, elephant Q-tips, prairie crocus and kitten ears, the pasque flower greets spring with showy lavender tepals surrounding bright yellow clusters of stamens, the pollen-bearing parts of the plant. The entire plant is covered with soft white hairs, which insulate it from early spring sub-freezing nighttime temperatures. Clusters of over a dozen single-flowered stems can be found emerging from winter dormancy near the edge of coniferous forests, often right through late-lying snow.

Both the common and scientific names of the pasque flower refer to its blooming around the time of the ancient pagan rites of Easter, the Jewish holiday of Passover, and now tied to Christ's resurrection. Pasque is a variation of the French word *pasche*, for the Passover holiday. *Pulsatilla* is thought to be derived from the Italian verb *pulsare*, meaning to "throb" or "pulse," and alludes to the Passion or suffering of Christ on the cross. Many species of pasque flowers are found throughout Europe, as well as in the plains and mountainous regions of western North America. *Patens* means "spreading," for the wide open blooms.

"Courage is not the towering oak that sees storms come and go; it is the fragile blossom that opens in the snow."

– Alice M. Swaim

Like many other mountain wildflowers, pasque flowers can be seen throughout the season by following the retreating snow. When the flowers at Cement Creek (8,500') are sporting their feathery seedheads, new blooms will just be emerging a thousand feet higher up Slate River in early June. They can be found all the way up to treeline, where they may be blooming beneath the krummholz as late as August.

Legend of the Pasque Flower

Pasque flowers are the state flower of South Dakota, where a Blackfoot Indian legend tells how the plant got its lavender petals, bright golden center, furry leaves and stem. A young boy went out on his three-day vision quest to seek visions that would prepare him to be a man. Cold, lonely and scared, he sat on a hilltop, hoping for the Great Spirit to bring him his dream. Beside him was a single white flower waving in the wind. Each night as the sun set, the flower spoke to him and provided comfort, telling the boy of his gifts to the world: a kind heart, wisdom and leadership.

On the last day of the vision quest, the boy said to the flower, "Little brother, three nights you have comforted me in my loneliness and brought me visions. Tell me now three of your wishes that I may ask the Great Spirit to grant them to you."

The flower spoke again and asked that it might have the purple blue of the mountains in its petals, a golden sun to hold close to its heart and a fur coat to keep warm on cold spring days. From that day on, the pasque flower has been blessed with these gifts.

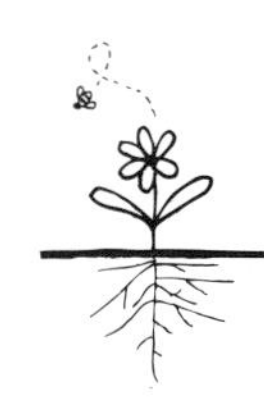

COLUMBINE *Aquilegia* spp.

These flowers are paradoxically named after both the dove and the eagle. One nomenclator with imagination dubbed the flower columbine, after the Latin *columba*, meaning "dove." If you squint at a flower you may see a flock of doves sipping from a bath. The scientific name, *Aquilegia*, is given for the resemblance of the long spurs of the flower to the sharp talons of *Aquila*, the eagle. A lesser known, but probably more accurate, interpretation of the generic name is in the translation of *aqua* (water) and *legere* (to collect), referring to the nectar found in the base of the spurs. This nectar attracts pollinators of the columbine: butterflies, moths and hummingbirds. Other insects, especially certain bees, "steal" the nectar by biting the ends of the spurs, thereby not trading the favor for pollination.

> *"I will be the gladdest thing under the sun!*
> *I will touch a hundred flowers and not pick one."*
> – Edna St. Vincent Millay

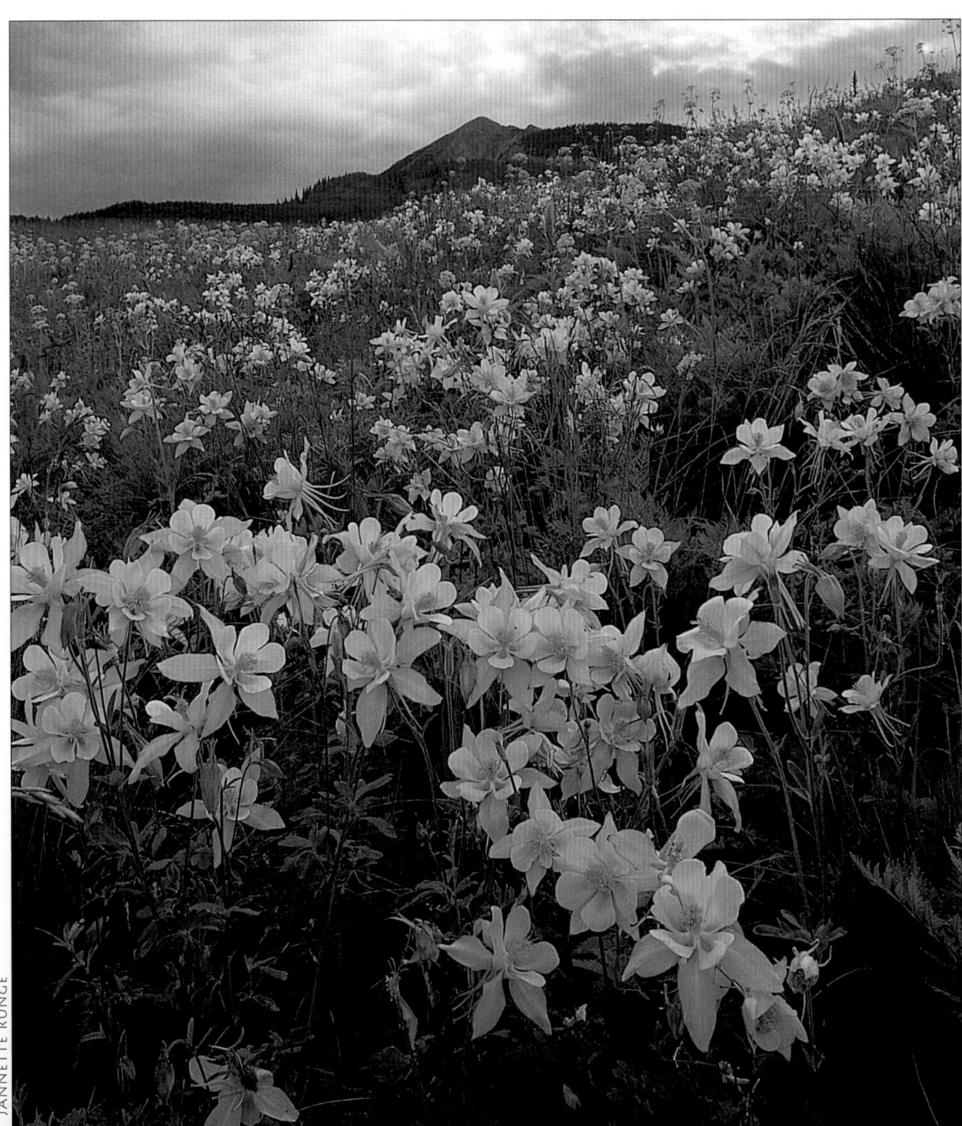

JANNETTE RUNGE

Blue Columbine *Aquilegia coerulea*

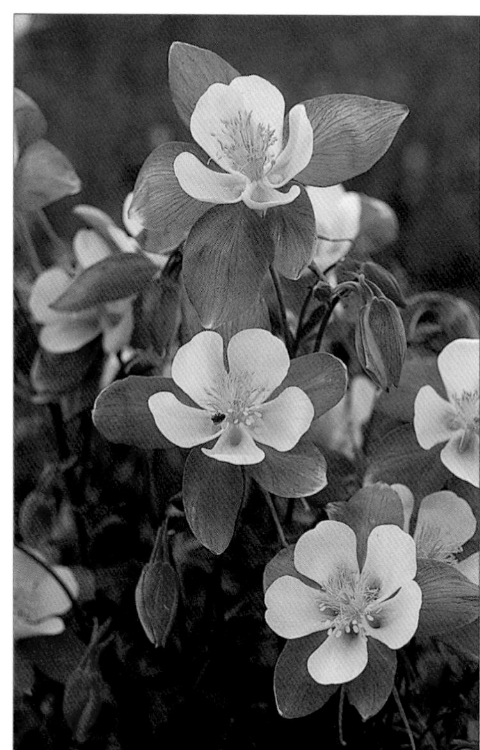

The blue columbine was declared the official state flower of Colorado on April 4th, 1899. Some say that the blue represents the Colorado skies; the yellow center of the flowers, gold ore; and white, the snow-capped mountains. In 1925, the state assembly made it unlawful to dig up the plant and limited the gathering of buds, blossoms and stems to twenty-five in one day. This is a rather generous helping by today's standards, which would be to pick none at all.

Flower folklore passes the wisdom that blue columbines are a symbol of unfaithfulness in women and a deserted lover in men. Therefore, it is bad luck to give columbines to a woman and insulting to give them to a man. This should be further incentive to leave these beautiful flowers where they grow.

Red Columbine *Aquilegia elegantula*

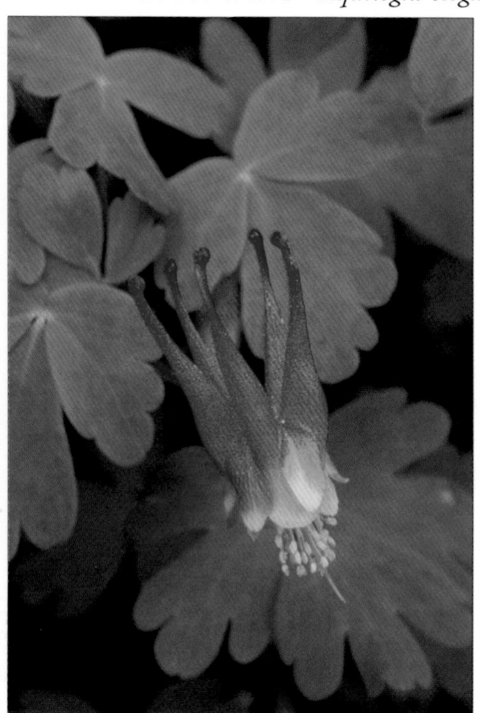

Another common native columbine is the elegant red columbine or rockbells. These flowers have yellow sepals and red petals, and prefer to grow in shady forests, moist rocky ledges and streamsides. As is typical of red flowers, these are primarily pollinated by hummingbirds.

Gardeners have hybridized columbines to create dozens of varieties and colors. Since there are no genetic barriers between species of *Aquilegia*, you might find a hybrid in the wild as well.

MARSH MARIGOLD *Caltha leptosepala (Psychrophila leptosepala)*

In low spots where snowmelt accumulates to form shallow ponds and rivulets, you will find marsh marigolds with their large white flowers and glossy heart-shaped leaves. As with many mountain wildflowers, you can see these plants all the way from valley floors to the alpine tundra as the summer progresses. If you're willing to get your feet and knees wet, it's worth bending down to take a whiff of their ephemeral, sweet fragrance.

Because they are often found growing right through or near the edge of snowbanks, an alternate scientific name for marsh marigolds is *Psychrophila*, meaning "cold-loving." This species, *C. leptosepala,* is so named because of its slender (*lepto*) white sepals, which look like showy petals.

Curiously, some other common names for marsh marigolds are cowslip, elkslip and horse blobs. Cowslip literally means "cow dung," or more precisely, a pasty or slippery dung, which is abundantly produced in wet meadows and pastures where marsh marigolds grow and cattle graze. This less than flattering name is also used for several other wetland wildflowers, such as primroses, bluebells and shooting stars. A more attractive name sometimes used is meadowbright.

JANNETTE RUNGE

Tall Larkspur *Delphinium barbeyi*

One of the most abundant and colorful wildflowers of mountain meadows is the deep blue or purple tall larkspur, which grows up to four feet high and often dominates entire hillsides. Known in gardening circles by its Latin name, *Delphinium*, the larkspurs are named commonly and scientifically for the distinctive spur that harbors nectar in these flowers. In bud, the spur looks somewhat like a leaping dolphin, *delphinus* in Latin. This species honors William Barbey, who was a Swiss botanist of the early 19th century.

Larkspur is well known by ranchers for its lethal effect on cattle. Larkspur poisoning causes some of the most severe losses of livestock in the western U.S. All parts of the plant are toxic. An animal must eat about 3% of its body weight in larkspur to be affected mortally; this is about twenty to twenty-five pounds for cattle. Curiously, sheep seem to be unaffected by larkspur alkaloids, so another management technique is to send sheep out to graze a pasture before bringing on the cattle.

Aside from being poisonous to livestock, the flowers provide abundant nectar for hummingbirds and pollinating insects, mostly bumblebees. Near the town of Gothic, where tall larkspur is one of the most common wildflowers of mid-summer, researchers have documented that the abundance of larkspur blooms and wildflowers in general, correlates with the number of feeder visits by hummingbirds. In a good year, hummers hang out in the meadows and slurp sugars from the flowers. In a dry year, they'll opt for the second-rate sugar water we provide them.

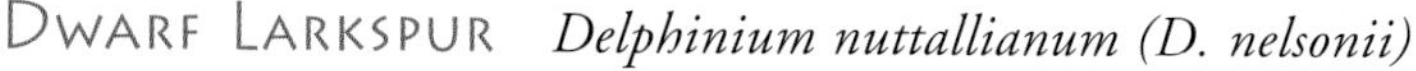

Dwarf Larkspur *Delphinium nuttallianum (D. nelsonii)*

DAVID INOUYE

Dwarf larkspurs grow to a foot tall, and have fewer, more-loosely arranged flowers than the tall larkspur. The arrival of hummingbirds in May is coincident with the early blooms of dwarf larkspur in lower elevation sagebrush areas and on up into the high mountain meadows. For both species of larkspur, a snowy winter is followed by abundant flowering. See page 8 for a photo of a prolific dwarf larkspur bloom south of the town of Crested Butte.

Thomas Nuttall was an enthusiastic 19th century botanist, explorer and a professor at Harvard who collected extensively throughout North America. Aven Nelson was professor of botany and founder of the Rocky Mountain Herbarium at University of Wyoming in Laramie.

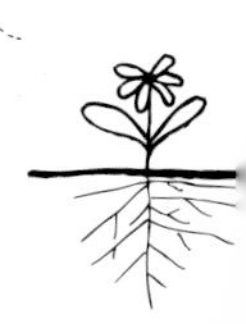

Buttercups *Ranunculus* spp.

There are at least eight species of buttercups found in the southern Rockies. All share the character of shiny yellow or white petals and tend to grow in wet soils. Although they are important forage for wildlife, buttercups are poisonous to most people and can cause blistering and inflammation of the mouth and skin, hence another common name, blisterflower. Also known as goldcups, butterflowers and crowsfoot, these plants are common around the world, with over four hundred species recognized. The name crowsfoot comes from the shape of many species' leaves. Children all over the world play the game of checking to see if someone likes butter, by seeing if the golden yellow flowers reflect off their chins.

Buttercups are easily confused with cinquefoils, members of the Rose Family, which also have bright yellow petals. Cinquefoils are usually found in drier habitats and also lack the glossy shine of buttercup petals. Check the leaves too; cinquefoils usually have compound leaves (separate leaflets), whereas buttercup leaves are usually only lobed.

Marsh Buttercup *Ranunculus alismifolius*

DAVID INOUYE

The caltha-flowered or marsh buttercup is often found growing right along with the marsh marigolds in sunny wet meadows as shown above, or in aspen forests before the trees have leafed out. Like the marsh marigolds, they tend to appear shortly following snowmelt wherever they grow. These buttercups look like miniature versions of the yellow Eastern species of marsh marigold and, like them, have eight to ten showy petals and broad leaves; *Caltha* is the old Latin name for marsh marigolds. Other buttercups usually only have five petals.

Water Crowfoot *Ranunculus aquatilis (Batrachium circinatum)*

Water crowfoot is an aquatic buttercup that forms floating mats along slow streams or in small ponds. The leaves are very thin, finely divided and mostly submerged. These plants provide excellent habitat for aquatic insects, which in turn provide food for many species of birds and fish. They are also a great place for tadpoles and frogs to take cover and feed.

Alpine Buttercup *Ranunculus adoneus*

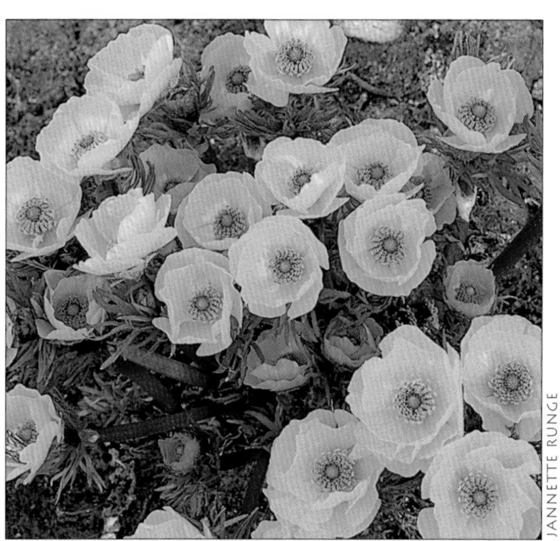

JANNETTE RUNGE

Alpine buttercups are common above treeline in low-lying snowmelt basins. The large, showy yellow flowers are commonly pollinated by flies, which tend to be more cold-hardy than bees, and so are more common flower visitors above treeline. The finely-dissected leaves and numerous petals help distinguish this species from other buttercups. The Latin name, R. adoneus, honors the most handsome of Greek gods, Adonis. The young man was torn between two lovers and thus, like the plant, spent half his years in the underworld with Persephone, and the other half above ground with the beautiful Aphrodite.

Sagebrush Buttercup *Ranunculus glaberrimus*

WENDY BROWN

Sagebrush buttercup is one of the earliest flowers to bloom in the Elk Mountains each spring, and is so abundant in some places that it colors the hillsides gold. Look for them as early as mid-April growing along with spring beauties (p. 151) in Slate River Valley or the Jack's Cabin area, growing among the sagebrush. In the photo shown here, the petals have an unusual notch in the tips, but most have un-notched petals.

Meadow Rue *Thalictrum fendleri*

Be sure not to confuse the columbines with this leafy look-alike, meadow rue, or false columbine. Walk through any aspen forest and you'll probably be wading in it. Meadow rue leaves are nearly identical to those of the columbine, but the flowers lack colorful sepals and petals. Look carefully and you'll find the inconspicuous flowers, which are wind pollinated, therefore not requiring a showy display to attract insects or birds. Some meadow rues are dioecious, meaning they have separate "male" (staminate) and "female" (pistillate) plants. Male flowers form tiny, yellow tassels of stamens. The female flowers have stiff, white pistils that resemble a starburst. A dwarf alpine meadow rue (*T. alpinum*) is monoecious (having staminate and pistillate flowers separate, but on one plant) and can be found growing among sedges and rushes in marshy places. A third species, few-flowered meadow rue (*T. sparsiflorum*), looks very similar to Fendler's meadow rue and also grows in aspen stands.

Rue is the name of a medicinal plant (*Ruta graveolens*) found in Europe, which is used homeopathically to treat tendonitis. Although the two plants are not taxonomically related, meadow rue carries the name because the leaves look similar to the leaves of rue. *Thalictrum* is an ancient name of unknown origin. *T. fendleri* was named after Augustus Fendler, a 19th century botanist who collected specimens in the Western U.S.

> *"Plants invite observation. They stay there, hold still, and are patient with our sensory frailties. We don't feel pressed to catch a fleeting glance of them."*
>
> – Reinhard F. Stettler

Fungi

Although fungi bear some resemblance to plants because of their non-sensory and somewhat stationary lifestyles, they are actually part of an entirely different kingdom of life. Ranging from yeasts and molds, to mushrooms and slime molds, the fungi are as diverse and complex as true plants. Truly extreme botanizing would include understanding the common fungi of a region. In the Elk Mountains, the bright red common amanita is probably the most spectacular of fungi. These highly poisonous mushrooms appear in the shade of spruce-fir forests in the late fall of a wet summer.

Globeflower *Trollius albiflorus (T. laxus)*

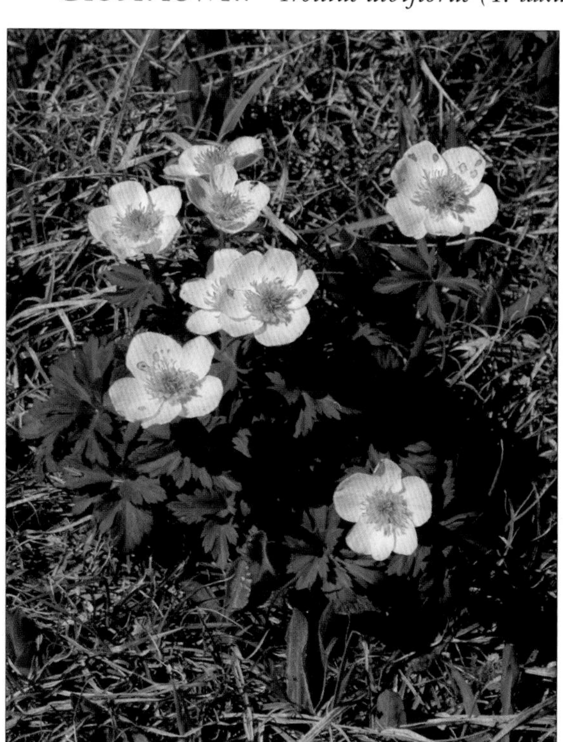

Trollius is derived from the German name for the flower, *trollblume*, which simply means "globe-like flower." Other species of these wildflowers are very common in European mountains; over a dozen species are found around the world. *Albiflorus* translates simply to "white flower."

Like its look-alike and co-habitant, the marsh marigold (p. 162), globeflowers emerge in marshy places soon after snowmelt. The globeflower is easily distinguished by its lobed leaves and cream-colored flowers in contrast with the shiny, heart-shaped leaves and bright white flowers of the marigold.

This species also resembles Narcissus anemone (p. 157), which may grow nearby in drier soils. The anemone has more petals and is also taller with narrowly lobed leaves.

Rose Family ROSACEAE

Our native flora has a diverse collection of roses ranging from the delicate mauve-pink flowers of prairie smoke to the brilliant yellow-flowered shrubby cinquefoil. Over two dozen species of plants in the Elk Mountains are in the Rose Family, many of them bearers of delicious fruit, such as serviceberry, wild raspberry, wild strawberry and chokecherry, as well as the wild rose, which produces vitamin C-rich rose hips.

Members of this family are cultivated around the world to stock fruit stands with apples, strawberries, apricots, plums, pears, peaches, nectarines and cherries. Others have been dubbed the "queen of flowers" because of their romantic beauty and heavenly fragrance. Many of our native species are available commercially for flower gardens and landscaping. The wild members of the Rose Family bear little resemblance to those in a rose garden and few smell so sweet. But they all share characteristics of numerous stamens and a hypanthium, the shallow bowl-shaped base of the flower which matures to form the fleshy fruit.

SERVICEBERRY *Amelanchier alnifolia*

The plump, deep-blue fruit of the serviceberry is worth collecting in the fall, if you can beat the birds. Like the wild rose, these huge (up to twelve feet high) shrubs are common along rivers and streams, especially at lower elevations (7,500-8,500 feet). They are also common in open dry sagebrush country wherever water is close to the surface. The species growing nearby in the Gunnison Basin is *A. alnifolia*, with serrated leaves resembling those of the alder (*Alnus* spp.). Serviceberry is one of the first plants to flower in the spring, filling the air with sweet perfume from its cherry-like white blossoms.

In addition to being important to wildlife, the fruits can be used to make pies and jams and are great trail snacks. Native Americans used these berries, along with other wild fruits, dried buffalo meat and fat, to make pemmican cakes. The Cree name for this plant is *mis-ask-quah-toomina*, which early white settlers shortened to "saskatoon," another common name for the shrub. Because the berries begin to ripen in June, they are also called juneberry.

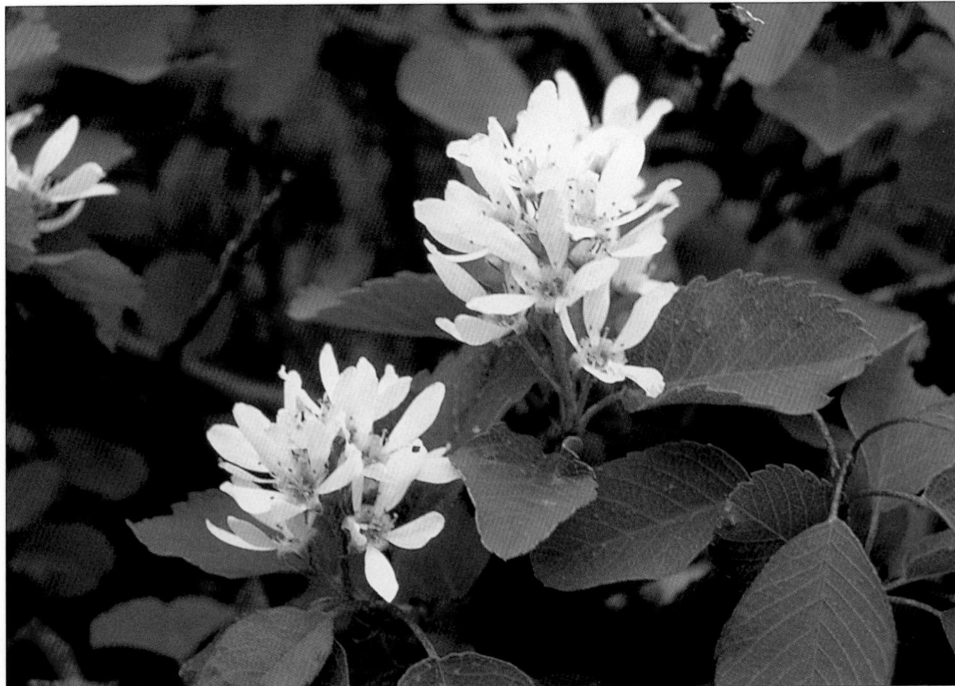

Mountain Dryad *Dryas octopetala*

The mountain dryad, also known as alpine rose or white mountain avens, is found on exposed slopes and ridges of the arctic and alpine tundra all over the world, forming vast carpets of leathery leaves. This plant is especially abundant on calcium-rich soils, preferring limestone ridges.

The large white flowers (one to two inches in diameter) of the dryad hug the ground and are easy to recognize by the eight petals (hence the Latin, *octopetala*) and numerous stamens characteristic of the Rose Family. In fruit, the stem elongates to allow the feathery seed puffs to be carried off by the wind.

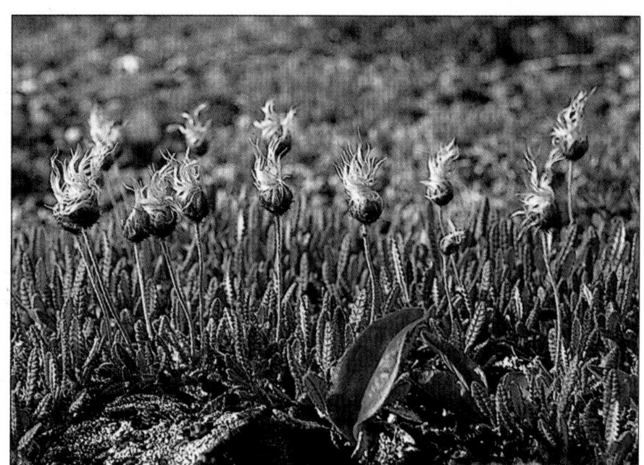

The thick leathery leaves, woolly hairs on the underside of the leaves, woody stem, mat-like growth and evergreen habit are classic adaptations to the exposed climate of sun, wind and cold on the tundra. The leaves are an important food for ptarmigans. Such a beautiful plant is honorably dubbed "a goddess of the mountains," a dryad being the wood nymph of Greek and Roman mythology.

Berries

Many bright-colored and succulent berries lure birds and mammals, as well as humans. By eating the berries, animals not only ensure a wide distribution of the seeds in their droppings, but also unwittingly perform a necessary scouring of the seed coat as the seed passes through their digestive tracts. For many seeds, this is needed so that germination is able to take place in the spring.

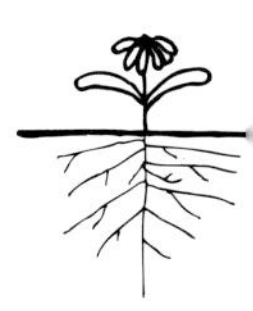

Alpine Avens *Geum rossii (Acomastylis rossii)*

In mid-summer, dry alpine fields are brightened by yellow blooms of alpine avens waving in the wind. The flowers are often covered with flies, their primary pollinators. Feathery leaves form thick mats on both arctic and alpine tundras. In the fall, the fern-like leaves of alpine avens rival the red, orange and purple colors of Eastern U.S. deciduous forests. *Acomastylis* is Greek for "without a hairy style," as opposed to other close relatives, whose styles become feathery plumes in fruit (see mountain dryad, p. 169 and prairie smoke, p.171). This species is named after Sir James C. Ross, a 19th century British arctic explorer.

Pika Food

Pikas, also known as conies or rock rabbits, are tiny relatives of cottontails. Unlike other members of the rabbit family, pikas have short round ears and no visible tail. During the summers, pikas gather over thirty species of alpine and subalpine plants from the meadows that surround the talus slopes where they shelter. Plants are carefully piled and dried in the sun, then stored beneath the talus where it will stay dry over the winter. A single pika will harvest up to two bushels of hay, weighing nearly fifty pounds. One of the dominant species collected by pikas is alpine avens, which has been found to make up to 30% of their stash. These miniature haystacks are the pikas main source of energy to sustain them through the winter, since they do not hibernate or store a thick layer of fat as do their compatriots, the marmots.

Prairie Smoke *Geum triflorum (Erythrocoma triflora)*

Prairie smoke sometimes lends the landscape a pink hue, blooming early in the summer along with the deep-purple dwarf larkspur (p. 163). The soft, rose-colored flowers hang down, usually in groups of three to a stem. When they go to fruit the stems turn up to display a puff of seeds resembling miniature versions of Dr. Seuss' truffula trees. Each strand of the smoke-like puff is actually an elongated style (female part) of the flower. This inspires other names for the plant, including old man's whiskers, pink plumes and fairy duster. *Erythrocoma*, means "red mane," also alluding to the fluffy pink seedhead. Prairie smoke is one of the most widespread plants of the area, being found in drier sagebrush habitats from 7,000 to 12,000 feet.

JANNETTE RUNGE

Ocean Spray *Holodiscus dumosus (H. discolor)*

The panicles of small white flowers inspired the common name for this large shrub. Ocean spray thrives on sunny talus and scree slopes below treeline. South and west-facing slopes of Crested Butte Mountain and south-facing slopes along Cement Creek Road are loaded with this species, which is an important browse plant for mule deer and elk. The Latin name means "bushy plant with rose flowers." Also known as rock spirea or cream-bush, this species makes a good ornamental for native plant gardens. The flowers have a musky smell.

Pollinators

The evolution and reproductive lives of wildflowers are intimately tied to the lives of pollinators who depend on them for food or other resources. The form and color of many flowers can help us to predict what types of pollinators are most likely to visit.

Bee Flowers

Bees and flowers are highly co-evolved, resulting in some of the most complicated flower/pollinator relationships, flower forms and biochemistry. Bees are most attracted to blue, purple, and yellow flowers, but also see patterns in the ultraviolet range that are invisible to us. Bee flowers often have a "landing pad" and may have a wide throat for the bee to crawl into, which facilitates pollination as the bee walks over or under the stamens and stigmas. Penstemons are classic bee flowers.

There are over 4,000 North American species of bees and over 20,000 worldwide. Unfortunately, competition with the imported European honeybee has rendered many native species rare or endangered. Except for honeybees and bumblebees, most bees are solitary rather than social.

Fly Flowers

Flies are especially attracted to bright yellow flowers that have numerous, well-exposed pistils and stamens, such as buttercups and cinquefoils. Flies are also attracted to flat-topped and open bowl-shaped flowers where it is easy for them to walk around, collect pollen and nectar and incidentally get their bellies dusted with pollen. Compared to bee-pollinated flowers, flowers that attract flies generally have little scent, although some tropical flowers have evolved a "rotting meat" scent, drawing flies that usually lay eggs in carrion.

Hummingbird Flowers

The model hummingbird flower has a long narrow corolla, copious nectar, and is often red. Flowers like Indian paintbrush and fairy trumpets fit the mold, but hummingbirds will visit flowers and feeders regardless of their color, as long as there is a good supply of nectar and the right fit for their beak. Glacier lilies, columbines, larkspur, and corydalis are other hummingbird favorites in the Rocky Mountains.

Butterfly Flowers

Butterflies are often host specific, being partial to plants that their larvae, or caterpillars, prefer to feed on. Their long slender tongues can reach into narrow tubular corollas. Pictured here is a Parnassian, the name of a group of butterflies common in arctic and alpine regions around the world. These butterflies are partial to members of the Stonecrop Family, but this one was caught feeding on a pink flea-bane (*Erigeron elatior*).

Ivesia *Ivesia gordonii*

Ivesia has some of the smallest flowers of the native roses, scarcely 1/8 inch in diameter, but growing in small bundles large enough to attract pollinators. The long (4-8 inches), narrow fern-like leaves grow into large clumps on dry, exposed rocky outcrops near treeline and on the alpine tundra. Occasionally you'll find ivesia growing in rocky areas at lower elevations down to 7,000 feet. Eli Ives, a professor at Yale University and George Gordon, a British horticulturist, are both commemorated in the naming of this species.

Rock Rose *Petrophyton caespitosum*

This is one of my favorite plants because it is so tough and softly beautiful at the same time. The small, thick leaves form extensive mats that grow right on the surface of limestone rocks, which seem to be the exclusive habitat for rock rose. Accordingly, the Latin name, *Petrophytum caespitosum*, means "rock-plant that grows in mats." Tough woody roots work their way through cracks in the rock to soak up moisture and nutrients in this soil-less environment. Rock rose doesn't bloom until late in the summer, putting out dozens of spikes of tiny, pale-pink, fragrant flowers. They often grow on vertical cliff faces, but are also found in easy-to-access places wherever there are outcrops of limestone. Look on cliffs along the Cement Creek Caves trail (p. 200). This species is also common around seeps and springs of desert canyons in the southwest, including the Grand Canyon.

Shrubby Cinquefoil *Potentilla fruticosa (Pentaphylloides floribunda)*

Shrubby cinquefoil grows in moist soils from sagebrush to tundra, but is most abundant near streams and wetlands. Although the stems and leaves are important winter food for wildlife, thick stands of this shrub are an indicator of over-grazing where livestock roam, since they'll eat most other plants before nibbling the bitter cinquefoils. In mid-summer, the round, robust shrubs are covered with bright yellow flowers, giving them another common name, yellow rose. The leaves are generally five-lobed (*penta-* means "five," *phylloides-* means "leaflets"). These leaves are smaller and thicker than those of the herbaceous cinquefoils, or potentillas.

Showy Cinquefoil *Potentilla gracilis* var. *pulcherrima*

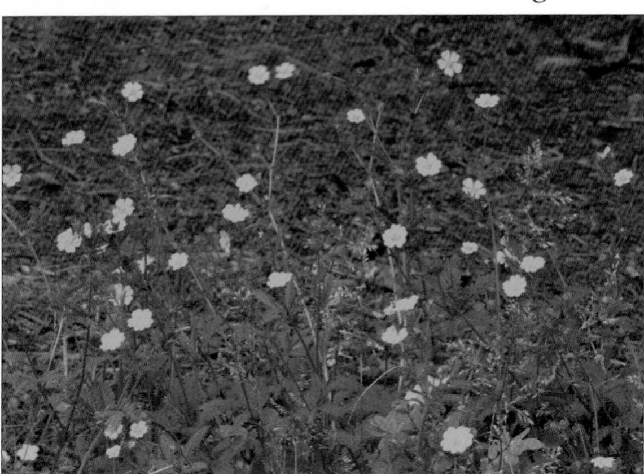

The leaves of some cinquefoils strongly resemble those of marijuana (*Cannabis sativa*). For reasons other than its look-alike, *Potentilla* means "little potent one," indicating this plant's importance in herbal medicine. Teas, tinctures and washes made from the leaves help reduce inflammations, including sore throats, sunburn and saddle sores. If you put some leaves in your boots on a long hike, they are reputed to help prevent blisters.

Cinquefoils are found literally everywhere in the Rocky Mountains. There is a species for every habitat, ranging from the large gangly silvery cinquefoil (*P. hippiana*) growing in the sagebrush zone, to the petite snow cinquefoil (*P. nivea*) found on gravely meadows above treeline. All have bright yellow, five-petaled flowers. Most are also good pioneer species, growing well in poor soils. Although the common name, cinquefoil, means "five leaflets," only a few species actually have only five; leaflets range from three to fifteen, and the leaves may be palmately or pinnately compound. Many have long white hairs on one or both sides of the leaves.

Michael Moore, author of *Medicinal Plants of the Mountain West,* aptly describes the genus as "a botanist's nightmare of crossbreeding." There are over five hundred species of *Potentilla* on the planet, comprising nearly a quarter of the species in the entire Rose Family. Around thirty are found in the Rocky Mountains; eighteen species occur in the Gunnison Basin. The most common in the Elk Mountains are silvery cinquefoil (*P. hippiana*) and showy cinquefoil (*P. gracilis*), both abundant along roadsides in sagebrush and mountain meadows. The silvery cinquefoil has pinnately compound leaves, while showy cinquefoils leaves are palmate.

Chokecherry *Prunus virginiana (Padus virginiana)*

Chokecherry grows from a low shrub to a twenty foot tall tree, depending on how much moisture it has access to. The deep purple berries live up to their name, as they are extremely bitter and astringent. However, with the addition of lots of sugar, these berries make excellent preserves. The musky-smelling, cream-colored flowers bloom in long catkins in early spring, about the same time as serviceberry (p. 168). The berries, twigs and leaves are important forage for wildlife. Near Crested Butte, chokecherry is most noticeable along Brush Creek Road and around the Almont Campground along Highway 135.

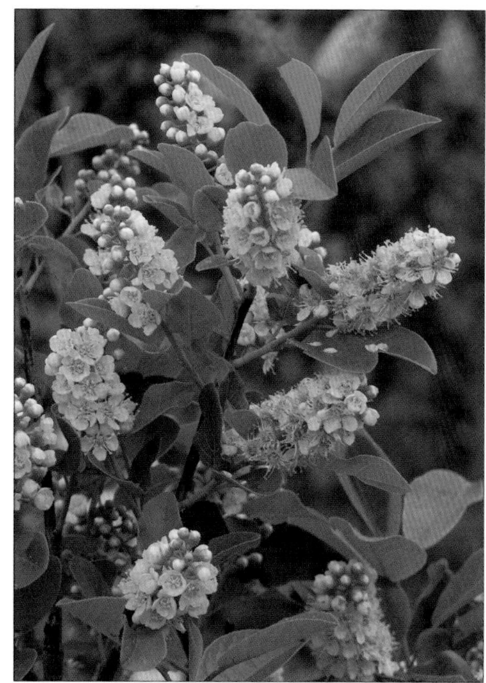

"To be overcome by the fragrance of flowers is a delectable form of defeat."

– Beverley Nichols

Wild Rose *Rosa woodsii*

The captivating fragrance of the wild rose is the perfect anecdote for a noseful of musky chokecherry blossoms. These prickly shrubs are common in moist meadows and along streams from lower montane to subalpine. Depending on the elevation and exposure, they can grow into sprawling shrubs over six feet tall, or small plants barely knee-high. In the fall, the delicate pink flowers become shiny red rose hips, which are important food for animals ranging from grouse to bears. The fruits are somewhat tasteless, mealy, and full of seeds, but are somewhat sweeter by mid-winter after they have frozen and thawed a few times. Although this species of wild rose does grow near forests, their true namesake is an English botanist named Joseph Woods.

Sibbaldia *Sibbaldia procumbens*

These inconspicuous plants are worth mentioning because they are one of the most common species in alpine tundra around the world. They tend to thrive in areas of late-lying snow, and have thus been a useful indicator for highway engineers who may wish to avoid areas prone to deep drifts. The leaves resemble wild strawberries, but the tiny yellow flowers are reminiscent of a popular European ornamental, *Alchemilla*, commonly known as ladies' mantle, and also a member of the Rose Family. The genus honors Robert Sibbald, who was a 17th century Scottish botanist. *Procumbens* means "prostrate," since these plants grow no more than a couple of inches above the ground.

Mountain Ash *Sorbus scopulina*

MARY ELLEN HARTE

White sprays of flowers on mountain ash, along with pinnately compound leaves, are easily confused with elderberry , a member of the Honeysuckle Family (p. 83). One way to distinguish the two is to look for alternating leaves (not to be confused with *leaflets*, which are opposite) and branches on the ash; elderberry leaves and branches are opposite.

Both shrubs also produce bright orange-red berries in the fall, a popular food for wildlife and birds. Mountain ash is common on sunny slopes and roadsides in rocky, well-drained soils. In the fall, the leaves and berries of these tall deciduous shrubs add a splash of color to autumn in the high mountains.

Madder Family RUBIACEAE

Without this family, many of us would have difficulty starting the day or pulling all-nighters: coffee (*Coffea arabica*) is a product of the Bedstraw or Madder Family. This is a huge family, with over 9,000 species found around the world. Most of these plants are subtropical and tropical shrubs and trees. The family's Latin name, Rubiaceae, was given for a bright red, or ruby-colored, dye made from the roots of madder (*Rubia tinctorum*). Other notable species include cinchona tree (*Cinchona* spp.), the bark of which is used to produce quinine for treatment of malaria, and gardenias (*Gardenia* spp.), which are cultivated as ornamentals. The most common North American genus, and the most common in Colorado, is the bedstraw group.

NORTHERN BEDSTRAW *Galium boreale (Galium septentrionale)*

There are over sixty common names in the U.S. alone used for this plant genus. Cleavers, catchweed, scratchweed and goose grass are just a few. Most refer to the annoying, but useful, trait of tiny hooked bristles on the stems, leaves and seeds of bedstraws, which causes them to stick to clothing. This is a great way for the plant to disperse its seeds, which catch on animal fur as well, thereby spreading them around the forests and countryside. The plant is also honored as supposedly having been the lining for baby Jesus' manger. Common folk have used it to stuff mattresses, or as bed ticking, since it is an effective flea repellent. The scientific name, *Galium*, means milk, alluding to its use by Greek shepherds to curdle milk and make cheese.

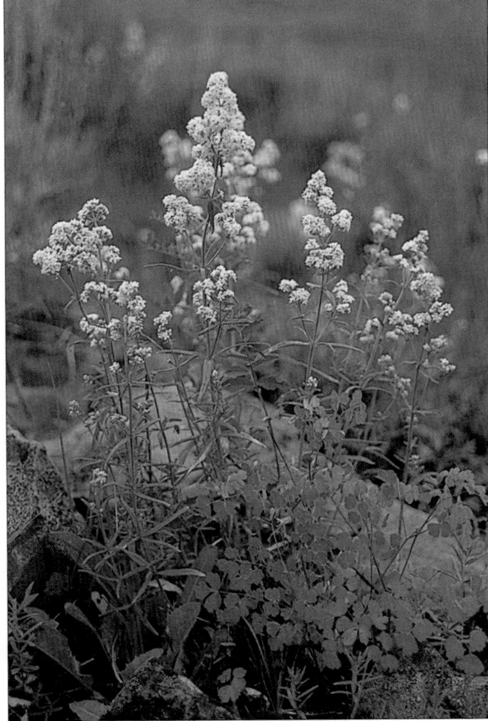

Over four hundred species of bedstraw are found around the world. All share the characteristics of four-sided stems, tiny four-petaled tubular flowers and whorled leaves (with three to six leaves per node), as well as being covered with bristly hairs. Most have white flowers, but there are a few yellow-flowered species. In addition to its use as bedding, the seeds can be roasted and brewed to make a coffee substitute, and the roots make a beautiful red dye. Tea or tincture made from the whole plant can be used medicinally as a diuretic and to treat urinary tract infections.

There are five species in the Gunnison Basin. The most common is northern bedstraw, a robust plant found in meadows, shrublands and open forests from sagebrush to tundra. The flowers are especially sweet-smelling, more so than the foliage of fragrant bedstraw (*G. triflorum*) that grows in moist, shaded aspen and coniferous forests. Yellow bedstraw (*G. verum*), two-leaved bedstraw (*G. bifolium*) and three-cleft bedstraw (*G. trifidum*) are less common.

Willow Family SALICACEAE

The Willow Family may not have bright showy blooms, but everyone enjoys soft, gray pussywillows, which are the flower buds of willows. Aspens and cottonwoods are also members of the Willow Family, and dangle their flowers from leafless branches in early spring. The long clusters of flowers are called catkins, after their resemblance to a cat's tail.

Members of the Willow Family are dioecious, which is a Greek word meaning "two houses." One "house," or plant, produces males, or pollen-bearing flowers and the other "house" produces female, or seed-producing flowers. All members of this family contain salicin, a precursor to aspirin. Long before aspirin became available in little white tablets, indigenous peoples around the world discovered that willow and aspen bark tea were among the best remedies for relieving pain, for reducing fevers and inflammation, and for use as an antiseptic poultice or wash.

NARROW-LEAF COTTONWOOD *Populus angustifolia*

Cottonwood groves line major drainages in the lower mountains, creating riverside forests that are a haven for deer and dozens of bird species, including bald eagles, great blue herons and owls. The rough, furrowed bark and massive trunks contrast with the straight, white columns of its cousin, the aspen. In spring, the bright-red male catkins are visible against the blue sky, dangling from the branches before the leaves emerge. In fall, the gold of cottonwood leaves rivals the shimmering colors of aspen on the hillsides. In summer, the female plants produce volumes of fluffy seeds, creating a downy blizzard in July.

Aspen *Populus tremuloides*

GALE PICKETT

Lying in a cool grove of aspens will revive any tired soul. The gentle flutter of quaking leaves emulates the sound of water running over rocks in a creek. The trees vibrate like living paintings of pointillists, each leaf a dab of paint. Native Americans considered the aspen to be a spirit tree since its leaves seem to shake by themselves, trembling in the slightest breeze. The physical reason for this has to do with the perpendicular orientation of the leaf blade relative to the flattened petiole, or leaf stem.

Aspens, also known as "quakies" in local lore, have soft, gray catkins similar to willows. Although they do produce seed, it is very rare for aspen seeds to germinate. Most often, these trees reproduce asexually by sending out suckers, resulting in forests of "clones" that are really all the same tree connected by modified underground stems called rhizomes. Individual clones are most easily recognized in the fall, when the trees in a clone tend to turn color at the same time and also turn the same shade of yellow or orange. Suckering is stimulated by disturbance, so that aspens are often the first trees to colonize an area after fire, avalanche, windthrow or logging. Aspens generally begin to be replaced by coniferous trees after a hundred years or so in the absence of massive disturbances, although some aspen forests are climax communities. One candidate for the largest living organism in the world is an aspen clone in Utah's Wasatch mountains that covers 106 acres, has about 47,000 trunks, weighs more than 6 million tons, and has been named "Pando" ("I spread") by the scientists who studied it.

The smooth, white bark of aspens is often an irresistible surface for travelers to record their thoughts and passing. Native Americans probably communicated to each other with "dendroglyphs," or marks on aspen and other trees. Today, the carvings of shepherds, ranchers and explorers are part of the local mountain history. Unfortunately, tree carving can lead to increased fungal and bacterial infections, causing severe damage to individual trees and entire clones.

Wild creatures also leave their marks as they pass through the forests. Bears leave claw marks; deer and elk rub the velvet off their antlers and mark their territories on the trees; elk, porcupines, hares and voles chew on aspen bark for food. Aspen is a major food source for beavers, as well as an important building material.

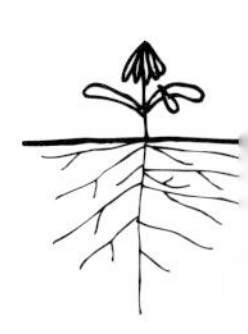

WILLOW *Salix* spp.

The Latin name for willow, *Salix*, and for the family, is derived from *salire*, meaning "to leap," describing the way willows and their cousins proliferate in their wetland or mountain habitats. Willows are important elements of wetlands, some of the most biologically productive ecosystems in the mountains, and unfortunately, the most abused. Willows play a role in the wetland functions of water purification, water storage and bank stabilization, as well as providing food and shelter for innumerable wildlife species. This includes many insects that are attracted by sweet willow nectar and pollen, although the wind takes care of most of the pollinating.

In addition to medicinal uses, willow twigs have been prized and propagated for millennia to use in basketry. The Old English word, *welig*, meaning "to twist or bend," is the origin of the name for these plants, because of how easily they can be shaped and woven.

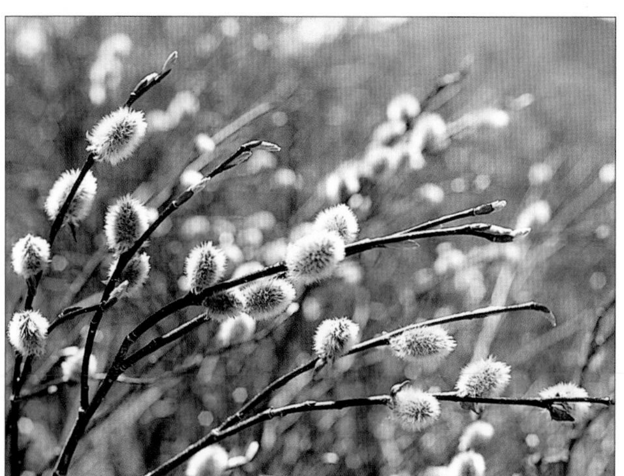

There are over five hundred species of willows on Earth, with nearly two dozen species growing in the Elk Mountain region. Two of the most common are mountain willow (*S. monticola*), growing mostly at lower elevations and on valley bottoms, and planeleaf willow (*S. planifolia*), shown left, which thrives along streams and in wet meadows all the way up to the alpine tundra. The mountain willow is easily recognized by its bright yellow twigs. Planeleaf willow has reddish-purple twigs. Be forewarned however, that willow identification is considered by some to be, at best, a fine art and at worst, incredibly confusing. Twig color is only a loose guide to species. Hybridization further complicates matters.

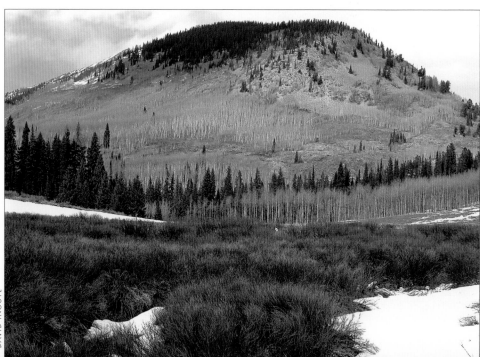

DAVID INOUYE

Two species of alpine willow are common on the tundra, forming vast, creeping mats rather than shrubs or trees. Snow willow (*S. reticulata*), shown below, is distinguished by its intricately veined or "reticulated" leaves that have blunt tips. Arctic willow (*S. arctica*) has smoother leaves with pointy tips. Both are important food for ptarmigan all year round; an ounce of dried willow buds provides over 100,000 calories!

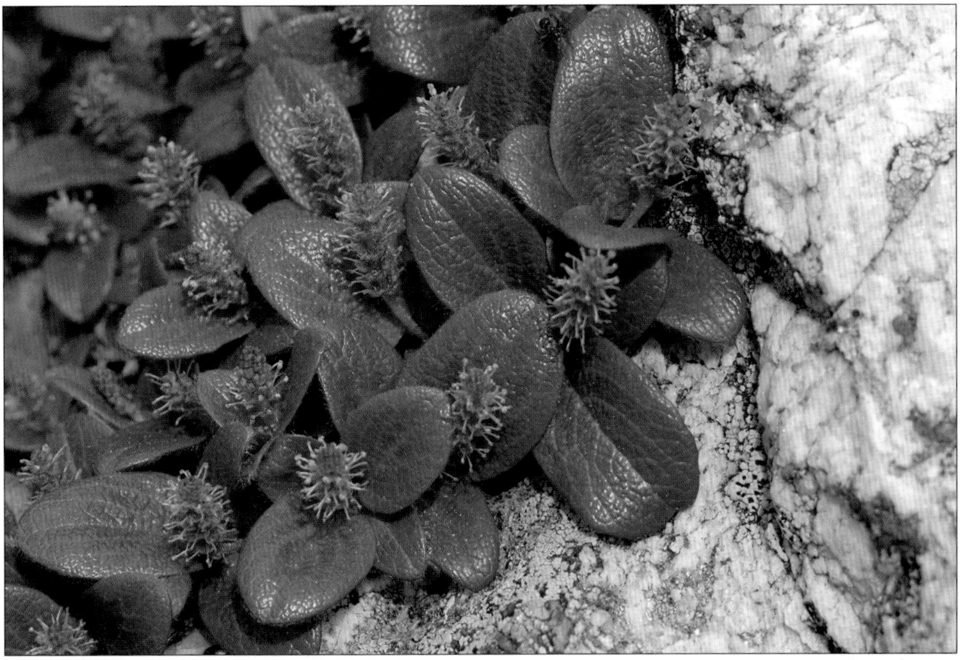

A federally endangered butterfly, the Uncompahgre fritillary, depends on snow willow for part of its life cycle. The small black and orange butterflies lay their eggs on the willows, which then hatch into caterpillars. For two summers, the caterpillars feed on the willows before metamorphosing into butterflies. Certain alpine peaks in the southern Rockies are the only known habitat in the world for the Uncompahgre fritillary.

> *"...they spring up so rapidly; they are so salient. They have hardly made two shoots from the sand in as many springs, when silvery catkins burst out along them, and anon golden blossoms and downy seeds, spreading their race with incredible rapidity."*
>
> – H.D. Thoreau

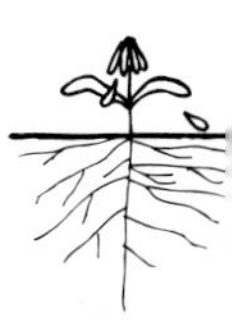

Saxifrage Family SAXIFRAGACEAE

Saxifrages, meaning "rock breakers," were originally named under the archaic medicinal Doctrine of Signatures for the kidney-shaped leaves of many species. By this belief, the resemblance of a plant to various body parts was supposed to indicate what ailments the plant would cure. Kidney and gall stones were treated with tinctures and teas made from saxifrage leaves, probably with very little effect. Many plants in this family grow on cliffs and in exposed arctic and alpine habitats, where the deep roots of some saxifrages do have an influence in breaking up the stones.

ALUMROOT *Heuchera parvifolia*

You'll probably notice the leaves of alumroot before you notice the flowers. Masses of basal leaves grow in rocky areas, from dry vertical cliffs at lower elevations to sheltered rocky areas of the alpine tundra. In the fall, the leaves turn deep red. The tall (up to two feet), slender flowering stems bear dozens of tiny whitish-green flowers, inspiring the Latin name, *parvifolia*, meaning "small flowered." The genus was named in honor of J.H. Heucher, a German botanist (1677-1747).

Alumroot tea has been proven effective in helping to relieve diarrhea and other gastrointestinal disorders. Its astringent qualities also make it useful for healing cuts and abrasions. A showy, red-flowered cousin called coral bells (*H. sanguinea*) is commonly used in rock gardens.

WHITE-FLOWERED BISHOP'S CAP *Mitella stauropetala*

MARY ELLEN HARTE

Bishop's cap is usually found growing in moist, mossy places by small streams in spruce-fir forests where you might expect to see a fairy or a leprechaun. The thread-like stem rises from a small group of basal leaves to display dozens of tiny flowers, the size and shape of perfect five-sided snowflakes.

Two species are common in the Elk Mountains, and are often found growing in the same elfin hollow. The green-flowered bishop's cap, *Mitella pentandra*, has more intricately branched petals than its white-flowered cousin. The genus name, *Mitella*, is Latin for "turban," or the diminutive of miter, a type of hat worn by high priests. The little saucer-shaped flower becomes filled with dark seeds when it turns to fruit.

Spotted Saxifrage *Saxifraga bronchialis (Ciliaria austromontana)*

Thin, crowded mounds of needle-like leaves found on spotted saxifrage make it easily mistaken for a moss. These plants thrive in very diverse habitats, from shaded, dripping cliffs in Douglas-fir forests, to exposed areas of the alpine tundra. Each of the five white petals on the flowers are dotted with purple, orange and yellow, acting as nectar guides for pollinating insects.

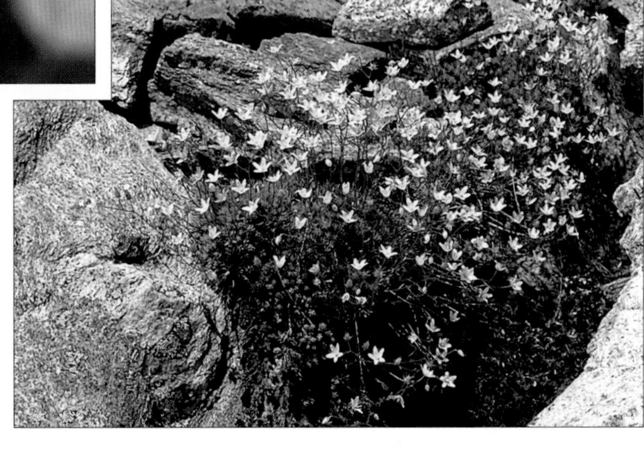

There are about 250 species of *Saxifraga* around the world, which is about half of the entire family; a dozen species are found in the Elk Mountains. This species is also referred to as *Ciliaria austromontana* meaning "thin-leaves, plant of southern mountains." The Latin name, *S. bronchialis*, indicates its use as a treatment for bronchitis.

Brook Saxifrage *Saxifraga odontoloma (Micranthes odontoloma)*

The leaves of brook saxifrage look like they've been carefully cut out with pinking shears to make a perfect zig-zag edge. Thin, loosely-branched flowering stalks rise from the crowded basal leaves, so that the small pink and white flowers almost look like they are suspended in the misty air where they grow. Look for brook saxifrage in bloom from mid- to late-summer in wet, shady places along streams in spruce-fir forests. The Latin name, *Micranthes odontoloma*, means "tiny flowers, toothed borders."

Snapdragon Family SCROPHULARIACEAE

You may remember playing with snapdragons (*Antirrhinum majus*) as a child, squeezing the flowers to make them "talk." Most of the wildflowers in this family have a similar shape, which is very specialized for pollination by bees. The tubular flowers have landing pads, often with stripes, or nectar guides, and stamens and stigmas positioned precisely for efficient transfer of pollen. The Latin name for the family, Scrophulariaceae, affectionately known as "Scroph," comes from the shape of the flower, which is "scrofulous." This is a fancy word for "swollen neck," since the flower tube is usually inflated from the base. "Scrofula" is also a medical term for tuberculosis of the lymph glands. The flowers are sometimes called figworts, also referring to their form or "figure."

This is a large and diverse family, with over 3,000 species worldwide. According to one taxonomist, the range of variation in flower form and color in the Snapdragon Family is exceeded only by orchids. Recent DNA analysis indicates that many of the genera traditionally included in this group may actually be more closely allied with the Plantain Family (Plantaginaceae). In Colorado, the common mullein (*Verbascum thapsus*) and figwort (*Scrophularia lanceolata*) are the only "true scrophs," according to the new systematics. Indian paintbrush and louseworts are more closely related to the Broomrapes (p. 138). However, this book is presented in the historic family concept with the understanding that all of these groups are very closely related.

INDIAN PAINTBRUSH *Castilleja* spp.

Of all the flowers blooming in the mountains, perhaps the most exquisite are the Indian paintbrushes, also known as painted cups, flame flower and squaw feather. The scientific name for Indian paintbrush genus, *Castilleja*, is in honor of 18th century Spanish botanist and explorer, Domingo Castillejo, who probably first studied these flowers in the southwest deserts of North America.

WENDY BROWN

Over two hundred species grace the Earth, mostly in the Western U.S., but also in such un-western places as Florida and New Hampshire. In the southern Rockies, six species thrive and are found from the driest of sagebrush hills up to the alpine tundra.

The actual flowers of paintbrushes are quite inconspicuous and usually green. Colorful, leafy bracts and sepals enclose the long narrow corolla, or petals, of the flowers. Look straight down at the plants and you can see the pointed corollas poking out among the color-drenched bracts.

Many paintbrushes are semi-parasitic on sagebrush, deriving some of their nutrients and water from the deeply rooted shrubs. In high mountains where sagebrush is lacking, paintbrushes parasitize grasses, lupines and other plants. This is the main reason you rarely find Indian paintbrushes in any of the carefully tended gardens in mountain towns. Even though they can photosynthesize and produce some of their own food, paintbrushes will not thrive without a host. Some horticulturists are beginning to discover how to cultivate them using fringed sage as a host plant.

How the Paintbrushes Got Their Colors

The legend of the Indian paintbrush explains that the extraordinary colors of these flowers are derived from a gift of the Great Spirits to a young Native American artist trying to capture the shades of the sunset. The Great Spirits presented the boy with brushes of every color of the evening sky, which he casually discarded after he had finished his masterpiece. The brushes transformed to flowers, which have since flourished throughout the mountains and deserts of North America.

The scientific story is equally fascinating, involving various biochemical and natural processes such as anthocyanin, evolution, pollination and hybridization. For Indian paintbrushes, co-evolution with their primary pollinators, hummingbirds, has resulted in the predominantly red colors of the genus. Long-tongued insects such as moths and butterflies are attracted to white and yellow species. Cross-pollination, or hybridization, between different species has expanded the range of color produced by chemical pigments called anthocyanins so that the paintbrushes truly do emulate a beautiful western sunset.

Crimson Paintbrush *Castilleja angustifolia (C. chromosa)*

Crimson paintbrush is one of the most brilliantly red and earliest blooming paintbrushes, abundant on sagebrush slopes near Almont and further south in the Gunnison Basin from early May to June. *Angustifolia* means "narrow," for the slender leaves and lobes of the flower bracts. The stems are more purple than green. This species is common throughout the Great Basin Desert.

Wyoming Paintbrush *Castilleja linariifolia*

The color of Wyoming paintbrush is more on the orange end of the red spectrum compared to the crimson paintbrush. These are tall, often many-branched plants with long slender leaves, most commonly associated with sagebrush. This species and the scarlet paintbrush look very similar, and are most easily distinguished by habitat.

Scarlet Paintbrush *Castilleja miniata*

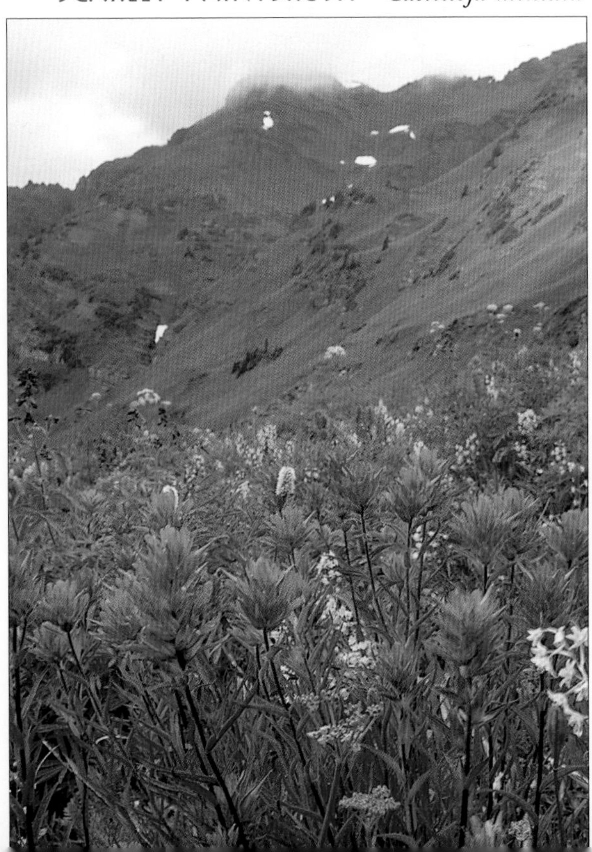

At higher elevations, scarlet paintbrush thrives in mountain meadows and aspen forests. This species often hybridizes with the pale yellow sulphur paintbrushes and rosy paintbrush to create swarms of the most intense shades of pink, red, orange and magenta flowers. Scarlet paintbrush tolerates drier, rocky meadows and forests than the rosy and sulphur paintbrushes. *Miniata* means "vermillion," or bright red.

Tundra Paintbrush *Castilleja occidentalis*

Near and above treeline, look for clumps of tundra paintbrush in talus and alpine meadows. This species is covered with short, soft hairs and has yellow flowers. These flowers are actually more yellow than the sulphur paintbrushes (p. 188), which have very pale or almost white bracts.

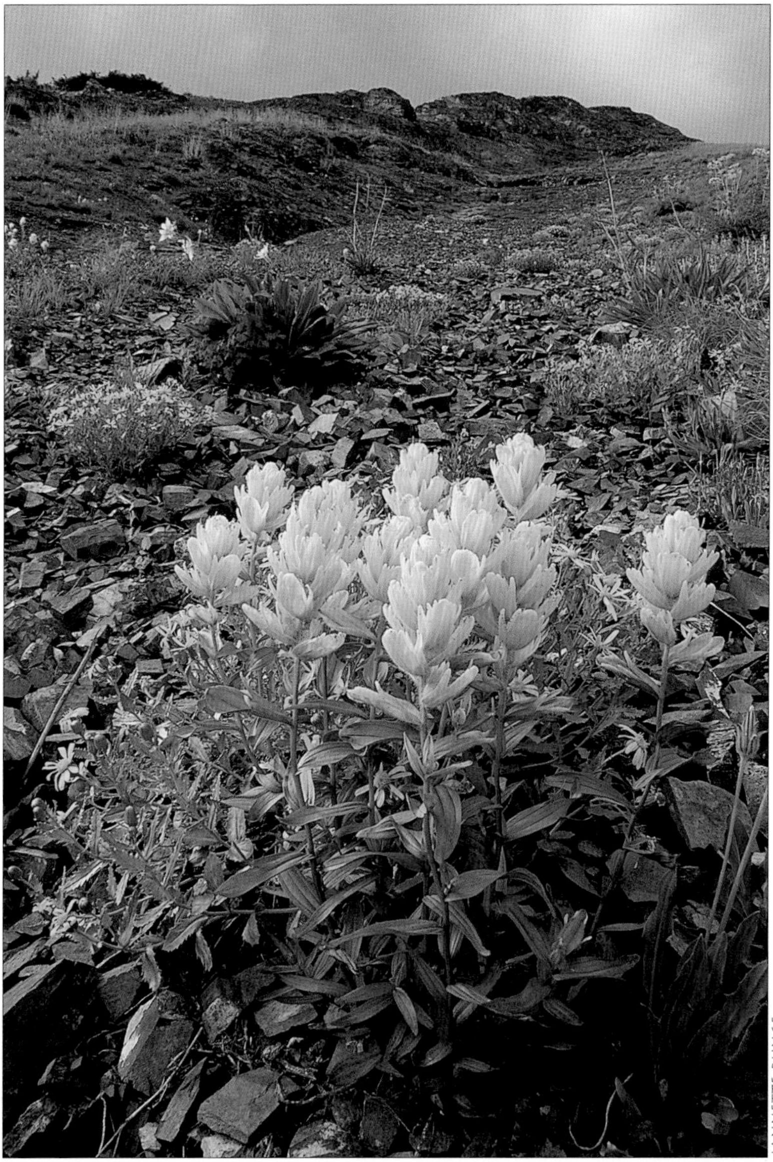

JANNETTE RUNGE

"Everybody needs beauty as well as bread, places to play in and places to pray in, where nature may heal and cheer and give strength to body and soul alike."

– John Muir

Rosy Paintbrush *Castilleja rhexifolia*

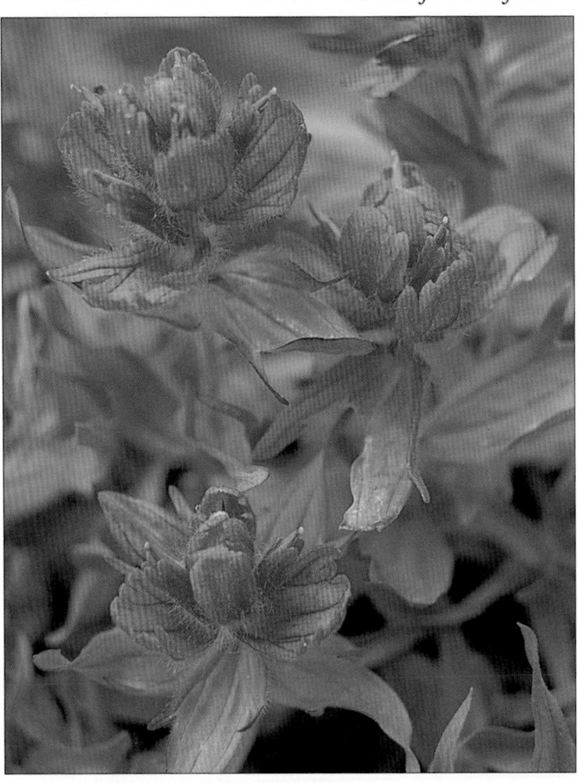

Rosy paintbrush may be the most spectacular floral display in the Rocky Mountains. The bracts range from pale pink to bright fuchsia to almost maroon colors and are even more varied in hybrid swarms with sulphur and scarlet paintbrush. They are most common in moist meadows in subalpine areas around 10,000 to 12,000 feet elevation.

Sulphur Paintbrush *Castilleja sulphurea*

Although named for the color yellow, this species is closer to white or pale green than yellow. The stems, leaves and bracts are also hairless in comparison with the tundra paintbrush. Sulphur paintbrush is common in mountain meadows, aspen and mixed conifer forests, often side by side with the scarlet paintbrush.

Butter-and-eggs *Linaria vulgaris*

Non-native Species

These beautiful and tenacious plants have yellow flowers to match their name and were brought from Europe for their ornamental and medicinal values. Unfortunately, they are so prolific that they have been listed as a noxious weed throughout the United States. Butter-and-eggs spreads by rhizomes as well as seeds, invading any disturbed or open land where it is introduced.

Toadflax is another common name for these sweet-smelling flowers because they open wide like a toad's mouth when squeezed at the base, much like a snapdragon. The slender stems and leaves are easily confused with flax (*Linum* spp.) when the plant is not flowering. This resemblance may have been what suggested the use of toadflax in a solution for starching linens during the Middle Ages.

Scottish custom says that if you walk around a patch of butter-and-eggs three times, you can break any spell that has been cast on you. Drinking a tea of the dried leaves and flowers is also reputed to be a cure for the curse of hepatitis and other liver problems.

Monkeyflower *Mimulus guttatus*

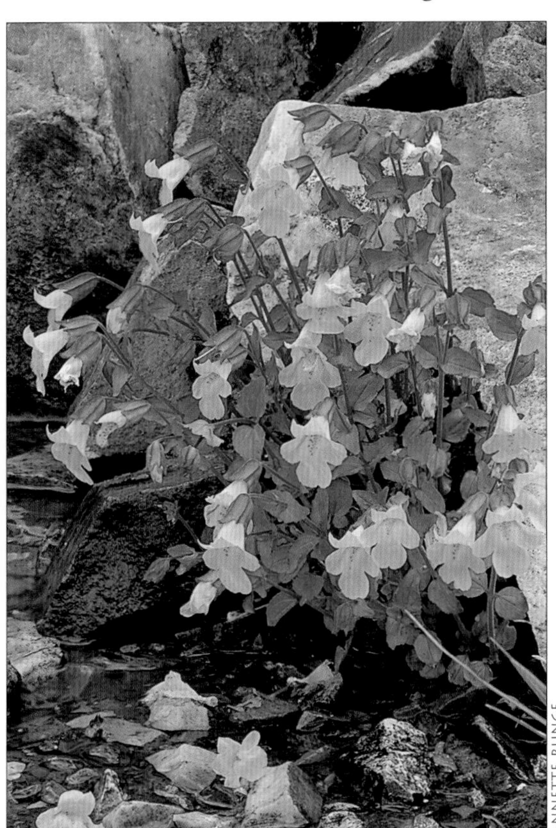

Jannette Runge

Lush clumps of red-spotted yellow monkeyflower are found around springs, along creeks and in marshy places. A case of the blues is easily cracked at the sight of these cheerful flowers, with faces that look like those of playful little monkeys. *Mimulus guttatus* translates to "mask with spots." Look for a tiny annual species, Suksdorf monkeyflower (*M. suksdorfii*), growing in moist areas near sagebrush in early summer, scarcely three inches high with quarter inch long flowers. Monkeyflower leaves are edible as pot herbs or salad greens.

"The Earth laughs in flowers."
– R.W. Emerson

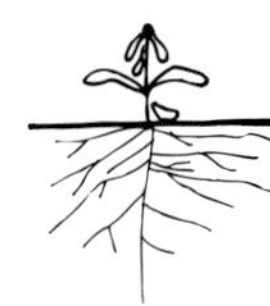

Lousewort *Pedicularis* spp.

Over four hundred species of lousewort are found worldwide; eight species are common in the southern Rockies. Most have fern-like leaves and flowers with curved "beaks," suggesting two other common names, fern-leaf and parrot's beak. Those species that grow in shaded forests are sometimes called wood betony, because they resemble betony (*Stachys* spp.), plants in the Mint Family. Like their cousins the Indian paintbrushes, louseworts are semi-parasitic, and most closely related to the broomrapes (p. 138) in the new understanding of the Snapdragon Family.

Pedicularis means "of lice." Folklore tells that livestock that eat the plants become infested with lice; conversely, some people believe that washing with a tea made of lousewort will help repel the same pests. Although the louseworts have little effect on infestations of lice, a tincture or tea made from the dried leaves and flowers is useful as a mild sedative.

Bracted Lousewort *Pedicularis bracteosa*

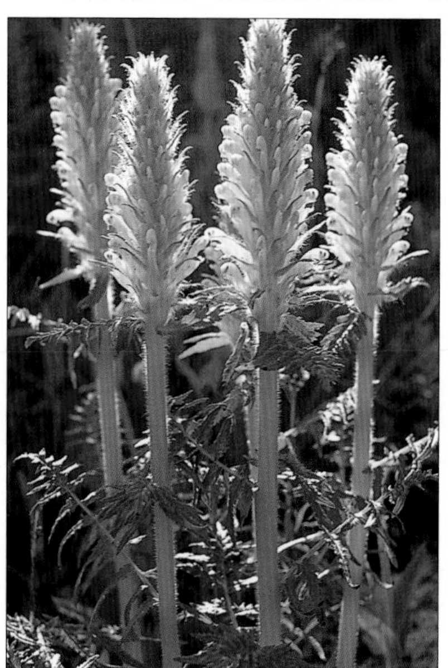

Bracted lousewort are common in mountain meadows and openings in aspen or spruce-fir forests, growing up to three feet tall. The blunt-beaked flowers are pale yellow. The large leaves are deeply divided, and easily mistaken for ferns when the plant is not in bloom or when nipped off by deer and elk that eat them. These plants may be confused with giant lousewort, *Pedicularis procera*, which grows in similar habitats, but is taller, more robust and has pale yellow flowers streaked with red.

Elephantella
Pedicularis groenlandica

Bright pink elephantella flowers look just like the heads of tiny little pachyderms, complete with big ears, trunk and a wide, rounded forehead. Herds of elephantella bloom along streams and in sunny wet swales and marshes throughout the summer, from montane to alpine tundra. The leaves are deeply lobed and fern-like. These flowers have no nectar, but are buzz-pollinated by pollen-collecting bumblees (see p. 154).

The Latin name means "lousewort from Greenland," where they also occur. Marsh lousewort *(P. crenulata)*, is another pink-flowered lousewort found in wet meadows, but lacks the long trunk, and has crenulate (rounded teeth) rather than fern-like leaves.

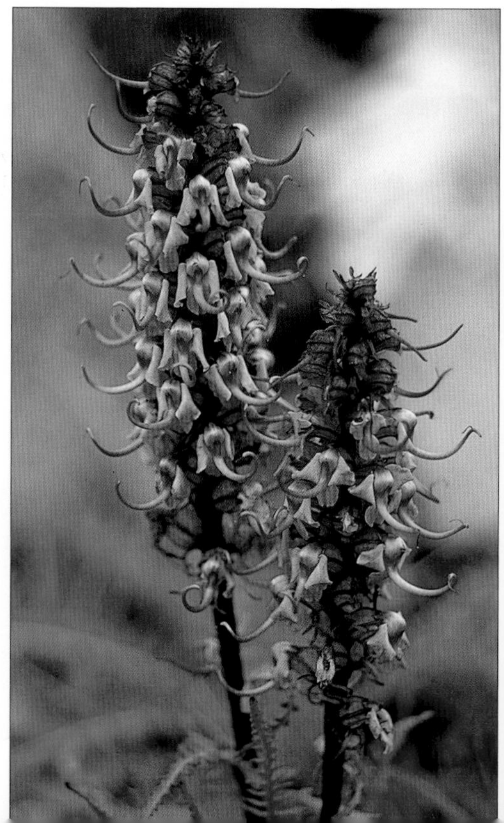

Parry's Lousewort *Pedicularis parryi*

This pale yellow-flowered lousewort is common in dry gravelly soils of subalpine meadows and alpine tundra. The leaves are fern-like, with deep lobes. Some people compare the shape of the flower to the head of a goose. Charles Parry was a 19th century Colorado botanist and explorer (see p. 101 for more on Parry). Look also for the pink-flowered alpine lousewort (*P. sudtica* ssp. *scopulorum*) on the tundra, where it grows in moist soils.

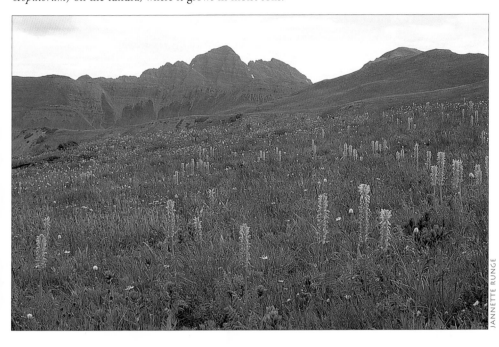

JANNETTE RUNGE

Curly Lousewort *Pedicularis racemosa*

Curly lousewort is a shade-lover, most commonly found in dry soils of spruce-fir forest. The creamy-white colored flowers have a distinctive twist that suggests another common name, ram's horn. The leaves are crenulate, with rounded teeth on the edge rather than deep divisions like many of the other lousewort species. Stems are often red or maroon colored.

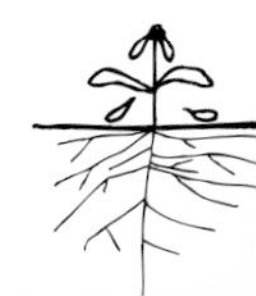

PENSTEMON *Penstemon* spp.

Among the showiest of alpine flowers are the penstemons. There are over 275 species in the world, all but one native to North America. Nine of the more than sixty species found in Colorado are considered rare, due mostly to very specific habitat requirements. In the Elk Mountain region you can find a dozen different penstemons, ranging from the mat-like creeping penstemon to the robust Rocky Mountain penstemon that grows to three feet tall. The flowers are easy to recognize, with tubular shaped corollas similar to garden snapdragons.

Most penstemons have blue or purple flowers, but there are also species with red, white and yellow flowers. Enthusiastic gardeners who call themselves "penstemaniacs" have cultivated dozens of hybrid varieties. There is even an American Penstemon Society, which you can join for only $10 a year. Some herbalists claim that penstemons are potent medicinal plants, said to be useful for treating a myriad of problems, including toothaches, rattlesnake bites, labor pain and venereal disease.

CREEPING PENSTEMON *Penstemon crandallii (P. caespitosus)*

Creeping penstemon forms low mats up to three feet in diameter and is most common on dry, rocky slopes from 7,000-10,000 feet, often in association with sagebrush.

SCREE PENSTEMON *Penstemon harbourii*

Scree penstemon grows in lush clumps and loose mats on alpine scree and boulder fields, as on the Yule Pass trail (p. 203). This is one of Colorado's endemic species, meaning that it is found nowhere else in the world, although it is fairly common within its limited distribution. The lavender-blue flowers are large and showy. J.P. Harbour was a 19th century Colorado plant collector.

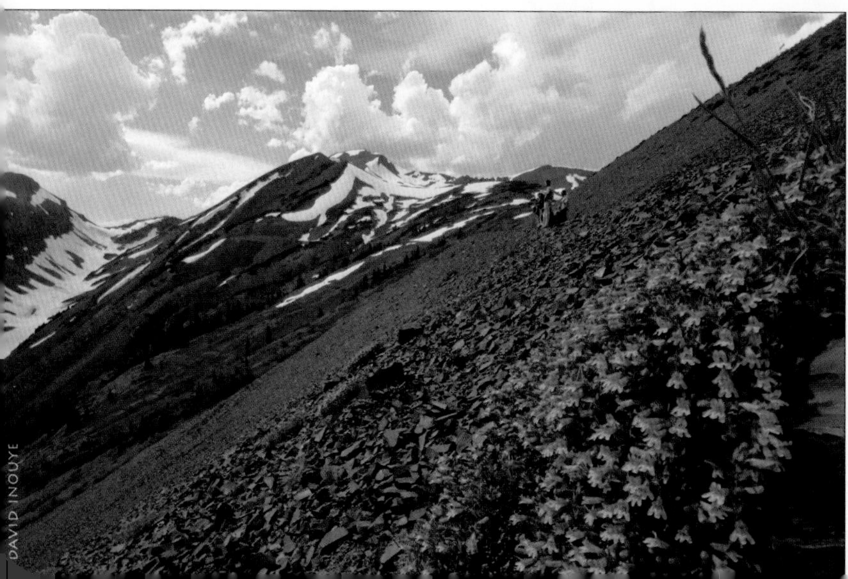

DAVID INOUYE

Grand Mesa Penstemon *Penstemon mensarum*

The Grand Mesa penstemon, named for its first discovery on Grand Mesa east of Grand Junction, Colorado, has hairless fertile stamens and is a brilliant electric-blue. *Mensarum* means "of the mesa." This species is quite common in the upper drainages of the Gunnison Basin, but endemic to the region. It thrives in disturbed areas along roadsides and trails near mountain meadows and upper elevation sagebrush.

If you peer inside the flower, you will find some beautiful architecture in the stamens for which the plant is named. There are two interpretations of the generic name. Most common is that *Penstemon* is a contraction of *pente* and *stamen*, meaning "five stamens." Another is that *pen* means "almost," referring to the sterile stamen ("almost a stamen") and often covered with hairs, earning the plants another common name, beardtongue.

Clustered Penstemon *Penstemon procerus (P. confertus* ssp. *procerus)*
Rydberg's Penstemon *Penstemon rydbergii*

Rydberg's and clustered penstemon are both found in moist soils near sagebrush and have clusters of small blue flowers all around the stem. The clustered penstemon has flowers about half the size of its cousin. *Procerus* means "tall," although this species is rather petite. Per Axel Rydberg was a Swedish immigrant and a prominent botanist in Colorado. Rydberg published several books on Rocky Mountain flora.

Rocky Mtn. Penstemon *Penstemon strictus*

Early in the summer, Rocky Mountain penstemon is the dominant blue flower lining the roadsides and painting blue patches on the sagebrush hills. *Strictus* means "straight," probably for the rigid stems. This is the most common and widespread, as well as tallest, of penstemons in the southern Rockies. The fertile anthers of these flowers are covered with long, white hairs. The hairy anthers are an easy way to distinguish Rocky Mountain penstemon from its cousin, Grand Mesa penstemon, which has hairless anthers, but a hairy sterile stamen or "stamenode."

Whipple's Penstemon *Penstemon whippleanus*

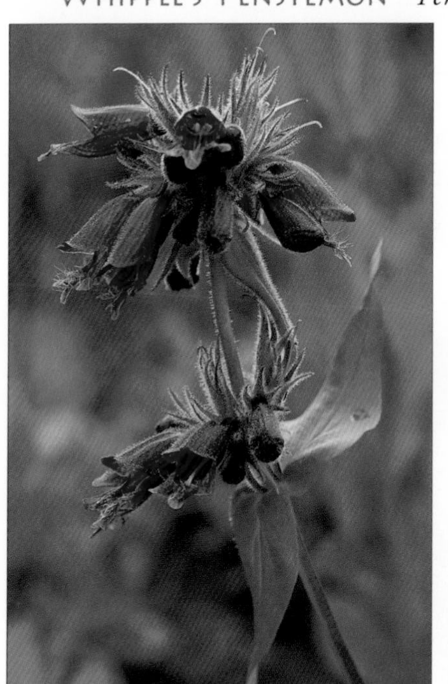

Whipple's penstemon is common in subalpine and alpine habitats, from dry forests to rocky ridges. They range in color from deep burgundy to cream-colored with purple stripes. The outsides of the flowers are covered with tiny glandular hairs, making them sticky and pleasantly fragrant. The species honors Lt. Amiel W. Whipple, who was a survey director for the transcontinental railroad.

Nettle Family Urticaceae

Nettles are a large, mostly tropical and subtropical family of plants with about a thousand species worldwide. Ramie, or Chinese silk plant (*Boehmeria nivea*), is a type of nettle cultivated for the long, strong bast, or stem fibers to make fine fabrics, rope and paper.

Stinging Nettle *Urtica dioica*

One of two representatives of this family in Colorado is stinging nettle, somewhat homely-looking plants common in wet meadows, streamsides and roadsides. Nettles are notable for their stinging hairs that contain formic acid, the same chemical in the sting of bees and ants. The plants are the host for an orange-winged species of butterfly called a "comma" (because of black marks on its wings), whose caterpillars do not seem to be deterred by the stinging hairs. The wind-pollinated flowers are clustered in long staminate or pistillate catkins that dangle from the axils of opposite leaves. The stems are square, like members of the Mint Family, and also contain strong bast fibers like the nettle's Asian cousin, ramie. Young plants can be steamed to remove the formic acid, making nutritious edibles high in vitamins and minerals. Nutritious broth or tea can also be made from nettles, which are often combined with clover and mint as a tonic.

Valerian Family VALERIANACEAE

Perhaps the best known member of the Valerian Family is Himalayan spikenard (*Nardostachys jatamansi*) which is cultivated and wild harvested in the Himalayan mountains for the strong-smelling oils in the large root. The Latin word *valere*, means "to be strong" or "to have value." The healing ointments made from the root are considered to be both strong and valuable.

This is the same ointment that is mentioned in the Bible in stories of Mary anointing Jesus:

"... there came a woman having an alabaster box of ointment of spikenard very precious; and she brake the box, and poured it on His head." Mark 14:3

"Then took Mary a pound of ointment of spikenard, very costly, and anointed the feet of Jesus, and wiped his feet with her hair: and the house was filled with the odour of the ointment." John 12:3

Both spikenard and valerian are popular remedies around the world used as an herbal nerve tonic and sedative, a preferred remedy for insomniacs and those who suffer from emotional stress. Raw dried root, gel capsules and tinctures to be used for these purposes are available at many natural food stores. Contrary to popular belief, the plants are not the source of Valium, a synthetic tranquilizer that has similar, but stronger and potentially addictive effects.

There are over two hundred species of valerian found in north temperate zones and in South America. In the southern Rockies there are three common species. Some characteristics they all share are opposite, lobed leaves, clusters of tiny, tubular white flowers and seeds that have parachutes like dandelions. All three are possessed of a stinky root as well, which to most people smells exactly like a pair of sweaty socks that have been worn for several weeks in the backcountry, although the flowers are pleasantly fragrant.

ALPINE VALERIAN *Valeriana acutiloba (V. capitata)*

Alpine valerian grows on rocky slopes near treeline, at the edge of high-elevation forests and onto the alpine tundra. The ball-like clusters of pinkish-white flowers bloom in the middle of summer. This is the smallest of the three species of valerian native to the southern Rockies, usually growing six to ten inches high.

Edible Valerian *Valeriana edulis*

In moist mountain meadows and near wetlands, you'll come across these tall, robust plants, sometimes up to four feet high. The long, thick taproot is edible when roasted, if you can stand the flavor, which is close to its rank smell. Some describe the flavor to be like chewing tobacco, giving the plant another common name, tobacco root.

DAVID INOUYE

Western Valerian *Valeriana occidentalis*

Western valerian is one of the first wildflowers to bloom in the lower mountain meadows, and is the white flower in handsome displays that include purple Nelson's larkspur and yellow groundsels. They often grow side-by-side with their edible cousins shown above, but can tolerate drier soils. This species grows all the way up to subalpine territory, where it comes close to populations of its smaller cousin, alpine valerian, shown left.

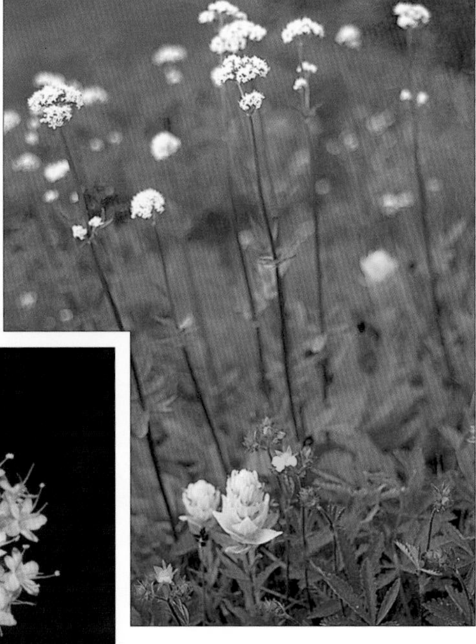

Violet Family VIOLACEAE

Symbols of modesty and simplicity, violets are replete with lore and legend. The ancient Greeks dedicated violets to the goddess Persephone and regarded them as symbols of the immortal soul of the plant world. Greek mythology tells us of the origin of violets as well. When the jealous queen of the gods, Hera, caught her husband, Zeus, flirting with Io, she turned the lovely maiden into a heifer. Beleaguered by her fate, Io wept. Her tears were turned into violets by Zeus as an expression of his love for her. Fortunately for Io, she regained her human form after being driven to Egypt under the hundred watchful eyes of the giant beast Argus, who was ordered by Hera to guard her.

The association of violets with love is also found in French folklore. A gift of violets is believed to turn the thoughts of a loved one towards the bouquet's bearer. Pansies, the domestic cousin of our native violets, derive their name from the French word *pensee*, meaning "a thought," more specifically, a thought of love.

The Romans had yet another use for violets. Garlands of these flowers were believed to dispel the effects of wine and spirits and thereby prevent drunkenness. Violet leaves and flowers are also flavorful additions to a dinner salad and are rich sources of vitamins A and C. Eating violets is probably a more effective remedy for drunkenness than wearing them around your neck!

VIOLETS *Viola* spp.

Although named after the color purple, native violets also come in white, yellow and blue. You'll find them as one of the dominant early flowers of mountain meadows, quietly blooming in the aspen forest or nestled among the grasses near streamsides. Of about nine hundred native species in the family worldwide, nearly half are in the genus *Viola*, and a few are tropical shrubs and trees. Eight native species of violets grow in the southern Rockies. The plants are identified as much by variations in leaf shape as by flower color. The seeds are dispersed by ants, which are attracted by the small "elaiosomes," or food bodies, attached to each seed.

HOOKED VIOLET *Viola adunca*

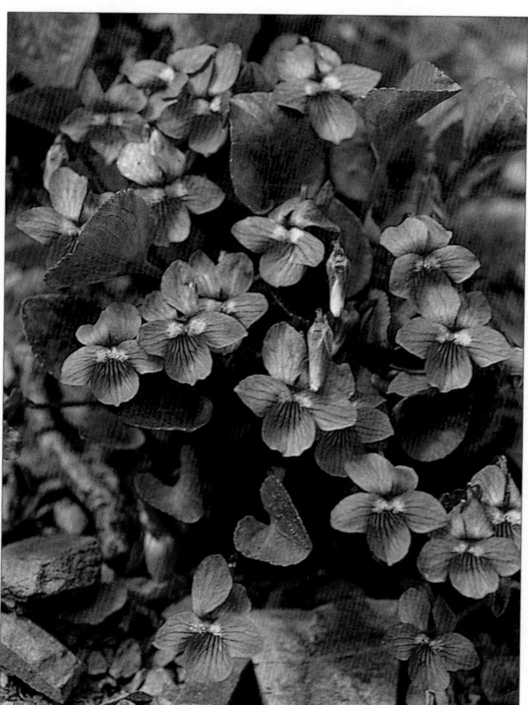

The most common blue or purple species is the hooked violet. They are equally at home on subalpine ridges, near streams and marshes, on open forest floors or tucked among the sagebrush. Look for the little nectar-bearing spur or hook (*adunca* means "hooked") poking out the back of the flower. Although they are generally regarded as spring flowers, they may bloom into late August. Leaves are rounded with tiny indentations along the edges.

Canadian Violet *Viola canadensis (V. scopulorum)*

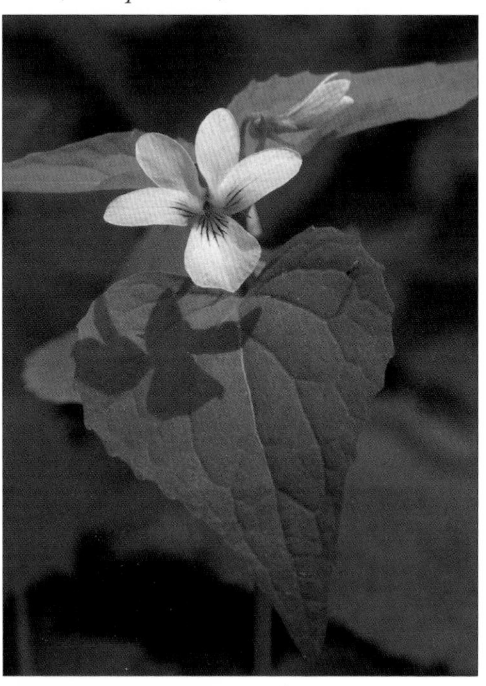

White Canadian violets prefer the shade of aspen or mixed conifer forests and bloom in early to mid-summer. The leaves are distinctively heart-shaped. They may grow between four and twelve inches tall, depending on local soil and light conditions, and often form extensive patches several feet in diameter.

Most violets are equipped with radiating lines or nectar guides, helping pollinating insects to hone in on the violet's sweet rewards. But the plants have a back-up system for seed production, known as cleistogamy, meaning "closed flower." Usually produced after the showy, open flowers on the same plant have passed on, cleistogamous flowers form low to the ground, sometimes beneath the soil, and produce seed by self-pollination. Though this results in inbreeding, it does ensure reproduction and is a common breeding strategy among early-season wildflowers that have to contend with the vicissitudes of spring weather.

"He is happiest who hath power to gather wisdom from a flower."
–Mary Howitt

Canary Violet *Viola praemorsa*

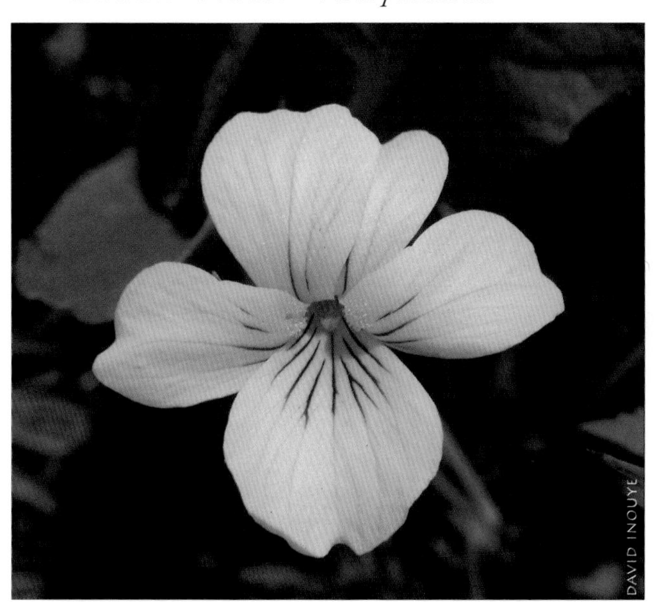
DAVID INOUYE

The most abundant, or at least most noticeable of the violets, is the yellow canary violet which grows in robust clumps among sagebrush and near aspen groves. The species name, *praemorsa*, means "appearing to have been nibbled upon," perhaps because they are valued as food for wildlife. They are one of the earliest spring wildflowers in the mountains. The leaves are long and prominently veined.

A Dozen "Wild" Flower Trails

The Crested Butte area offers hundreds of trails and many off-trail destinations where you can begin your quest for wildflowers Here are a dozen great trails that will help you find some of the best wildflower displays the area has to offer, plus some tips on where to find certain special species. Please respect private property wherever you choose to explore.

Almont to Crested Butte

Jack's Cabin/Almont Triangle

The Almont Triangle is a thirteen square mile piece of land bounded by Highway 135, Taylor River Road and Jack's Cabin Road. During snowy months it is closed to human activity as a winter wildlife area. This is where hundreds of elk, mule deer and a herd of bighorn sheep hang out, grazing on the shrubs and seeking shelter in aspen and pine groves. In the summer, this is one of the most beautiful sections of sagebrush habitat around. The best access is off the Jack's Cabin Road, twelve miles south of Crested Butte or five miles north of Almont. Drive three and a half miles up this road to the top of a low pass, where there is a parking area on the north side near a telephone pole. From there you can hike north or south of the road on old jeep roads.

Lambert's locoweed, mariposa lilies, broomrape, mountain ball cactus and arrowleaf balsamroot are some of the sagebrush-loving plants you'll find. It's easy hiking around here, with about two miles of road on the north and six miles on the south, but many acres of open country to wander around in. See pages 12 and 100 for photos of this area.

Cement Creek/Walrod Gulch

Cement Creek is named for the limestone bluffs that crop out all along the drainage. This trail winds along the south-facing slope above the creek, beginning two miles from Highway 135 on the Cement Creek Road, seven miles south of Crested Butte. A moderate set of switchbacks takes you to the top of The Caves, a bluff that offers some spelunking. Keep going up to a fork in the trail and take the right fork to Walrod Gulch. Here there is an old road that leads you back to Cement Creek Road. Loop back to the trailhead on the roadside trail for about two miles.

There are oodles of serviceberries and wild roses along this sagebrush and mountain meadow loop. Look around on the bluffs for rock rose, which blooms in late August and September. The early spring display of mule's ear sunflower is unparalleled. This is a moderate seven-mile hike.

Brush Creek

Turn onto the Brush Creek Road three miles south of town at the sign to Crested Butte Country Club. Follow the road about three miles to a parking area on the left, just before you cross a bridge over the East River. An old road heads east from this parking area across mountain meadows on the southeast flank of Crested Butte Mountain.

Because of the south-facing aspect, this is one of the first meadows in the area to reach peak bloom. A trail branches off into aspen forest and loops back to the road. Sagebrush and wetlands can also be explored from this trail. This is an easy three-mile round-trip hike. A photo on page 107 shows a view of the Brush Creek area.

Crested Butte Mountain

The easiest access to alpine tundra near Crested Butte is on Crested Butte Mountain, where you can take the Silver Queen lift nearly to treeline. Lift tickets are available at the CBMR ticket office or hotels at the base of the mountain. Follow the trail from the top of the lift on a beautifully maintained trail through spruce-fir forest. Treeline is about one steep mile up, and beyond is alpine tundra. The peak's summit is at 12,162 feet.

You'll find many species of strictly alpine flora here beginning in mid-July, including sky pilot, moss campion and alpine sunflower. The lift will save you a walk to the bottom as well, but it is worth sauntering through the lush meadows full of columbines, fireweed and lupines along the mountain road. In the fall, the roadside raspberries are the biggest and juiciest anywhere near here!

Upper Loop

The Upper Loop Trail extends for about four miles along the west flank of Crested Butte Mountain. The south end begins off of the Brush Creek Road, three miles south of town and about two more up the road. The north end can be accessed from Hunter Hill Road in Mt. Crested Butte. The trail is also bisected by Tony's Trail, which begins near the end of the road extending east from Elk Avenue in the town of Crested Butte.

The trail rambles through coniferous and aspen forests, sagebrush meadows and crosses some avalanche paths. This is a great trail to look for red columbine and coralroot orchids, both shade-loving plants. Mountain lover dominates the understory in both aspen and Douglas-fir forests. Out in the open, you'll find mountain ball cactus blooming in June on a rock outcrop overlooking the town of Crested Butte.

Peanut Lake Road/Woods Walk

At the north end of town, follow Butte Avenue west to Peanut Lake. You can explore past Peanut Lake about as far as you want to go into the wilderness on the Lower Loop trail, or catch a trail heading south near the old, cement mining tower (affectionately known by locals as "The Gronk") leading back towards Crested Butte. The Crested Butte Land Trust is restoring the mining area just north of Peanut Lake with native plants.

Wetlands, sagebrush, aspen forest and mountain meadows provide early season displays close to town. This is one of the first places to find glacier lilies and spring beauties in mid-May, and one of the last places to find bottle gentians in late September. The view of Paradise Divide (see pages 17 and 151) from the Peanut Lake Road is spectacular any time of year.

North of Town

Poverty Gulch/Daisy Pass

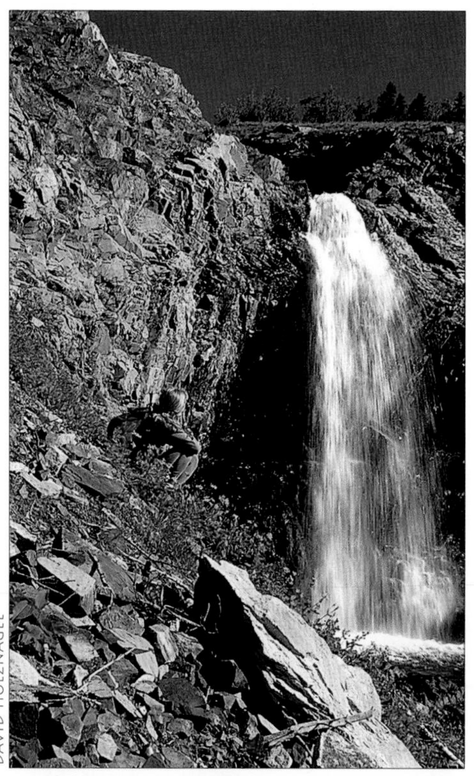
DAVID HOLZNAGEL

Drive about eight miles up the Slate River Road, a short mile north of Crested Butte, until you see a sign for the loose group of cabins called Pittsburgh. Take a left at the first junction in the road and park near the creek. Cross Slate River and head up the old road. This is an old mining road and branches about one and a half miles up the Gulch. Either fork is worthwhile. If you take a right, you'll be heading toward Mineral Point and Augusta Peak, the two dominant mountains. To get to the top of Daisy Pass, take a left. From there it's a stiff 2,000 foot climb to the pass, where the trail drops into Democrat Basin. A ten-mile shuttle loop can be done by dropping into the Basin and hiking out along the Oh-be-Joyful Road.

Poverty Gulch is filled with corydalis, a lush endemic plant found growing along the creek. This is also where you'll find the giant lady fern, growing among the krummholz at the head of the Gulch. Because this trail is so high and shadowed by Schuylkill Mountain, the wildflowers don't really get going until early July, but when they do, it's one of the best!

Rustler Gulch

About four miles past the town of Gothic, home of the Rocky Mountain Biological Laboratory, there is a trailhead on the right leading into Rustler Gulch. This is a moderate hike taking you four miles or so through incredible mountain meadows and on up to the alpine tundra. There are three creek crossings, so be prepared to take your shoes off or get your boots wet.

The lower trail is lush with chiming bells, tall larkspur and aspen sunflower. On south-facing slopes near outcrops of red sandstone, you can find colonies of sweet-smelling little bee balm. Near treeline you'll find some brilliant fields of rosy paintbrush and Parry's primrose growing along the creeks. See page 10 for a mid-summer view high in Rustler Gulch.

West Maroon Trail

The hike between Aspen and Crested Butte is an annual trek and sort of a spiritual quest for many. Thirteen miles of trail take you over West Maroon Pass in the Maroon Bells-Snowmass Wilderness and right past the legendary Maroon Peaks. From trailhead to pass is a 2,000 foot elevation gain. On the Crested Butte side, the trailhead is located about nine miles past Gothic over Schofield Pass.

Depending on the snow year, Schofield Pass may or may not be open, so there's an extra one or two miles of hiking along the road if it isn't cleared for vehicle use. If you only have one day to hike, this should be the one. The wildflowers are usually at their peak in July. Photos on pages 3 (Contents), 15, and 186 were taken from the West Maroon Trail.

Yule Pass

Anyone suffering acrophobia might be better off avoiding this trail, but for the adventurous hiker, this very exposed old mountain road offers some of the best botanizing and scenery in the Elk Mountains. Numerous alpine endemics thrive in the scree here, and the west side of the pass is outrageously beautiful.

First, you'll need to navigate the Slate River Road beyond Pittsburg, which winds and climbs up to Paradise Divide. From the Divide, the rocky wagon road, now navigable only by foot, skirts the mountains west to Yule Pass. With the aid of the Oh-Be-Joyful, Snowmass Mountain, and Marble USGS topographic maps, avid hikers can reach the gem-like Yule Lakes. To the lakes and back from Paradise Divide is a nine-mile trek. To Yule Pass and back is about four and a half miles. See page 192 for a view from the Yule Pass trail.

West of Town

Green Lake/Irwin Road

Eight miles west of Crested Butte on the Kebler Pass Road, take a right and follow signs to the Irwin Lake Campground. A stroll around the lake will take you through lush wetlands, spruce forest, meadows and mountain sagebrush. The wetlands and streams along the trail are full of marsh-loving plants like elephantella, globeflowers, bog orchids, sedges and rushes. Look carefully and you'll find two kinds of bishop's cap nestled in shaded areas beneath the spruce trees. This is an easy one mile walk, but could take you three hours because there is so much plant diversity.

For the energetic hiker, the peaks and ridges that rise above Lake Irwin are accessible from the old mining road that climbs from the lake for about three miles to another alpine waterhole, Green Lake. Along the way, you'll be rewarded with some beautiful waterfalls and lush subalpine meadows. Most vehicles can get at least a mile up this road; from then on, four-wheel-drive is recommended. This is one of the best and most accessible alpine hikes in the area.

Dark Canyon/Dyke Trail

This is the trail to hike for fall aspen colors. Drive about ten miles up the Kebler Pass Road from town. The trailhead is on the right at Horse Ranch Park. The trail cruises through what is reputed to be one of the largest contiguous aspen forests in North America. Along the trails you will find many interesting inscriptions carved in the tender bark of aspen trees, left mostly by sheepherders as far back as 1918. From here you can link to a network of trails that run through the Raggeds Wilderness Area. For a short hike, the Dark Canyon overlook is a good destination, about two miles up the trail.

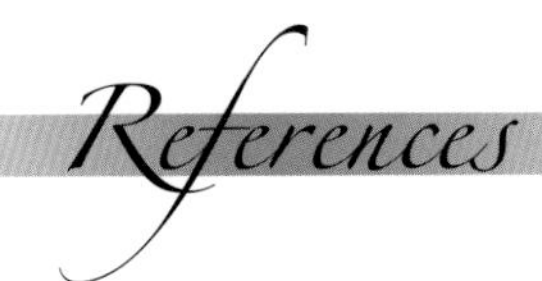

References

Barrell, Joseph. 1969. *Flora of the Gunnison Basin: Gunnison, Saguache, and Hinsdale Counties, CO.* Natural Land Institute, Hinsdale, IL.

Benedict, A.D. 1991. *A Sierra Club Naturalist's Guide: The Southern Rockies.* Sierra Club Books, San Francisco, CA.

Blanchan, Neltje. 1904. *Nature's Garden: An Aid to Knowledge of Our Wildflowers and Their Insect Visitors.* Doubleday, Page, and Co., NY.

Briggs, D. and Walters, S.M. 1984. *Plant Variation and Evolution.* Cambridge Univ. Press, Cambridge.

Buck, P. and Frase, B. 2003. *Vascular Plants of the Gothic Area.* Rocky Mountain Biological Laboratory, Gothic, CO.

Carter, J.L. 2006. *Trees and Shrubs of Colorado.* Johnson Books, Boulder, CO.

Craighead, J., Craighead, F., and Davis, R. 1963. *The Peterson Field Guide Series: A Field Guide to Rocky Mountain Wildflowers.* Houghton Mifflin Co., Boston, MA.

Cronquist, A., A.H. Holmgren, P.K. Holmgren, and J.L. Reveal. 1989. *Vascular Plants of the Intermountain West,* USA New York Botanical Gardens, Bronx, NY.

dePaola, T. 1988. *The Legend of the Indian Paintbrush.* G.P. Putnam's Sons, New York.

dePaola, T. 1996. *The Legend of the Bluebonnet.* The Putnam and Grossett Group, New York.

Duft, Joseph F. and Moseley, Robert K. 1989. *Alpine Wildflowers of the Rocky Mountains.* Mountain Press Pub. Co., Missoula, MT.

Fischer-Rizzi, Suzanne. 1990. *Complete Aromatherapy Handbook: Essential Oils for Radiant Health.* Sterling Pub. Co., New York.

Galen, Candace. July, 1985. *The Smell of Success.* Natural History Magazine.

Gledhill, D. 1985. *The Names of Plants.* Cambridge Univ. Press, Cambridge.

Guennel, G.K. 1995. *Guide to Colorado Wildflowers, Volume 2, Mountains and Volume 1, Plains and Foothills.* Westcliffe Pub. Inc., Englewood, CO.

Gunnison River Watershed Integrated Weed Management Plan. 1996. Gunnison Basin Weed Commission.

Hall, Denis B. 1999. *Hiking in Heaven: A Crested Butte Trail Guide.* Wildbird Publishing, Crested Butte, CO.

Harrington, H.D. 1967. *Edible Native Plants of the Rocky Mountains.* Univ. of NM Press.

Hartman, R.L. and B.E. Nelson. 2001. *A Checklist of the Vascular Plants of Colorado.* Rocky Mountain Herbarium, Univ. of WY, Laramie.

Heywood, V.H. 1993. *Flowering Plants of the World.* Oxford Univ. Press.

Huggins, Janis L. 2004. *Wild at Heart: A Natural History Guide dedicated to Snowmass, Aspen, and the Maroon Bells Wilderness.* WHO Press, Basalt, CO.

Inouye, D. W. 1984. *Ants and the aspen sunflower.* Natural History 93:48-53.

Langenheim, Jean H. 1962. *Vegetation and Environmental Patterns in the Crested Butte Area, Gunnison County, Colorado.* Ecological Monographs, Vol.32, No. 3, pp. 250-285.

Long, John C. 1965. *Native Orchids of Colorado.* Denver Museum of Natural History, Denver, CO.

Mallary, K. and Day, S. 1992. *Wildflowers: A Collection of U.S. Commemorative Stamps.* U.S. Postal Service.

McIntyre, Anne. 1996. *Flower Power.* Henry Holt and Co., New York.

Moore, Michael. 1979. *Medicinal Plants of the Mountain West.* Museum of New Mexico Press.

Neal, Bill. 1992. *Gardener's Latin.* Robert Hale Ltd., London.

Nelson, Ruth A. 1992. *Handbook of Rocky Mountain Plants.* Roberts Rinehart Pub., Niwot, CO.

Paige, K.N. June, 1988. *The Wiliest Wildflower in the West.* Natural History Magazine.

Porter, C.L. 1967. *Taxonomy of Flowering Plants.* W.H. Freeman and Co., San Francisco, CO.

Prather, T. 1982. *Geology of the Gunnison Country.* B&B Printers, Gunnison, CO.

Rare Plants of Colorado. 1997. The Colorado Native Plant Society, Falcon Press Pub. Co., Helena, MT.

Richards, A.J. 1986. *Plant Breeding Systems.* George Allen and Unwin, Boston, MA.

Strickler, Dee. 1990. *Alpine Wildflowers: Showy Wildflowers of the Alpine and Subalpine Areas of the Northern Rocky Mountain States.* The Flower Press, Missoula, MT.

Tarr, Mary Anne. 1996. *Timber, Talus and Tundra: Hiking Trails And Mountain Peaks of the Gunnison Basin.* Uncompahgre Books, Gunnison, CO.

Taylor K. 1999. *Floristic Inventory of the Northern Gunnison Basin.* M.S. Thesis, University of Wyoming, Laramie.

Taylor, R.J. 1992. *Sagebrush Country: A Wildflower Sanctuary.* Mountain Press Pub. Co., Missoula, MT.

Weber, William A. 1992. *Catalog of the Colorado Flora: A Biodiversity Baseline.* University Press of Colorado.

Weber, William A. and Ronald C. Wittmann. 2001. *Colorado Flora: Western Slope.* University Press of Colorado, Boulder, CO.

Webster's New World Dictionary of American English. 1988. Neufeldt, V. and Guralnik, D.B., eds. Webster's New World, New York, NY.

Wingate, J. L. 1990. *Rocky Mountain Flower Finder: a guide to wildflowers found below tree line in the Rocky Mountains.* Nature Study Guild, Berkeley, CA.

Zomlefer, Wendy B. 1994. *Guide to Flowering Plant Families.* Univ. of North Carolina Press, Chapel Hill.

Some Useful Websites

Database for North American Wildflowers: http://plantwatch.sunsite.ualberta.ca

Dictionary of Botanical Epithets: http://www.winternet.com/~chuckg/dictionary.html

Southwest Colorado Wildflowers: www.swcoloradowildflowers.com

Medicinal Plant Information: www.botanical.com

University of Wyoming, Rocky Mountain Herbarium: www.rmh.uwyo.edu

Trail Maps of the Region

Aspen-Crested Butte-Gunnison: Recreation Topo Map, Latitude 40, Inc.

Crested Butte-Taylor Park Colorado Trails: Recreation Topo Map, Latitude 40, Inc.

Crested Butte-Pearl Pass Colorado, USA: Topographic Map, National Geographic/Trails Illustrated.

Gunnison Basin Public Lands: US Forest Service Series Map, USDA.

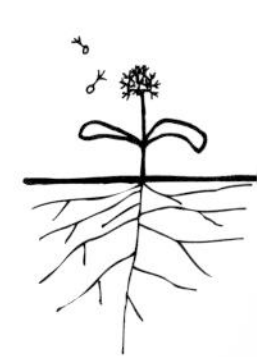

Borage 67 | Borage 68 | Borage 70 | Borage 70 | Buttercup 16

Buttercup 163 | Flax 127 | Gentian 109 | Gentian 109 | Bellflower

Bellflower 79 | Iris 114 | Iris 115 | Pea 98 | Phlox 1

Phlox 145 | Phlox 146 | Snapdragon 193 | Snapdragon 194 | Snapdragon 1

Alder 66 | Pine 28 | Pine 30 | Pine 27 | Rush 1

Sedge 90 | Sunflower 57 | Birch 66 | Buttercup 166 | Fern

erns & Allies 25
Ferns & Allies 25 
Grass 140 
Grass 141 
Grass 141 

eather 93
Hemp 80 
Nettle 195 
Orchid 136 
Parsley 32 

arsley 32
Parsley 36 
Parsley 36 
Saxifrage 182 
Willow 181 

orage 69
Borage 71 
Buttercup 158 
Gentian 109 
Harebell 78 

lint 117
Mint 118 
Mint 119 
Snapdragon 192 
Snapdragon 192 

unflower 42
Sunflower 49
Sunflower 49
Violet 198

Borage 71 | Buttercup 156 | Buttercup 163 | Gentian 108 | Gentian 11

Gentian 110 | Snapdragon 194 | Sunflower 55 | Buckwheat 148 | Buttercup 1

Phlox 143 | Snapdragon 185 | Snapdragon 186 | Stonecrop 88 | Sunflower

Agave 31 | Borage 69 | Buckwheat 150 | Buckwheat 148 | Buttercup 1

Buttercup 162 | Buttercup 165 | Buttercup 167 | Currant 112 | Currant 1

Dogwood 87 | Evening Primrose 134 | Fumitory 105 | Gentian 107 | Gentian 1

eranium 111

Heath 93

Honeysuckle 83

Honeysuckle 83

Lily 120

ily 121

Lily 123

Lily 123

Lily 124

Lily 126

1adder 177

Mallow 128

Mustard 72

Mustard 74

Mustard 75

rchid 136

Orchid 137

Parnassus 139

Parnassus 139

Parsley 34

arsley 35

Pea 96

Pea 97

Pea 101

Pea 102

hlox 144

Phlox 144

Pink 84

Pink 84

Primrose 153 | Primrose 153 | Purslane 152 | Rose 168 | Rose 16

Rose 171 | Rose 175 | Rose 176 | Saxifrage 182 | Saxifrage 18

Saxifrage 183 | Sedge 91 | Snapdragon 191 | Sunflower 38 | Sunflower 3

Sunflower 39 | Sunflower 42 | Sunflower 44 | Sunflower 46 | Sunflower 4

Sunflower 44 | Sunflower 48 | Sunflower 49 | Sunflower 55 | Valerian 19

Valerian 197 | Valerian 197 | Violet 199 | Barberry 65 | Buckwheat 14

Buttercup 164
Buttercup 165 
Buttercup 165 
Cactus 76 
Evening Primrose 134 

Fumitory 104
Honeysuckle 82 
Lily 122 
Mustard 73 
Mustard 73 

Mustard 75
Parsley 33 
Rose 170 
Rose 173 
Rose 174 

Rose 176
Snapdragon 187 
Snapdragon 188 
Snapdragon 189 
Snapdragon 189 

Snapdragon 190
Stonecrop 89 
Sunflower 40 
Sunflower 40 
Sunflower 43 

Sunflower 45
Sunflower 45 
Sunflower 45 
Sunflower 50

Sunflower 52
Sunflower 53
Sunflower 54
Sunflower 56
Sunflower 56

Sunflower 58
Sunflower 59
Sunflower 59
Sunflower 60
Sunflower 60

Sunflower 60
Sunflower 61
Sunflower 62
Sunflower 63
Sunflower 63

Sunflower 64
Violet 199
Water Lily 130
Broomrape 138
Buckwheat 147

Buckwheat 147
Buckwheat 149
Buckwheat 149
Buttercup 157
Cactus 77

Caper 81
Currant 113
Evening Primrose 132
Geranium 111
Heather 92

Heather 94

Heather 94

Honeysuckle 82

Mustard 75

Mustard 74

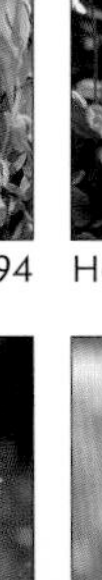

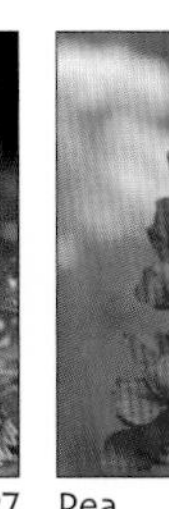
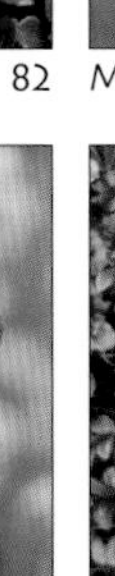

Orchid 135

Pea 97

Pea 100

Pea 101

Pea 101

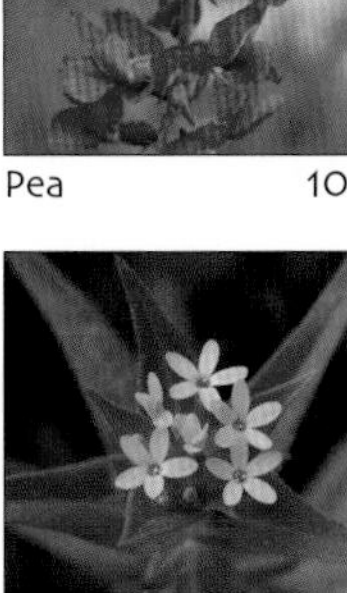

Pea 102

Pea 103

Phlox 142

Phlox 143

Pink 85

Primrose 154

Primrose 155

Purslane 151

Purslane 152

Rose 171

Rose 173

Rose 175

Snapdragon 188

Snapdragon 190

Staff Tree 86

Stonecrop 89

Sunflower 39

Sunflower 43

Sunflower 48

Key to Plant Families in this Book

Choose the description in each pair of the key that best fits the plant you are trying to identify. Follow the numbers through the key to arrive at the plant family to which your plant belongs.

1A. Woody shrubs or trees — 2
1B. Herbaceous or grass-like plants — 12
1C. Ferns or other spore-producing plant — FERNS & ALLIES (p. 24)

2A. Trees with needle-like leaves, seeds in woody cones — PINE (p. 26)
2B. Shrubs or trees with broad leaves, or seeds not in woody cones — 3

3A. Plants with thorns or spines on twigs or stems — 4
3B. Not thorny or spiny — 5

4A. Flowers small, tubular, producing a pea-sized black or red berry — CURRANT (p. 112)
4B. Flowers large, showy, with 5 pink petals; leathery red fruit — ROSE (*Rosa woodsii*) (p. 175)

5A. Flowers in catkins, i.e. long tassels of minute flowers — 6
5B. Flowers not in catkins — 7

6A. Trees or low-growing shrubs of riparian or marshy areas; leaves round to oval, with distinctly toothed edges; cone-like fruit — BIRCH (p. 66)
6B. Trees or shrubs; leaves may be long and narrow or broad with a pointed tip, usually smooth-edged — WILLOW (p. 178)

7A. Low-growing shrub, usually not more than 1 foot high — 8
7B. Upright shrub, usually more than 1 foot high — 9

8A. Leaves edged with tiny teeth; flowers 4-petaled, salmon-pink, tiny (<1/4") — STAFF TREE (p. 86)
8B. Leaves with smooth edges; flowers bell-shaped — HEATHER (p. 92)

9A. Leaves alternate; flowers yellow or green, in small clusters or heads —10
9B. Leaves opposite; flowers larger with distinct petals — 11

10A. Flowers clustered in heads, with ray and/or disc flowers — SUNFLOWER (*Artemesia,* p.41; *Chrysothamnus, Ericameria,* p. 45)
10B. Flowers each with five distinct petals — ROSE (p. 168)

11A. Flowers showy, tubular, in pairs — HONEYSUCKLE (p. 82)
11B. Flowers small, white, in clusters; shrubs with bright red stems — DOGWOOD (p. 87)

12B. Grass or grass-like plant — 13
12C. Herbaceous, with broad leaves and/or showy flowers; not grass-like — 15

13A. Stems triangular — SEDGE (p. 90)
13B. Stems round — 14

14A. Stems hollow, with nodes — GRASS (p. 140)
14B. Stems pithy, smooth, without nodes — RUSH (p. 116)

15A. Flowers in heads, appearing to be one flower, but composed of many small disk and/or ray flowers — SUNFLOWER (p. 37)
15B. Flowers not in heads — 16

16A. Parasitic plants lacking chlorophyll (not green) — 17
16B. Not parasitic (green) — 18

17A. Plants of pine or aspen forest community — ORCHID (p. 135)
17B. Plants of sagebrush community — BROOMRAPE (p. 138)

18A. Plants aquatic, wholly or partially submerged — 19
18B. Plants not aquatic, though may grow near or in water, not submerged — 20

19A. Plant with large, round floating leaves, large yellow flowers — WATER LILY (p. 130)
19B. Plant with finely divided leaves, wholly or partly submerged, small white flowers — BUTTERCUP (*Ranunculus aquatilis,* p. 165)
19C. Plants with small, lanceolate floating leaves; flowers pink, in clusters — BUCKWHEAT (*Polygonum amphibium,* p. 149)

20A. Plant a vine — HEMP (p. 80)
20B. Plant not a vine — 21

21A. Stems and/or leaves succulent, or somewhat thick, juicy — 22
21B. Stems and leaves not succulent — 24

22A. Plant armed with spines — CACTUS (p. 76)
22B. Plant without spines — 23

23A. Leaves opposite or basal; usually low-growing or spreading plants — PURSLANE (p. 151)
23B. Leaves alternate; plants upright — STONECROP (p. 88)

24A. Flowers obviously irregular; not radially symmetrical — 25
24B. Flowers regular; appearing radially symmetrical — 33

25A. Leaves compound (with many leaflets) — 26
25B. Leaves simple, entire, toothed, or lobed — 28

26A. Spur present on back of flower; sepals 2 — FUMITORY (p. 104)
26B. Spur absent; sepals 4 or 5 — 27

27A. Flowers like a sweet pea, stamens enclosed — PEA (p. 95)
27B. Flowers with 4 petals, long protruding stamens — CAPER (p. 81)

28A. Flowers tubular, or with a long "snout" — 29
28B. Flowers not tubular or with a snout — 30

29A. Stems always square; leaves opposite, usually with minty or sage-like fragrance; flowers pink, lavender, or blue — MINT (p. 117)
29B. Stems sometimes square; leaves opposite or alternate, no fragrance — SNAPDRAGON (p. 184)

30A. Flowers similar to garden violets or pansies — VIOLET (p. 198)
30B. Flowers not like violets — 31

31A. Flowers small, in ball-like clusters; flowers tubular and irregular on close inspection; leaves opposite — VALERIAN (p. 196)
31B. Flowers not in ball-like clusters; leaves opposite, alternate or basal — 32

32A. Flowers blue/purple; leaves deeply lobed — BUTTERCUP (p. 156 or p. 163)
32B. Flowers variously colored, often with sac-like lower petal; leaves not lobed — ORCHID (p. 135)

33A. Leaves with parallel veins, often flat, grass-like; flower parts in 3's or 6's — 34
33B. Leaves with netted or branching veins, leaves various; flower parts in 4's or 5's — 36

34A. Ovary inferior; flower parts attached to the top of the ovary — IRIS (p. 114)
34B. Ovary superior; flower parts attached below the ovary — 35

35A. Leaves basal, stiff, pointed; flowers large, white, thick-petaled — AGAVE (p. 31)
35B. Leaves various, not stiff; flowers various, but not thick-petaled — LILY (p. 120)

36A. Petals united, flowers usually conspicuous — 37
36B. Petals separate, or flowers small and inconspicuous — 46

37A. Leaves basal — 38
37B. Leaves on stem — 39

38A. Flowers with short tube flaring to five petals — PRIMROSE (p. 153)
38B. Flowers without a short tube — HEATHER (p. 92)

39A. Leaves opposite or whorled — 40
39B. Leaves alternate — 41

40A. Flowers tiny, white or greenish; leaves whorled — MADDER (p. 177)
40B. Flowers larger, variously colored, often blue or purple; leaves whorled or opposite (some members of this family appear to have separate petals, but on close inspection, they are united at the base) — GENTIAN (p. 106)

41A. Leaves simple — 42
41B. Leaves lobed or compound — 44

42A. Slender plants with bell-shaped flowers and pointed petals; fruit a single capsule — BELLFLOWER (p. 78)
42B. Plants more robust than above; flowers with rounded petals — 43

43A. Leaves broad, sometimes hairy or glandular — BORAGE (p. 67)
43B. Leaves short, stiff, needle-like; not hairy or glandular — PHLOX (p. 142)

44A. Stamens many (>10), united in a tube around the style — MALLOW (p. 128)
44B. Stamens fewer, not united around the style — 45

45A. Corolla a long narrow tube flaring to 5 petals; flowers not in spiral cymes — PHLOX (p. 142)
45B. Corolla a short broad tube; flowers often arranged in spiral cymes — BORAGE (p. 67)

46A. Flowers small and inconspicuous — 47
46B. Flowers showy, though individual flowers sometimes small and arranged to present as one large "flower" — 48

47A. Leaves opposite; plants with stinging hairs; flowers long, greenish clusters dangling from leaf axils — NETTLE (p. 195)
47C. Leaves basal — SAXIFRAGE (p. 182)

48A. Individual flowers small (<1/4"), clustered or arranged to present as a larger inflorescence — 49
48B. Individual flowers larger, not clustered to present as a larger inflorescence — 50

49A. Leaves simple — BUCKWHEAT (p. 147)
49B. Leaves compound — PARSLEY (p. 32)

50A. Petals in 4's — 51
50B. Petals in 5's — 52

51A. Inferior ovary (petals and sepals attached above ovary) — EVENING PRIMROSE (p. 132)
51B. Superior ovary (petals and sepals attached below ovary) — MUSTARD (p. 72)

52A. Leaves stiff, leathery, holly-like with sharp pointed lobes — BARBERRY (p. 65)
52B. Leaves not as above — 53

53A. Stamens numerous (>10) — 54
53B. Stamens as many or twice as many as petals — 55

54A. Floral parts attached to a shallow cup-like hypanthium — ROSE (p. 168)
54B. Floral parts attached directly to the flower stalk (pedicel) — BUTTERCUP (p. 156)

55A. Flowers light blue; plant slender, of open meadows — FLAX (p. 127)
55B. Flowers not blue — 56

56A. Leaves compound or deeply lobed — GERANIUM (p. 111)
56B. Leaves simple — 57

57A. Leaves chiefly basal; flowers white — PARNASSIA (p. 139)
57B. Leaves opposite; flowers variously colored — PINK (p. 84)

If you haven't placed your plant in a family with this key, there is a large possibility that the family is not covered in this book. For a more thorough and precise key, consult Weber's *Colorado Flora: Western Slope (2001)*. For another useful simple key, consult the *Rocky Mountain Flower Finder (1990)* by Janet Wingate.

Index of Plant Families and Species

Common names in plain text; *Latin species names in italics*; Plant Families In All Caps.

Kathy Carr TECHNICAL DIRECTOR

Kathy Carr is a third-generation Gunnison native who loves spending time outdoors, especially in the mountains and her garden. Her mountain biking companions know not to "tailgate," as she brakes for wildflowers. Her husband, Gale Pickett, documents their adventures with photographs, some of which appear in this book. Kathy has worked in the printing industry since 1985, gaining knowledge in all facets of the offset printing process and specializing in graphic design and pre-press preparation.

Leanne Canty ARTISTIC DIRECTOR

Leanne Canty is an independent artist and owner of Rendezvous Gallery in Crested Butte, CO. She earned a degree in art and graphic design from Rocky Mountain College of Art and Design in Denver, and is also an accomplished calligrapher. Leanne specializes in botanical illustration, and is a professional framer, as well as a lover of wildflowers. Her artwork and designs reflect her uniquely calm, refreshing and often whimsical outlook on life.

Wendy Brown NATURALIST AND PHOTOGRAPHER

Wendy has worked at Rocky Mountain Biological Laboratory in Gothic, CO since 1985 as a field biologist. Her research is focused on the ecology and taxonomy of aquatic insects and spiders, but she also works as a research technician for many other scientific studies at the lab. This leads her deep into the mountains where she loves everything except the lightning. Compelled by the beauty surrounding her, she enjoys the art of photographing wildflowers.

Mary Ellen Harte NATURALIST AND PHOTOGRAPHER

Dr. Mary Ellen Harte is a biologist who has been spending summers at Rocky Mountain Biological Laboratory in Gothic, Colorado since 1982. As a naturalist and educator, Mel has produced a weekly summer radio program, *Nature Notes*, which focuses on the natural history of the Rocky Mountains, and also leads tours for the Crested Butte Wildflower Festival. She has also produced a CD, *"What's that Wildflower? A Photographic Guide to the Wildflowers of the Western Colorado Rockies,"* that contains nearly 1,000 digital photos of wildflowers.

Katherine Darrow Author, Botanist and Photographer

Katherine Darrow has been roaming the western U.S. with her camera and notebook for thirty years, settling every now and then to teach, study, do research, and raise her two children, Brooke and Orion. Kathy earned a B.A. in Biology with a minor in art at Colorado College and an M.S. in Botany at CSU in Fort Collins. She has taught environmental education for Yosemite Institute, Bear Creek Nature Center in Colorado Springs, and Colorado Outward Bound School. She has also worked as botanist, environmental consultant, and research assistant for the National Park Service, U.S. Forest Service and Rocky Mountain Biological Laboratory in Gothic, Colorado.

An avid mountaineer, river runner, skier, hiker and backpacker, Kathy is happiest in the backcountry. Her natural history writing and photographs have been published in regional newspapers and magazines. This is the second edition of *Wild About Wildflowers,* which was first published in 1998. Kathy currently lives in the Sonoran desert of Arizona.

David Inouye Plant Ecologist and Photographer

Dr. David Inouye is a professor of biology at the University of Maryland where he is the director of the graduate program in Sustainable Development and Conservation Biology, and teaches courses in ecology and conservation biology. David has been conducting field studies on plant population and pollination biology in the Rocky Mountains since 1971, and is a primary researcher at Rocky Mountain Biological Laboratory in Gothic, Colorado. His long-term studies of flowering phenology and plant demography are being used now to provide insights into the effects of climate change at high altitudes. As part of his research, David especially enjoys capturing images of plants and their pollinators.

Jannette Runge Photographer

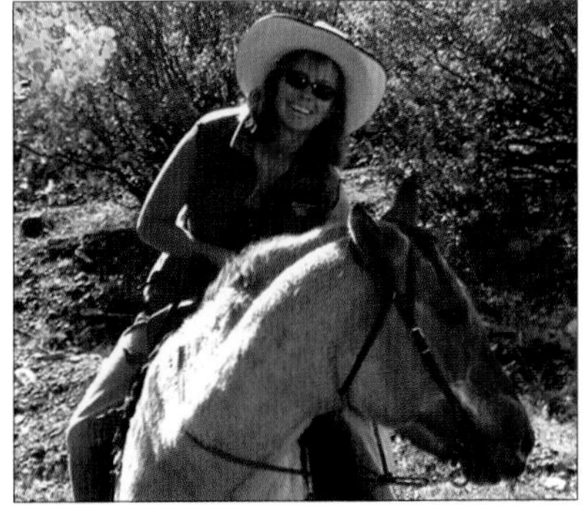

Jan was born and raised in Colorado, and has lived in Gunnison County for over thirty years. Few people know the backcountry of southwestern Colorado as well as Jan does. One of the secrets of producing her gorgeous landscape and wildflower photos is that she spends most of her summers backpacking and horsepacking in the wilderness, where she can begin and end each day in the best light, and take time to discover unique compositions. Jan's photographs are published in many regional and national magazines. Fans and colleagues agree that she is a master of her art.

A PORTION OF THE PROFITS FROM THE SALE OF THIS BOOK WILL BE DONATED TO THE FOLLOWING NON-PROFIT ORGANIZATIONS THAT HELP TO EDUCATE AND CONSERVE HABITAT FOR NATIVE PLANTS.

Crested Butte Land Trust

One of the reasons that Crested Butte can continue to claim the distinction of Wildflower Capital of Colorado is due to the dedication and vision of the Crested Butte Land Trust, a land preservation group established in 1992. Through generous donations, grants, and fundraisers, the Land Trust has been able to preserve nearly 3,000 acres of open space through direct purchase and conservation easements. Among those lands are the corridor connecting the town of Crested Butte to the Oh-Be-Joyful Wilderness and over 1,200 acres of pristine wetlands in the Slate River Valley. Numerous smaller projects ensure that the trails, views and acres of wildflowers that surround Crested Butte are not lost to development. For more information about the Crested Butte Land Trust, visit their website at www.cblandtrust.org or call (970) 349-1210.

Rocky Mountain Biological Laboratory

During the late 1880s, Gothic, Colorado (eight miles north of Crested Butte) was a thriving silver-mining town attracting hopeful prospectors from all over the country. Twenty years after the mines were abandoned, in 1928, Dr. John C. Johnson, a biology professor at Western State College in Gunnison, purchased the land and the historic buildings that were left behind to pursue his dream of creating a biological field research station. Now the town of Gothic sees an annual boom and bust cycle. The Rocky Mountain Biological Laboratory (RMBL) swells to an active community of over one hundred and fifty students and researchers each summer and diminishes to a handful of hearty residents in the winter.

RMBL is nationally recognized for its excellence in education and research, attracting students and scientists from around the world. At 9,500', it is one of only a few high-elevation biological research stations in the country, complete with insect, plant and mammal collections, a weather station, library and other laboratory facilities. Among the topics of research are studies on the life history and behavior of local wildlife, such as marmots, salamanders, hummingbirds and butterflies; trends and effects of global warming; and pollination biology. In addition to rigorous academic courses offered each summer, RMBL offers a nature study series for children, weekly historic walks and wildflower tours. For more information about RMBL and its summer programs, visit their website at at www.rmbl.org, or call (970) 349-7231.

Gunnison Ranchland Legacy Project

The Gunnison Ranchland Conservation Legacy was established in 1996 to "create a legacy for future generations by preserving ranching and conserving ranchlands in the Gunnison Country." Acting on behalf of landowners in conjunction with established land trusts, the GRLP facilitates the placement of conservation easements on agricultural lands. Ranch families benefit by knowing their land is available for agriculture forever. The permanent protection of large expanses of hay meadows, riparian areas and sage uplands also benefits the wildlife and native plants that depend on these undeveloped spaces. Local residents and visitors benefit from the assurance that these beautiful agricultural open spaces will never be developed. For more information, visit their website at www.gunnisonlegacy.org or call (970) 641-4386.

Crested Butte Wildflower Festival

Since 1986, the Crested Butte Wildflower Festival has celebrated the peak wildflower season in the East River valley and spectacular mountains surrounding the town. The Festival's mission is to educate the public about the local flora, to promote natural landscaping and to share an appreciation for and promote the preservation of wildlands.

The week-long celebration offers daily hikes on local trails and tours of town gardens. Workshops on topics including medicinal plants, cooking with native plants, landscaping, wildflower identification, drawing and photography are among the dozens of special events. The Festival also provides an opportunity for local artists to showcase their work in the annual wildflower art exhibit and poster contest. For more information and a schedule of events for the annual Wildflower Festival, visit their website at www.crestedbuttewildflowerfestival.com or call the Crested Butte Wildflower Festival office at 970-349-2571.